BLINDSIGHT IS 2020

Reflections on Covid Policies from Dissident Scientists, Philosophers, Artists, and More

GABRIELLE BAUER

BLINDSIGHT IS 2020

Reflections on Covid Policies
from Dissident Scientists,
Philosophers, Artists, and More

GABRIELLE BAUER

BROWNSTONE
INSTITUTE

CONTENTS

A TALE OF TWO STORIES

The story went like this: There is a virus going around and it's a bad one. It's killing people indiscriminately and will kill many more. We must fight it with everything we've got. Closing businesses, closing schools, canceling all public events, staying home...whatever it takes, for as long as it takes. It's a scientific problem with a scientific solution. We can do this!

There was another story simmering under the first one. It went like this: There is a virus going around. It's nasty and unpredictable, but not a show stopper. We need to take action, but nothing so drastic as shutting down society or hiding out for years on end. Also: the virus is not going away. Let's do our very best to protect those at higher risk. Sound good?

The first story traveled far and wide in a very short time. People blasted it on the nightly news and shouted it to each other on Twitter. They pronounced it the right story, the righteous story, the true story. The second story traveled mainly underground. Those who aired it in public were told to shut up and follow the science. If they brought up the harms of closing down society, they were reminded that the soldiers in the World War 1 trenches had it much worse. If they objected to placing a disproportionate burden on children and youth, they were accused of not caring about old people. If they breathed a word about civil liberties, they were told that freedumbs had no place in a pandemic.

The first story was a war story: an invisible enemy had invaded our land and we had to pour all our resources into defeating it. Everything else—social life, economic life, spiritual life, happiness, human rights, all that jazz—could come later. The second story was an ecological story: a virus had entered and recalibrated our ecosystem. It looked like we couldn't make it go away, so we had to find a way to live with it while preserving the social fabric.

The two stories continued to unfold in tandem, the gulf between them widening with each passing month. Beneath all the arguments about the science lay a fundamental difference in world view, a divergent vision of the type of world needed to steer humanity through a pandemic: A world of alarm or equanimity? A world with more central authority or more personal choice? A world that keeps fighting to the bitter end or flexes with a force of nature?

This book is about the people who told the second story, the people driven to explore the question: Might there be a less drastic and destructive way to deal with all this?

As a health and medical writer for the past 28 years, I have a basic familiarity with infectious disease science and an abiding interest in learning more. But my primary interest, as a journalist and a human taking my turn on the planet, lies in the social and psychological side of the pandemic—the forces that led the first story to take over and drove the second story underground.

Many smart people have told the second story: epidemiologists, public health experts, doctors, psychologists, cognitive scientists, historians, novelists, mathematicians, lawyers, comedians, and musicians. While they didn't always agree on the fine points, they all took issue with the world's single-minded focus on stamping out a virus and the hastily conceived means to this end.

I have selected 46 of these people to help bring the lock-down-skeptical perspective to life. Some of them are world famous. Others have a lower profile, but their fresh and powerful insights give them pride of place on my list. They lit up my own way as I stumbled through the lockdowns and the byzantine set of rules that followed, bewildered at what the world had become. I see them as the true experts on the pandemic. They looked beyond the science and into the beating human heart. They looked at the lockdown policies holistically, considering not only the shape of the curve but the state of the world's mental and spiritual health. Recognizing that a pandemic gives us only bad choices, they asked the tough questions about balancing priorities and harms.

Questions like these: Should the precautionary principle guide pandemic management? If so, for how long? Does the aim of stopping a virus supersede all other considerations? What is the common good, and who gets to define it? Where do human rights begin and end in a pandemic? When does government action become overreach? An article in the *Financial Times*[1] puts it this way: "Is it wise or fair to impose radical limits on the freedom of all with no apparent limits in sight?"

Now that three years have gone by, we understand that this virus doesn't bend to our will. Serious studies (detailed in subsequent chapters) have called the benefits of the Covid policies into question[2-4] while confirming their harms.[5-8] We've entered the fifty shades of moral grey. We have the opportunity—and the obligation— to reflect on the world's choice to run with the first story, despite the havoc it wreaked on society.

I think of the parallel Covid stories as the two sides on a long-playing vinyl album (which tells you something about my age). Side A is the first story, the one with all the flashy tunes. Side B, the second story, has the quirky, rule-bending tracks that nobody wants to play at parties. Side B contains some angry songs, even rude ones. No surprise there: when everyone keeps telling you to shut up, you can't be blamed for losing patience.

Had team A acknowledged the downsides of locking up the world and the difficulty of finding the right balance, team B might have felt a tad less resentful. Instead, the decision makers and their supporters ignored the skeptics' early warnings and mocked their concerns, thereby fueling the very backlash they had hoped to avoid.

Side A has been dominating the airwaves for three years now, its bellicose tunes etched into our brains. We lost the war anyway and there's a big mess to clean up. Side B surveys the damage.

Many books about Covid proceed in chronological order, from the lockdowns and vaccine rollout through the Delta and Omicron waves, offering analysis and insight at each stage. This book takes a different approach, with a structure informed by people and themes, rather than events.

Each chapter showcases one or more thought leaders converging on a specific theme, such as fear, freedom, social contagion, medical ethics, and institutional overreach. There's oncologist and public health expert Vinay Prasad, who explains why science—even very good science—cannot be "followed." Psychology professor Mattias Desmet describes the societal forces that led to Covid groupthink. Jennifer Sey, whose principles cost her a CEO position and a million dollars, calls out the mistreatment of children in the name of Covid. Lionel Shriver, the salty novelist of *We Need To Talk About Kevin* fame, reminds us why freedom matters, even in a pandemic. Zuby, my personal candidate for world's most eloquent rapper, calls out the hubris and harms of zero-risk culture in his pithy tweets. These and the other luminaries featured in the book help us understand the forces that shaped the dominant narrative and the places where it lost the plot.

Along with the featured 46, I've drawn from the writings of numerous other Covid commentators whose sharp observations cut through the noise. Even so, my list is far from exhaustive. In the interest of balancing perspectives from various disciplines, I've left out dozens of people I admire and no doubt hundreds more I don't know about. My choices simply reflect the aims of the book and the serendipitous events that placed some important dissenting thinkers in my path.

To maintain the book's focus I've stepped away from a few subplots, notably the origin of the virus, early treatments, and vaccine side effects. These topics merit separate analyses by subject matter experts, so I respectfully cede the territory to them. And what they find under the hood, while obviously important, doesn't alter the core arguments in this book. I also steer clear of speculations that the lockdown policies were part of a premeditated social experiment, being disinclined to attribute to malice what human folly can readily explain (which is not to say that malfeasance didn't occur along the way).

In case it needs to be said, the book does not discount the human toll of the virus or the grief of people who lost loved ones to the disease. It simply argues that the path chosen, the Side A path, violated the social contract underpinning liberal democracies and came at an unacceptably high cost. If there's a central theme running through the book, it's exactly this. Even if lockdowns delayed the spread, at what cost? Even if closing schools made a dent in transmission, at what cost? Even if mandates increased compliance, at what cost? In this sense, the book is more about philosophy and human psychology than about science—about the trade-offs that must be considered during a crisis, but were swept aside with Covid.

The book also calls out the presumption that lockdown skeptics "don't take the virus seriously" or "don't care." This notion infused the narrative from the get-go, leading to some curious logical leaps. In the spring of 2020, when I shared my concerns about lockdowns with an old friend, the next words out of her mouth were: "So you think Covid is a hoax?" Some two years later, a colleague gave me a thumbs-up for hosting a woman from war-torn Ukraine, but not without adding that "I didn't expect it from a lockdown skeptic." (I give her points for honesty, if nothing else.)

You can take the virus seriously *and* oppose lockdowns. You can respect public health *and* decry the suspension of fundamental civil liberties during a pandemic. You can believe in saving lives *and* in safeguarding the things that make life worth living. You can care about today's older people *and* feel strongly about putting children first. It's not this or that, but this and that.

The pandemic is both a collective story and a collection of individual stories. You have your story and I have mine. My own story began in the Brazilian city of Florianópolis, known to locals as Floripa. I lived there for five months in 2018 and returned two years later to reconnect with the gaggle of friends I had made there. (It's ridiculously easy to make friends in Brazil, even if you're over 60 and have varicose veins.)

March was the perfect month to visit the island city, signaling the end of the summer rains and the retreat of the tourist invasion. I had a tight schedule: Basílico restaurant with Vinício on Monday, Daniela beach with Fabiana on Tuesday, group hike along the Naufragados trail on Wednesday, just about every day of the month packed with beaches and trails and people, people, people.

Within three days of my arrival, Brazil declared a state of emergency and Floripa began folding in on itself. One after the other, my favorite hangouts closed up: Café Cultura, with its expansive sofas and full-length windows, Gato Mamado, my go-to place for *feijão*, Etiquetta Off, where I indulged my sartorial cravings... Beaches, parks, schools, all fell like dominoes, the world's most social people now cut off from each other.

My friend Tereza, who had introduced me to *ayahuasca* two years earlier, offered to put me up in her house for the next month, amid her rabbits and dogs and assorted Buddhist and vegan lodgers. I would be lying if I said I wasn't tempted. But Prime Minister Trudeau and my husband were urging me to come home, and as much as I loved Brazil I couldn't risk getting stranded there. I hopped on a plane to São Paulo, where I spent 48 hours awaiting the next available flight to Toronto.

When I finally got home and flung open the front door, Drew greeted me with his right arm stretched out in front of him, his hand facing me like a stop sign. "Sorry we can't hug," he said, fear traveling across his face. He pointed to the stairs to the basement. "See you in two weeks."

There wasn't much natural light in the basement, but I did have my computer, which kept me abreast of the memes of the moment. Stay home, save lives. We're all in this together. Don't be a Covidiot. Keep your social distance. The old normal is gone. It felt alien and graceless and "off" to me, though I couldn't yet put my finger on why. Ignoring my misgivings, I slapped a "stay home, save lives" banner on my Facebook page, right under my cover photo. A few hours later I took it down, unable to pretend my heart was in this.

Every once in a while I would go upstairs to get something to eat and find Drew washing fruits and vegetables, one by one. Lysol on the kitchen counter, Lysol in the hallway, paper towels everywhere. "Six feet," he would mumble as he scrubbed.

The fourteen days of quarantine came and went, and I rejoined Drew at the dining table. On the face of it, the restrictions didn't change my life much. I continued to work from home, as I had done for the past 25 years. All my clients wanted materials on Covid—Covid and diabetes, Covid and arthritis, Covid and mental health—so business was brisk.

Even so, the new culture forming around the virus troubled me mightily: the pedestrians leaping away if another human passed by, the taped-up park benches, the shaming, the snitching, the panic... My heart ached for the young people, including my own son and daughter in their dreary studio apartments, suddenly barred from the extra-curricular activities and gigs that made university life tolerable for them. People said it was all part of the social contract, what we had to do to protect each other. But if we understand the social contract to include engaging with society, the new rules were also breaking the contract in profound ways.

Stay safe, stay safe, people muttered to each other, like the "praise be" in *The Handmaid's Tale*. Two weeks of this strange new world, even two months, I could countenance. But two months were turning into the end of the year. Or maybe the year after that. As long as it takes. Really? No cost-benefit analysis? No discussion of alternative strategies? No regard for outcomes beyond the containment of a virus?

People told me to adapt, but I already knew how to do that. Job loss, financial downturn, illness in the family—like most people, I put one foot in front of the other and powered through. The missing ingredient here was acquiescence, not adaptability.

I connected with an old-school psychiatrist who believed in conversation more than prescriptions, and scheduled a string of online sessions with him. I called him Dr. Zoom, though he was more of a philosopher than a medical man. Our shared quest to understand my despair took us through Plato and Foucault, deontology and utilitarianism, the trolley problem and the overcrowded lifeboat dilemma. (Thanks, Canadian taxpayers. I mean that sincerely.)

And then, slowly, I found my tribe: scientists and public health experts and philosophy professors and lay people with a shared conviction that the world had lost its mind. Thousands and thousands of them, all over the planet. Some of them lived right in my city. I arranged a meetup, which grew into a 100-strong group we called "Questioning Lockdowns in Toronto," or Q-LIT. We met in parks, on restaurant patios, at the beach, and between meetings stayed connected through a WhatsApp chat that never slept. Zoom therapy has its place, but there's nothing more healing than learning you're not alone.

To those who have traveled a similar path, I hope this book provides that same sense of affirmation. But I've also written it for the Side A people, for those who sincerely upheld the narrative and despaired at the skeptics. Wherever you fall along the spectrum of viewpoints, I invite you to read the book with a curious mind. If nothing else, you'll meet some interesting and original thinkers. And if their voices help you understand Side B, even a little, we all win.

THE FEAR FACTOR: LAURA DODSWORTH

Ask people how they felt in March 2020 and they'll probably tell you they were scared. My husband was scared. My Zoom shrink was scared. My writer friend from the wind-blown plains of Manitoba was scared. My New York cousin with the infectious laugh and big hair was scared. "I thought we were all going to die," she told me later.

A few oddballs, like Laura Dodsworth, were not scared. A UK journalist, photographer and filmmaker, Dodsworth had previously distinguished herself through her books about men, women, and body parts. One of her books inspired a documentary, *100 Vaginas,* which a reviewer described as "an extraordinary and empowering spread of the legs."[1]

When Covid-19 came along, Dodsworth grew alarmed—not at the virus, but at the fear swirling around it. She watched the fear grow legs and wings and wrap itself around her country. What troubled her most was that her government, historically charged with keeping people calm during times of crisis, seemed to be amplifying the fear. The media, which she had expected to push back against government edicts, gave the fear train an extra shove. Whatever had happened to "keep calm and carry on?"

Dodsworth understood why a government might want to keep

people afraid at this time: a scared populace would happily comply with the Covid restrictions, which presumably would keep everyone safer. It was for the public's own good. But was it ethical to use fear in this way?

In her book *A State of Fear*,[2] published in 2021, Dodsworth argues that it isn't.

It's hard to dispute her contention that the UK government and media chose fear over fortitude. She gives example after example in her book, starting with the evening of March 23, 2020, which she calls "fright night." On that evening, then-prime minister Boris Johnson described the coronavirus as "the biggest threat this country has faced for decades," adding that "all over the world we are seeing the devastating impact of this invisible killer." A day later, the BBC declared the UK on a "war footing" with the virus. "Heartbreak as healthy 21-year-old dies from coronavirus—it's not just a virus," the *Daily Express* intoned the day after that. When Johnson himself caught Covid, the *Evening Standard* reported on the Cabinet's "shock at [his] condition" as he fought the "truly frightening" virus.

It didn't have to be this way. In his address to the nation, Johnson might have said something like, "we're taking this virus seriously and we want to keep everyone as safe as possible. But the virus doesn't pose an equal threat to everyone, and most of us have no reason to panic." The report on the death of the 21-year-old—always a tragedy—might have stated that "sadly, a young person succumbed to the virus, but everything we know so far suggests this is very rare." And Boris's own battle with the virus might have been presented as "a fight that the prime minister is thankfully winning and a symbol of hope for the country." But fear ruled the day, generating clicks and retweets and more fear.

The fear mongering catalogued by Dodsworth in her own country found echoes all over the world. Dan Andrews, premier of the Australian state of Victoria, raised the fear bar to new heights in a July 2020 address[3]: "No family. No friends. No holding hands. No goodbyes. Denied the last quiet moments that we all hope for. That's how dangerous and infectious this disease is." In case that didn't get the message across, he added: "You should be scared of this. I'm scared of this. We all should be." (It bears noting that it wasn't the disease, but the government policies, that led people to die alone.)

Anthony Fauci, the physician-scientist who advised the US on Covid-19 management during both the Trump and the Biden administrations, declared the virus his "worst nightmare" in a June 2020 CNN broadcast.[4] (In a juicy bit of irony, Fauci had called out Americans for their overblown fear of pandemics in 2017.[5]) In a bid to get more Germans vaccinated in 2021, then-chancellor Angela Merkel warned her constituents that by the end of the winter, "everyone in Germany will be vaccinated, cured or dead."[6]

On some occasions, the fearsome proclamations crossed the line between overheated speculation and outright falsehood. In a public broadcast on March 17, 2020, Michael Gove stated that "this virus doesn't discriminate,"[7] despite study after study revealing a risk gradient that tracked closely with age and other predisposing factors.[8] Drawing from the same playbook, Kamal Khera, a 31-year-old Canadian member of parliament who contracted and recovered from Covid, warned Canadians that the coronavirus does not discriminate based on age or health status, adding that "this virus is literally everywhere."[9]

Some of the fear seemed genuine to Dodsworth. But not all of it. As she watched Johnson deliver his "fright night" speech, "something seemed 'off' and that triggered alarm bells. At a basic level that was hard to pinpoint, it didn't feel genuine." Consultations with two mental health experts reinforced her sense that Johnson didn't quite believe his own words.

There is no way to prove that, of course. Dodsworth brought her own biases to the table, as we all do, and was angling for confirmation. But as the weeks and months rolled by and political leaders throughout the world began flouting their own rules, it became difficult to escape the conclusion that they did not, in fact, view the world outside their homes as a mortal danger.

We all remember the 2020 pandemic hypocrisy parade[10]: Chicago mayor Lori Lightfoot getting a haircut in April, when barbers and stylists were shut down; New York then-governor Andrew Cuomo skipping off to Georgia in July, despite strict guidelines to stay close to home; California senator Dianne Feinstein showing up maskless at the airport despite calling for a mask mandate... Rod Phillips, Ontario's finance minister at the time, not only flew down to the Caribbean during Ontario's second lockdown, but dropped a series of social media posts insinuating he was spending the time at home.[11] A video posted on Christmas Eve found him seated next to his living-room fireplace, a glass of eggnog in hand and a gingerbread house in the background. In fact, he was catching rays in St. Barts on that day and had recorded the video in advance. And the biggest whoopsie of all: in 2022, the so-called Partygate investigation revealed that groups of high-ranking UK government officials, including Boris Johnson himself, had been living it up at 10 Downing Street and elsewhere while public health restrictions prohibited most gatherings.[12]

Predictably, these acts triggered a hue and cry from the public. The general feeling was, "How dare you? The rules are for everyone, not just for the unwashed masses." Truth be told, I found the hypocrisy more amusing than outrageous. I could hardly blame politicians for stickhandling around rules that had never seemed proportionate in the first place—I only wished they offered the same largesse to their constituents.

Dodsworth devotes a chapter of her book to "nudge theory"—the use of human psychology to steer behavior in a given direction. A pioneer in the use of nudging, Britain launched the Behavioural Insights Team (colloquially known as the Nudge Unit) in 2010 and exported the model to numerous other countries. During Covid, Dodsworth learned from insiders, the nudging took the form of "hard-hitting emotional messages" to increase the sense of threat that would lead people to follow the mandates.

Some people view nudging as an acceptable tool, even a laudable one, in the service of protecting life and health. Not Dodsworth. She likens it to locking up cookies in a jar, a tactic that the parent of a toddler might reasonably employ but a government should not. The tactic can easily slip into the territory of "noble lies"—deceitful statements intended to bring about desired outcomes. But who gets to define what a desired outcome is? And where does the obligation to tell the truth begin and end?

Most would agree that "there are no Jews hiding in this house" constitutes a "good" lie, with no downside. But telling healthy young people they're in mortal danger from Covid-19 fills them with unnecessary anxiety and robs them of the ability to make informed decisions. And once they discover that the institutions they trusted misled them, they lose that trust. When the next wave or next variant or next pandemic comes along, they won't take the sky-is-falling warnings as seriously. At the very least, Dodsworth maintains, the nudge techniques used during Covid deserve a public airing.

Dodsworth would also like to see the purveyors of fear held to account. This has happened at least once: in May 2021, a group of individuals and organizations filed criminal charges against Martin Ackerman, head of the Swiss National Covid-19 Science Task force, for deliberately and successfully frightening the population in accordance with Art. 258 of the Criminal Code.[13] The list of complaints includes repeated publication of implausible Covid horror stories, systematic manipulation of ICU bed data, and false statements about hospitalizations and deaths. If nothing else, the threat of such charges may give other fearmongers a good scare—the perfect karmic retribution, if you ask me.

Despite a withering review from *The Times*,[14] *A State of Fear* quickly rose through the charts and became a bestseller. Evidently, Dodsworth and I were not the only two people to bristle at the institutional use of fear to achieve social ends. The reviewer dismissed Dodsworth's concerns as conspiracy talk, which told me he didn't get it. Dodsworth never presumed a nefarious Grand Plan devised by a posse of bad guys with thin moustaches. She simply argued that the end (compliance) didn't justify the means (fear).

She had me on her side from the earliest pages of her book, when she disclosed that she feared authoritarianism more than death, manipulation more than illness. On the day Johnson announced the UK lockdown, she "froze on the sofa." It wasn't the virus she feared, but the prospect of putting an entire country under house arrest.

Several people have asked me why, like Dodsworth, I never worried about what the virus might do to me. The short answer: reassuring data. (The long answer: Talk to my Zoom shrink. We're still trying to figure it out. I mean, panic is clearly contagious, so why didn't I catch it?) Early in the pandemic, I entered my vital statistics into the QCovid® risk calculator[15] to find out my chances of dying of Covid if I caught it. One in 6,500—those were the odds. Granted, I had no underlying health issues, but I was 63 years old. To hear it from the news headlines, I risked life and limb by grabbing a bag of pretzels at the convenience store. One in 6,500? I could live with that.

John Ioannidis's early studies reassured me still further. An epidemiologist at Stanford University, Ioannidis analyzed global data from March and April 2020 and concluded that deaths in people under 65 without extra risk factors "are remarkably uncommon," even in pandemic epicenters.[16] "Remarkably uncommon" sounded good to me, especially coming from an evidence-based medicine expert who counts among the most cited scientists in the world.

For the record, I'm no stranger to worrying. Every time my grown children get into a car, I pester my husband: *Why haven't they called yet? If everything were OK, they would have called by now. Do you think they're OK?* The coronavirus never took me to that place—perhaps because the rest of the world was carrying so much fear there was very little left for me.

My sense of kinship with Dodsworth grew stronger when she admitted, a few chapters into the book, that she had never liked the

Clap for Carers program, a 10-week initiative that drew everyone out of their homes on Thursday evenings to clap for the healthcare workers treating Covid patients. "It's not that I'm curmudgeonly, but something about the weekly ritual felt performative, forced, and, well, a bit Stalinist," she confessed. The Thursday-night pot-banging in Canada never sat well with me, either. On one occasion my husband convinced me to join him, but I could feel the stiffness in my arms, the falseness in my smile, as I whacked the rim of my skillet with a wooden spoon. I wasn't fooling anyone, least of all myself.

Dodsworth called the effort "controlled spontaneity" and wondered if government actors were somehow involved, manipulating the expression of solidarity behind the scenes. While I didn't share this suspicion, the we-the-righteous aura surrounding the pot banging left me with a similar discomfort. It also felt like a tacit endorsement of the government policies: *Here we are, all in this together, doing the best we can to deal with an unavoidable situation. Smile and keep banging.* People who bang pots together don't question policies together.

Dodsworth continues to write about the response to the pandemic. In an essay called "The Collective and the Self," she explores the tension between individual and group interests.[17] With the benefit of hindsight, the article catalogues the losses accrued over the previous two years. The lost jobs, the lost businesses. The mom-and-pop shops that disappeared after a decade of sweat equity. The lost math classes, lost swim meets, lost friendships. The women who gave birth alone. The people who died alone. The wreckage of lockdowns in the developing world, threatening people's ability to put food on the table. "Much of this was not necessary, and was not included in previous pandemic plans for good reason," Dodsworth writes.

During pandemics, she reflects, people have a strong impulse to seek the state's guidance on how to behave and even what to think. Governments reinforce this tendency, declaring that people must "act as one" to beat the offending pathogen into submission. Individuality becomes a "dirty word when the collective good and solidarity are extolled."

In Dodsworth's view, the individual should never get lost, even in a pandemic. When the collective takes over, the current of groupthink becomes too powerful to fight. People jettison their critical faculties and may even lose their basic humanity, like the nurse who reportedly refused to let a man sit with his dying wife "for the greater good." The insidiousness of groupthink may help explain why individualistic societies such as the Netherlands, Bhutan and the US produce more altruistic people than their collectivist counterparts, as discovered in a 2021 psychocultural study of the world.[18] To put it simply, bowing to the collective doesn't equate to caring.

The spell of groupthink also disposes people to accept all manner of government encroachment on their lives, and governments are all too happy to oblige. As Milton Friedman has said, "nothing is so permanent as a temporary government program."[19] This is not quite true, of course. Over the course of the pandemic, governments *have* lifted many restrictions, bit by bit. But the institutional template for lockdown now exists. That's what keeps people like Dodsworth and me awake at night.

Dodsworth calls the pandemic response "a beginning" toward totalitarianism, if not the full Monty. Still astonished that society so readily traded liberty for security—which was never assured in the first place—she exhorts us to reflect on the Covid story with a critical eye. "Recovery and healing *should* be accompanied by misgivings about what we have done, the prickle of conscience and desire to do better."

Do better? When the world shut down, many people viewed the strategy as the best—the only—possible course of action. People like Dodsworth and me were just fighting reality, they said. I remember the early days, when my friends were trying new bread recipes and my husband was scrubbing down our groceries while I paced the kitchen like a caged animal, muttering "this isn't right." Materially I had everything I needed to weather the lockdown gracefully: a warm house, flour and yeast, a blessedly patient husband. But my bones said no. Like Dodsworth, I chose to explore that "no"—and then write a book about it.

Dodsworth concludes her book by reminding us that perfect safety has never and will never exist, a fact of life on earth that Covid made people forget. If we don't accept this reality, we set the stage for "policies of fear that invade our humanity." She invites readers to help her "write the end of the story"—a more balanced and courageous end.

THE MADNESS OF CROWDS:
MATTIAS DESMET

To Mattias Desmet, the pandemic that crashed into 2020 was more of a state of mind than a material reality. Yes, there was a new contagious disease. Yes, we needed to take it seriously. Yes, it warranted some collective action. But the way people were behaving? That was the real virus. "From May 2020 onwards, I had the feeling that the core was not the biological problem," he has said. "It was a psychological problem."[1]

A professor of clinical psychology at the university of Ghent in Belgium, Desmet couldn't shake the sense that a mental disturbance was spreading through the world, making people behave in strange ways: with suspicion, hostility, sanctimoniousness, and very little common sense.

Carl Jung, one of Desmet's seminal influences, would likely agree with his disciple's assessment. In Jung's estimation, "it is not famine, not earthquakes, not microbes, not cancer, but man himself who is the greatest danger to man, for the simple reason that there is no adequate protection against psychic epidemics, which are infinitely more devastating than the world of natural catastrophes."[2]

Now hold on, you might say. The coronavirus was a nasty piece of work that demanded a vigorous collective response. People and governments behaved reasonably, under the circumstances. But Desmet saw nothing reasonable about a shopper in a grocery store screaming at another shopper for removing her mask to scratch her face. Or calling a snitch line after spotting someone sipping a coffee on the beach. Or depriving a dying parent of human touch.

In essence, Desmet was saying: "This virus is a nasty piece of work *and* the world has gone mad." He and other lockdown-critical people keep returning to this point: a real threat and a disproportionate response can coexist.

Desmet's dual training in psychology and statistics gave him a unique angle on the pandemic. The statistician in him began seeing red flags in May 2020, when new data from population studies suggested that early projections had overestimated the lethality of the virus. At the same time, global organizations were starting to sound alarm bells about the harms of lockdowns in the developing world, where cessation of economic activity could lead millions to starvation and loss of life. Instead of adjusting the strategy to the new information, governments and people doubled down: stay home, stay apart. Don't be selfish. More lockdowns, please.

At that point, Desmet "switched from the perspective of statistician to [that] of a clinical psychologist... I started to try to understand what psychological processes were going on in society."[3] The question burning in his mind: Why was the world clinging to a narrative that no longer fit the facts? His Eureka moment came in August 2020: "This was a process of large-scale mass formation." Having lectured about the phenomenon for years, he was "surprised it took me so long" to connect the dots.

In interview after interview, Desmet set about explaining mass formation to the world. (Somewhere along the way, his listeners tacked on "psychosis" to the term, but Desmet himself has stuck to the original wording.) After his September 2021 interview with UK podcaster Dan Astin-Gregory, which garnered over a million views and ten thousand shares,[3,4] other online influencers began popularizing the term. And then an even bigger moment arrived: on the last day of 2021, American physician and vaccine scientist Robert Malone brought up mass formation on the Joe Rogan Experience show.[5] All of a sudden the whole world was talking about Desmet and his hypothesis.

So what exactly is it, anyway? Desmet explains mass formation as the emergence, in society, of a mass or crowd of people that influences people in specific ways. "When an individual is in the grip of mass formation, they become radically blind to everything that goes against the narratives the group believes in," he says.[4] If the hypnotic state persists, they will "try to destroy everyone who doesn't go along with them, and they typically do it as if it is an ethical duty."

According to Desmet, four conditions must exist for mass formation to emerge: a lack of social connectedness (what political philosopher Hannah Arendt calls "social atomization"), a lack of meaning in many people's lives, a high level of "free-floating" anxiety in society (meaning anxiety without a specific object, unlike the anxiety you feel when a tiger is heading your way), and an undercurrent of societal aggression with no outlet.

As a clinical psychologist, Desmet was especially attuned to the social malaise preceding the pandemic, as evidenced by a "steady increase in the number of depression and anxiety problems and the number of suicides" and the "enormous growth in absenteeism due to psychological suffering and burnout."[6] In the year before Covid, "you could feel this malaise growing exponentially."

The final catalyst for mass formation is a narrative—ideally of the mythical sort, with heroes and villains. In his 2021 book *The Delusions of Crowds*,[7] a history of financial and religious mass manias over the past five centuries, William Bernstein notes how "a compelling narrative can act as a contagious pathogen that rapidly spreads through a given population" in the same manner as a virus. As the narrative spreads from person to person, from country to country, it spirals into "a vicious cycle for which we lack an analytical emergency brake." No matter how misleading the narrative, "if compelling enough it will nearly always trump the facts" because the human brain can't resist a good yarn. As Bernstein puts it, "we are the apes who tell stories."

The Covid narrative met all the criteria for triggering mass formation: a deadly plague, an "enemy against humanity" (to borrow WHO director-general Tedros Ghebreyesus's locution[8]), a call to join forces and fight it. A chance for heroism. The pandemic memes of the early days, telling social recluses they could finally claim hero status by eating potato chips and zoning out on their couch, tapped into this sensibility.

The narrative also gave people a focus for their anxiety, which they could now project onto a concrete (if invisible) enemy. Suddenly enlisted in a global army, they experienced what Desmet calls the "mental intoxication of connectedness."[3] Purpose, meaning, social bonds, now available to every malcontent. The scientists who brought the story to the public, in turn, were "rewarded with tremendous social power."[6] It's no surprise the narrative gripped both experts and ordinary citizens so tightly. But here's the rub: the social bonds fostered by mass formation do not occur between individuals, but between each person and an abstract collective. "That's crucial," Desmet says. "Every individual separately connects to the collective."[4]

This leads us to the concept of parochial altruism, sensitively explored in an essay by Lucio Saverio-Eastman.[9] Defined as "individual sacrifice to benefit the in-group and harm an out-group," this type of altruism undermines cooperation between groups and leads to pathological (rather than reasoned) obedience—hardly the ingredients for a truly caring global response to a pandemic. Instead of owning their thoughts and decisions, people in the grip of parochial altruism engage in outward projection, which Saverio-Eastman describes as "a deflection of individual responsibility onto the collective in-group or out-group."

This mindset explains why, despite all the talk of solidarity in the early weeks of the crisis, people would scurry away from a maskless tourist asking for directions. If someone fell on the sidewalk, other pedestrians refused to break the six-foot barrier to offer help. They let their parents die alone "to protect the elderly."

When people bond with an abstraction ("the greater good"), rather than with other people, Desmet says they lose their moral bearings. That's why mass formation erodes people's humanity, leading them to "report [others] to government, even people they loved before, out of solidarity with the collective."[4]

Ah yes, the tattle-tales. By April 2020, "social distancing snitches" in Canada were already clogging 911 emergency lines with hundreds of calls, including 300 complaints involving people in parks in a single day.[10] When polled about snitching, four in 10 Canadians said they intended to report anyone who flouted the Covid rules. After a resplendent spring day brought some Montreal rule breakers out of hiding, the local police set up a COVID-19 webpage to make snitching that much easier.

Generally derided as the conduct of petty bureaucrats with lack of agency in their lives, snitching became a badge of good citizenship in the early weeks of the pandemic. As psychologist Geneviève Beaulieu-Pelletier observes, snitching "gives people the impression that they have more control on [sic] their situation. It's a way of controlling our fear."[10]

Some might argue that snitching serves a unique social purpose in a pandemic, but encouraging people to turn on each other hardly promotes solidarity. On the contrary, it weakens the social bonds that Desmet views as crucial to our humanity. And once given free rein, the snitching impulse tends to run away with itself. People don't just report their neighbors for having raucous birthday bashes, but for sharing a coffee with a friend on a park bench or even for walking along a deserted beach. At that point, the snitches are no longer motivated by good citizenship, but by the naked impulse to control, which Desmet views as both a driver and outcome of mass formation. Under the spell of mass formation, people seek uniformity, and the nail that sticks out gets hammered in.

According to Desmet, unchecked mass formation can easily slip into totalitarianism, an idea he explores in his 2022 book *The Psychology of Totalitarianism*.[11] Just weeks after its publication, the book became an Amazon #1 bestseller in the privacy & surveillance category. (Note to book authors looking to turn a profit: get on Joe Rogan's show.) As Desmet explains in the book, every totalitarian regime begins with a period of mass formation. Into this tense and volatile mass steps an autocratic government and voilà, the totalitarian state clicks into place. "Nascent totalitarian regimes typically fall back on a 'scientific' discourse," he says.[6] "They show a great preference for figures and statistics, which quickly degenerate into pure propaganda." The architects of the new regime don't go around shouting, "I am evil." They often believe, to the bitter end, they are doing the right thing.

Some people get really jumpy at the suggestion that the Covid protocols bear any resemblance to a totalitarian regime. In Desmet's defense, he never alleges that we've landed there. He simply maintains that Covid created the right conditions for totalitarianism to creep in: a frightened public, a cry for strong government action, and the universal political impulse to hold on to power when given the reins. A 34-nation European organization called IDEA agrees that democracy has taken a beating since Covid, "with countries notably taking undemocratic and unnecessary actions to contain the coronavirus pandemic."[12]

Fortunately, during the pandemic's third year, countervailing forces began nudging most of the world away from Covid extremism. Even so, Desmet suggests we remain vigilant. A sneaky new variant could send us right back to where we started: scared, angry, lost to rational discourse, and begging to be locked down again.

Over 40 million people listened to Joe Rogan's interview with Robert Malone, turning mass formation into a household word. The media pushback was swift and merciless—and if I may, editorially sloppy. A commentary in *Medpage Today*,[13] written 12 days after the interview, exemplifies the low bar: "Malone posits that promoting messages encouraging people to get vaccinated against COVID-19, among other scientifically validated pandemic communications, is an attempt to hypnotize groups of people to follow these messages against their will."

A simple fact check can puncture that statement. Texas congressman Troy Nehls saw fit to preserve the full interview transcript on his website,[14] and everything Malone had to tell Rogan about mass formation appears on p. 38. For example: "When you have a society that has become decoupled from each other and has free-floating anxiety...and then their attention gets focused by a leader or series of events on one small point, just like hypnosis, they literally become hypnotized and can be led anywhere... This is central to mass formation psychosis and this is what has happened." A few more sentences, essentially more of the same, and he's done. Earlier in the interview he talks about the lack of transparency surrounding the vaccine data, but never once does he link the vaccination campaign to mass formation or group hypnosis. I read the whole transcript—twice—just to make sure.

Other pundits threw shade on the concept of mass formation itself, calling it scientifically unsound and unproven. A *Reuters Fact Check* article[15] reported that the term doesn't appear in the American Psychology Association dictionary and that, according to "numerous psychologists," it lacks professional legitimacy.

It's a disingenuous allegation. When you get down to it, mass formation is just another term for good old mob psychology. We may not have an instrument to measure it, but we've recognized the phenomenon for centuries. Scholars such as Freud, Jung, and Gustave Le Bon have all described it. Both *The Delusions of Crowds* and its 19th-century inspiration, *Memoirs of Extraordinarily Popular Delusions and the Madness of Crowds,* discuss it. In his book *Crowds and Power,* written in 1960, Nobel laureate Elias Canetti argues that fear leads people to devolve into pack behavior.[16] Fear of the virus did just that, leading people to set aside their basic humanity and common sense.

Remember the mother who put her 13-year-old son in the trunk of her car? The boy had tested positive for the virus and she was taking him for additional testing. To protect herself from exposure, she had him lie in the trunk while she drove him to the testing site.[17] "What she did is antithetical to every maternal instinct we have," says podcaster Trish Wood in a post-Rogan interview with Desmet.[18] "For a mother to put her own fear...above the care and comfort of a kid... I mean, really?"

Or how about this one? Paramedics wouldn't let a 19-year-old man with meningitis symptoms into the hospital until he tested negative for Covid. The staff was "so psychotically attached to the Covid narrative," to use Wood's phrasing, that they disregarded his obviously alarming symptoms. When his parents took him to the ER a second time, he was so weak they had to carry him to the car. Hospital staff refused to let him in, and the young man died.[19]

Can people read stories like this and *not* conclude the virus vigilantes were under a spell?

When in the thrall of mass formation, people become "radically intolerant to dissonant voices," Desmet says on various occasions. They certainly don't welcome the suggestion that they're being swept up by the crowd, and the strength of their numbers allows them to push the idea out of consciousness. That's why Desmet encourages those who take issue with the dominant narrative—about 10 to 30 percent of the population, by his estimate—to speak out. "If there is no dissonant voice anymore in society, then the process of mass formation becomes increasingly deep."[18]

It bears repeating: Desmet has never denied the biological reality of the virus or the threat it poses to public health. Nor does he ascribe evil motives to the people who responded in extreme ways. He simply sees the forces of crowd psychology at work. There's nothing surprising in any of this: When you mix a virus with a planet of frightened people, how could crowd psychology *not* kick in?

In fact, several other academics have circled around Desmet's mass formation hypothesis, using slightly different terms. In a 2021 journal article, a trio of academics concluded that "collective hysteria may have contributed to policy errors during the COVID-19 pandemic."[20] Within the psychotherapy community, Desmet finds a staunch ally in Mark McDonald, a child and adolescent psychiatrist based in Los Angeles. MacDonald traces the rash of mental health problems afflicting his patients in the post-Covid era—the stress, anxiety, depression, addiction, and domestic violence—to the climate of fear stoked by public health authorities and amplified by the media.[21] Like Desmet, he contends that people stopped thinking rationally when Covid arrived, and that the "mass delusional psychosis" that gripped the world has done more harm than the virus itself.

Whatever we call the phenomenon—mass formation, mob psychology, social contagion—Desmet says we can offset it by drawing on eternal principles of humanity. Like Jung, he invites us to reach beyond a purely rational and mechanistic world view—to cultivate a "resonant knowing" that awakens real empathy and connection between people.

THE MODERN-DAY SOCRATES:
ZUBIN DAMANIA (A.K.A. ZDOGGMD)

I f you haven't seen one of Zubin Damania's videos, you really
should—just because they're so damned entertaining. Damania,
a Stanford-trained doctor and digital influencer who goes by
ZDoggMD, has all the eloquence and charm to crush it on social
media. And crush it he does, with over 2.5 million Facebook followers, 481 thousand YouTube subscribers, and more than a billion
views of his shows and videos.[1] He calls himself "healthcare's
unfiltered voice" and "slightly funnier than placebo." While he
grounds his ideas in facts and data, his zany sense of humor and
propensity for bursting into song at random moments undoubtedly
boost his brand.

There he sits in front of the video camera, with his billiard-ball
scalp and ear-to-ear smiles, asking question after question like
Socrates on Mount Olympus. He doesn't just want the facts, he
wants the reasons. Why, why, why. Why has Covid polarized the
USA and other countries so much? Why do people come to blows
over masks? Where has the pandemic story gone astray? Like a
child, he confronts the simplest and toughest questions of all: Why
are we here? Why does being alive matter? What makes us human,
and how do we preserve it?

During the pandemic, ZDogg quickly distinguished himself as a doctor with slightly heterodox ideas but a whole lot of understanding and compassion for all sides of the debate. That's what made his message palatable to his listeners and added new acolytes to his already large and loyal fan base.

A personal chat with him endeared him to me all the more. We talked about the erosion of independent journalism, the new "secular religions," and how tribalism and technology converged to create the Covid wars. "These new algorithms are designed to maximize clicks," he told me. "They know what humans are about and they tap into that." And what would that be? "Humans respond to moral outrage, to in-groups and out-groups, to demonization. The algorithm figures out what winds us up and feeds us those stories. So we have different groups getting different 'truth streams.' If this goes on for some time, the groups can no longer talk to each other."

ZDogg's capacious grasp of human nature came to the fore in a May 2020 video called "Masks and the Moral Matrix."[2] I can't remember how I stumbled on the video, but it gave me a new angle on the questions that had been haunting me during Toronto's first lockdown: Why are so many people on board with this? What's wrong with them? What's wrong with me?

The video reviews the tenets of Moral Foundations Theory,[3,4] a framework conceived by a group of cognitive scientists and social psychologists led by Jonathan Haidt, author of the bestselling book *The Righteous Mind*. As Haidt sees it, our moral judgments arise from quick intuitions, rather than logical reflection; the reasoning gets tacked on later, as a post-hoc justification. Haidt likens people's moral intuitions to a taste or distaste for different foods—reflexive responses that have their roots in early life, possibly even in genetics, and short-circuit the logical part of the brain.

The theory, tweaked a little after its original iteration, posits that our moral inclinations fall along six separate axes: care/harm, liberty/oppression, fairness/cheating, loyalty/betrayal, authority/subversion, and sanctity/degradation.[4] Just as we all vary in our aptitudes for math or music, each one of us has a different mix of affinities to these moral spheres. It's Howard Gardner's multiple intelligences theory transposed to the moral realm. Because our moral impulses spring from the core of our personalities, Haidt argues, they tend to resist change, much as an adult is unlikely to walk back a distaste for cilantro or Muenster cheese.

ZDogg uses Moral Foundations Theory to explain the intense reactions—whether pro or con—to the Covid lockdowns and mandates. He begins his video by decrying the polarization that took root so quickly and firmly in the US after Covid appeared. Us and them. We goodies versus them baddies. It's a paradigm he flatly rejects: "Most Americans just really want what's best for their families, their communities and their country, right? Can we agree on that?" That's his baseline: most of us are fundamentally good people. So why do we have such different takes on elemental ethical issues? ZDogg says Moral Foundations Theory can explain it.

Take the care/harm foundation, the moral sense that compels us to protect ourselves and each other. Just about all of us have it, but it doesn't play out the same way in everyone. For example, we may differ in our intuitions about how far out to extend our compassion. Is it just me? Is it my family? My community? My country? All people on the planet? All conscious beings? Do I care enough to give ten percent of my income to charities? To go volunteer in a developing country for a year? To adopt children with special needs? ZDogg's point: ten different people, all of them "good," may differ significantly in their orientation to caring.

In his trademark down-to-earth style, ZDogg connects people's "moral palate" to their responses to the Covid measures. People with, say, active caring and authority tastebuds but a weak response to freedom may feel baffled and outraged that others would oppose stay-at-home or masking rules. If these rules make the world safer (or even *feel* safer) for other people, what on earth is the problem? People with dominant freedom tastebuds, on the other hand, see the demand to stay home and cover the face, especially if prolonged, as an assault on the most foundational of human rights. Every bit as baffled as the pro-mandate contingent, they wonder how others can place so little value on personal agency, a moral nexus they hold as dear as life itself. It's not that they don't care about other people: like most humans, they have loved ones they would die for. They're happy to sacrifice when their conscience calls them to do it. They also believe that, to the greatest extent possible, adults should have the freedom to author their own lives. Absent this authorship, life loses much of its value for them.

Unlike so many other observers of the Covid scene, ZDogg resists the temptation to rank the different flavors. He simply describes the moral foundations as interesting and idiosyncratic human features, like a long nose or wide hips. Just as white meat has no intrinsic superiority over dark meat, there is nothing inherently better about valuing, say, fairness over loyalty. They're just flavors.

Watching the video, and then reading *The Righteous Mind*, helped me understand the militant eagerness with which some people embraced lockdowns, masks, and the rest. Early in the pandemic, support for these measures became branded as the caring choice, ceaselessly reinforced in the media with such slogans as "stay home, save lives," "wearing is caring," and "my mask protects you, your mask protects me." Many people define themselves as caring above all else, whether or not they live a life of service. They also want to be *seen* as caring—that's the ego jumping in, eager to display its moral stripes. Breathing a word against lockdowns and masks would expose them to accusations of "not caring," thus threatening their very identity. Their psyche couldn't let that happen.

People with strong freedom tastebuds took an especially hard beating during the early months of the pandemic, having to dodge mud slings like "selfish idiot" and "freedumb lover" from both the mainstream press and the Twitter warriors. But seen through the lens of moral foundations, freedom carries no less value than any other moral inclinations. It's just one of several moral aptitudes, like an affinity for mountains or the open sea. Only those with sensitive freedom tastebuds can fully understand its allure. The salience of freedom on my own moral palate took me by surprise. Prior to Covid, I hadn't given freedom much thought. It was just there in the background, unobserved and unappreciated, like the water surrounding a goldfish. It only got my attention when it was taken away. I immediately recognized myself in ZDogg's description of people with reactive freedom tastebuds: without the taste of freedom on my tongue, life no longer made sense. (In case it needs to be said, I do not claim the "freedom to infect others" as a right, a specious debating point I'll cover in another chapter.) I also saw my passion for freedom as a form of caring—namely, caring about preserving the liberal democratic values the human family took so many centuries to establish.

People whose moral tastebuds vibe most strongly with fairness went in one of two directions when the world shut down: some invoked the fairness principle to support lockdowns—"we're all in this together"—while others bristled at the unfairness of lockdowns to the young and the poor. Pandemic or no pandemic, they could not countenance a mitigation strategy that would widen the inequality gap and mortgage young people's futures.

The loyalty foundation also cuts both ways. An outgrowth of our long history as tribal creatures, this foundation underpins the sense of patriotism and other forms of group identity. It gets activated during times that require group mobilization. When the pandemic hit, an active loyalty tastebud led people to assume the position of their chosen tribe: left or right, democratic or republican, progressive or conservative.

The authority foundation, which stems from our drive to organize into hierarchical structures, drives the impulse to respect traditions and defer to people in positions of authority. The exhortation to "listen to the experts"—a constant refrain throughout the pandemic—reflects this world view. While historians, philosophers, or simply shrewd observers may have important things to say about the Covid policies, people who feel most comfortable within hierarchies believe the world works better when everyone stays in their lane.

The sanctity foundation shines a light on the fear of contagion. Often associated with religion, this foundation inspires people to live in a more elevated, less carnal manner. It gives special status to the body, which it views as a temple to be safeguarded from pollution or contamination. Some sanctity-driven people may thus view the virus as an impurity, a defilement to be avoided at all costs.

As ZDogg points out, "you can have the same piece of evidence, the same news cast, the same show, and people with different moral matrices will pull out of them completely different conclusions." In his ideal world, Bob and Joe can get together and hash out their moral differences amicably. Bob tells Joe that he reacts strongly to anything that feels uncaring to him, so he gets miffed by people who object to staying home or wearing a mask. It's a reflexive response, he admits, based more on wiring than on reason. Joe tells Bob he understands, but his own moral palate tilts so strongly toward freedom that a pandemic strategy based on blanket rules and restrictions seems like a poor trade-off to him, even if it does reduce some risks. He also admits he's just wired that way. They end their discussion with a (touchless, for Bob's sake) high-five.

ZDogg talks from both sides of his mouth, in the best sense of the expression. He understands that complex issues don't have a tidy answer. He knows that humans come in different flavors and doesn't expect them to think in lockstep. His readiness to give people the benefit of the doubt reminds me of that old French saying, *tout comprendre c'est tout pardonner*. Understanding all is forgiving all.

Let's be honest: it's tedious to try to understand our ideological opposites. It's easier to call them evil and be done with it. But ZDogg invites us to undertake the more demanding spiritual task of understanding before judging. (Which is not to say we shouldn't seek justice when harmed. The rituals of justice can heal both the wronged and the wrongdoers.) He reminds us that, if we expect understanding from others, we need to return the favor. Thinking of people's responses to the Covid policies as moral flavors or reflexes helped remove some of the judgment from my own gaze. Although my palate still ached for freedom, I gained a glimmer of understanding for those who didn't mourn the loss of its sweet taste.

ZDogg returns to the theme of social division in an October 2021 video[5] titled "Covidians vs. Covidiots: an Alt Middle view." To those unfamiliar with the terms, they're both put-downs. "Covidiot" sprang up early in the pandemic to describe people who didn't take the protocols seriously. The restriction-averse contingent retorted with "Covidian," an insinuation that the zeal for restrictions had become a religion, complete with a god (Anthony Fauci) and rituals (masking, distancing, sanitizing) that adherents followed unthinkingly.

To get his audience warmed up, ZDogg breaks into song: "We getting fancy like Applebee's on a date night with the Bourbon Street steak and the Oreo shake." Without further ado, he dives into his subject: the thought processes behind the Covidiot and Covidian labels. To the pro-restriction people, the antis (Covidiots) lack a grip on material and social reality: they turn a blind eye to the threat of the pandemic, and their opposition to government regulations marks them as petulant toddlers. The antis, for their part, see the rule followers (Covidians) as fear-driven conformists who would happily hide in a bubble for the rest of their lives.

ZDogg calls these two positions the thesis and antithesis, respectively. The thesis views the pandemic as a dangerous disease and threat to humanity, which we must fight with all the tools at our disposal, no matter how disruptive. "The flavor of the thesis position is one of fear," he says. The antithesis sees Covid as a threat to elderly people and those with specific vulnerabilities, but a survivable nuisance to the majority. People in this camp are also driven by fear, only in this case it's "fear of loss of liberty, fear of increasing authoritarian control, fear of loss of autonomy and decision-making...and fear of economic damage."

Once again he invokes Moral Foundations Theory to explain people's allegiance to the thesis or the antithesis. Both sides view the world through different moral lenses: you see orange and I see blue. To bridge the gap, we need to recognize our own confirmation biases and take pains to understand the opposing arguments. We can then arrive at a synthesis, which he calls Alt Middle or rational discourse. "It sounds middle-of-the-road, but I see it as a radical viewpoint," he says. "We're trying to find truth, not win an argument."

Just two weeks later, ZDogg is back at it: trying to make sense of the Covid culture wars in a video called Covid Chill Chat.[6] Fresh off a six-day silent retreat, he radiates energy and calm. He tells us the retreat changed his life and will color the way he talks about the pandemic going forward. He will be more chill about it all.

Unmasked and silent, the people at the retreat connected on a deeper level than anything ZDogg had experienced on Zoom. He felt such deep love and connection with the group that he briefly considered ditching all his social media accounts. "When you spend time in silence with other human beings, you realize that a lot of the opinions we cling to so desperately come down to our ego," he told me. "It's a way to make our ego feel safe in a world where we feel separate."

ZDogg now has a new definition of Alt Middle: not getting overly attached to one's own views. Not taking things too seriously. Not allowing fear and media and the ego's constant chatter to generate internal strife. "You're in control of that," he says.

In other videos, ZDogg talks about lucid dreaming, awakening flow states, and the nature of reality. Oh yes, and mind-altering drugs. Rest assured the good doctor is no New Age woo spinner. But he's a curious guy—curious enough to wonder where mind-altering substances might take his synapses and his soul.

As it happens, I first tried LSD in the summer of 2020, when Covid culture was in full swing and I felt like a stranger in a strange land. Like ZDogg, I needed to understand. I hoped the LSD would help me quiet the *why, why, why* that had been knocking around my brain for the past four months.

I first learned that recreational drugs existed at age 10, after a classmate's presentation in school. My mother immediately began warning me against them. "Just say no," she said. Say no to what? To drugs. Why? They're bad. Why are they bad? Stop with the questions. She also said that people who took LSD ended up "jumping out of balconies." When I finally tried it, on that July afternoon, the subtle waviness in the air hardly lived up to my mother's depiction. Was *this* what had frightened and fascinated me for over five decades?

I felt lucid enough to take my paddleboard out on Lake Ontario. It was a windless afternoon, the water a twinkling mirror under my feet. As I paddled, the clouds smiled down at me, like giant cotton-ball emojis. I felt connected to all of it: the clouds, the squirrels darting between trees on the shore, my family, ZDogg. Saving lives meant nothing if it required us to jettison these connections. For a couple of weeks, sure. A couple of months, also fair. Anything more than that and we risked trading the fullness of life for some indeterminate, safer future that might never arrive. This is what some of us despaired about. In the mad frenzy to flatten the curve, something precious was being lost. As I paddled back to shore, the tears started. Big fat lysergic acid tears that bloomed into purple and green and yellow puddles on my board.

And then I smiled again, heartened at the thought that I had ZDogg as a traveling companion through this mess. I had the beginnings of a tribe. I didn't know it then, but the tribe would keep growing roots and tributaries and connect me with some of the coolest people I would ever meet. If the lockdowns had an upside, it was surely this.

FOCUSED PROTECTION: JAY BHATTACHARYA, SUNETRA GUPTA, AND MARTIN KULLDORFF

I f you express any misgivings about the Covid policies, people are quick to retort: OK, so what's *your* solution? How do *you* propose we should have handled the pandemic instead? Three experts came up with an answer, which they put into writing and co-signed in the Massachusetts town of Great Barrington on October 4, 2020.[1]

Nobody could fault their credentials. A public health expert focusing on infectious diseases and vulnerable populations, Stanford University professor Jay Bhattacharya doubles as a health economist. Sunetra Gupta, an epidemiology professor at Oxford University, specializes in immunology, vaccine development, and mathematical modeling of infectious diseases. Martin Kulldorff, a biostatistician and epidemiologist, ended an 18-year run as a Harvard University professor in 2021.

The strategy they proposed in the Great Barrington Declaration (GBD) flowed from a unique feature of the coronavirus: its unusually sharp and well-defined risk gradient. By the end of summer 2020, studies were confirming what the staff in every hospital already knew: "The risk [of dying of Covid] climbs steeply as the years accrue."[2] The CDC published an infographic that put this sharp gradient into relief: if you contracted the virus at age 75-84, your risk of dying from it was 3,520 times higher than if you caught it at age 5-17.[3] Chronic conditions such as obesity, heart disease, and diabetes also bumped up the risk, though not nearly as much as age.

So here we had a virus that posed a significant risk to some people and a very small risk to others. At the same time we had lockdown policies that, for all their egalitarian pretensions, divided people rather neatly along class lines. To the professional couple with a chef's kitchen and a subscription to four streaming services, lockdowns represented a chance to reconnect and revel in life's simple pleasures, like home-baked olive bread and Humphrey Bogart movies. To the newly landed foreign student, dizzy with loneliness under his basement ceiling, not so much. Essential workers, for their part, were expected to bear the risks deflected by the laptop class.

This confluence of circumstances made it impossible not to consider the question: Might we give low-risk groups back their freedom while protecting more vulnerable people? That's exactly what the GBD proposed. I've reproduced it here in abbreviated form[1]:

> *Current lockdown policies are producing devastating effects on short and long-term public health. Keeping these measures in place until a vaccine is available will cause irreparable damage, with the underprivileged disproportionately harmed.*

> *We know that vulnerability to death from COVID-19 is more than a thousand-fold higher in the old and infirm than the young. We know that all populations will eventually reach herd immunity and that this can be assisted by (but is not dependent upon) a vaccine. Our goal should therefore be to minimize mortality and social harm until we reach herd immunity.*

The most compassionate approach is to allow those who are at minimal risk of death to live their lives normally to build up immunity to the virus through natural infection, while better protecting those who are at highest risk. We call this Focused Protection. A comprehensive and detailed list of measures, including approaches to multi-generational households, can be implemented, and is well within the scope and capability of public health professionals.

Those who are not vulnerable should immediately be allowed to resume life as normal. Arts, music, sport and other cultural activities should resume. People who are more at risk may participate if they wish, while society as a whole enjoys the protection conferred upon the vulnerable by those who have built up herd immunity.

Outside the context of Covid, there was nothing radical about the proposal. It aligned with pre-Covid pandemic guidance from such organizations as the WHO and CDC, which advised against blanket restrictions and put a premium on minimizing social disruption.[4,5] It also capped off a growing unrest throughout the summer of 2020, when groups of experts in several countries began calling for a less aggressive approach to Covid—from Balanced Response in Canada[6] to New Zealand's Covid Plan B[7]—and exhorting their governments to restore a more normal life for the lower-risk majority. The GBD emerged as the culmination of these rumblings, the anti-lockdown appeal that finally got the world's attention. Quiet academics on the eve of its launch, Bhattacharya, Gupta and Kulldorff now had the global spotlight on their faces.

When the trio posted the document online, they invited supporters to co-sign it. The signature count grew very quickly for a few days—I know, because I watched the changing digits—and then screeched to a halt. The backlash began just four days after the GBD came out, when Francis Collins, then-director of the National Institutes of Health, called it the work of "three fringe epidemiologists" in an email to Fauci and other high-ranking colleagues.[8] Evidently concerned about the media buzz surrounding the Declaration, he requested a "quick and devastating take down [sic] of its premises." Collins got his wish when an article by Yale University epidemiologist Gregg Gonsalves appeared in *The Nation* that same day.[9] We're not going to follow "some notion of the survival of the young and the fittest," Gonsalves wrote—a rather elastic interpretation of "protect the vulnerable." A few days later, the *Lancet* published a GBD rebuttal statement known as the John Snow Memorandum.[10] Fauci himself described the GBD as "nonsense" and "dangerous."[11]

With Fauci's blessing to bash the GBD, media pundits and online warriors happily obliged. Outrage flared up in print and on social media: Murderers! Covid deniers! They don't care about the vulnerable! (Never mind that the whole strategy revolved around shielding the vulnerable.) "I started getting calls from reporters asking me why I wanted to 'let the virus rip,' when I had proposed nothing of the sort. I was the target of racist attacks and death threats," Bhattacharya recalls.[12] Rumors that the American Institute for Economic Research (AIER) was using the GBD trio to advance a libertarian agenda began to circulate. In fact, "AIER was kind enough to provide the venue for the meeting that led to the Great Barrington Declaration, but played no role in designing its content."[13] Jeffrey Tucker, AIER's senior editor at the time (and founder of the Brownstone Institute), explained to me that the group was "hoping to catalyze a discussion around the Covid policies. We had no idea where it would go or how big it would become."

The term "herd immunity" acquired dark undertones, with everyone forgetting that respiratory pandemics have ended with herd immunity throughout history.[14] The misreading of the term as a callous and individualistic concept continues to puzzle Gupta, who notes that "herd immunity is actually a deeply communitarian idea" because broad societal immunity "is what ends up protecting the vulnerable."[15]

Suddenly *personae non gratae,* the GBD partners sought vainly to defend themselves to an audience that had already blocked its ears. Gupta, a life-long progressive, was relegated to publishing her thoughts in conservative news outlets. "I would not, it is fair to say, normally align myself with the Daily Mail," she admitted in an article she wrote for the newspaper shortly after the GBD came out,[16] adding that she was "utterly unprepared for the onslaught of insults, personal criticism, intimidation and threats that met our proposal."

I had the opportunity to chat with all three members of the GBD team on separate group video calls. For the record, I cannot imagine a more sincere and gracious trio—the types of people my late mother would have called *mensches.* Had their critics spent an hour with them over nachos and craft beer, I'm confident the smear campaign against them would have fizzled right out.

Sometimes, a single word can make everything fall into place. The word "unpoetic," which Gupta used to describe the Covid response, had this effect on me. It was the word I had been searching for all along, the key to what the stay-home-save-lives people were missing. It's probably no coincidence that Gupta wears a second hat as an award-winning novelist,[17] giving her mind a respite from the biomedical world view.

"It's a crisis of pathos," she said when I asked her to elaborate. "It's a one-dimensional response to a multidimensional crisis. I call it an unpoetic response because it misses the soul of life, the things that give life meaning."

If Gupta found the pandemic response lacking in poetry, she also decried its *esthetics.* Sitting at a restaurant table, breaking bread with your unmasked friends while the masked server grinds fresh pepper over your linguini...the "unbearable feudal aspect of it" offended her egalitarian sensibilities.[15] "It echoes the caste system, [with] all sorts of rules about who can receive a drink of water from whom—all these completely illogical and highly unesthetic rules that are there to demolish the dignity of individuals."

That same word, feudal, underpins Tucker's analysis of the Covid restaurant closures. In one of his numerous essays,[18] he notes that "the tavern, the coffee house, and the restaurant had a huge role in spreading the idea of universal rights." The restaurant closures represented "a return to a pre-modern age in which only the elites enjoyed access to the finer things"—what Tucker calls a "new feudalism."

As the pandemic progressed, Gupta continued to delight me with her insights—like the notion of shared responsibility for viral transmission. "It is fruitless to trace the source of infection to a single event," she reflects in *The Telegraph*.[19] "In our normal lives, many die of infectious disease but we collectively absorb the guilt of infecting them. We could not function as a society otherwise."

Such a lovely way of putting it: *we collectively absorb the guilt.* Nobody has to worry about "killing grandma" because nobody *is* killing grandma. A pathogen enters our world and we divide its psychic weight among us, the burden made lighter for being shared. (It goes without saying that deliberately infecting someone falls into a different category, though I have yet to hear of anyone who seeks to do that.) But Covid culture "concentrated the blame that should have been dispersed within the community upon an individual," Gupta says. And for individuals like Gupta, who spoke out publicly against a strategy sold to (and bought by) the public as necessary, the blaming and shaming culture knew no pity.

I had some idea of what Gupta and her GBD collaborators were going through, having received my share of invective when discussing Covid policies online: *Go lick a pole and catch the virus. Have fun choking on your own fluids in the ICU. Name three loved ones you're ready to sacrifice to Covid—do it now, coward. Enjoy your sociopathy.*

None of these missives came from anyone who knew me personally, but after receiving enough of them I started to wonder if the shamers knew something I didn't.

"What if the lockdown lovers are right?" I asked Dr. Zoom on one occasion. "What if I *am* a sociopath?"

"You're not a sociopath."

"How do you know?"

"A sociopath wouldn't ask the question—plus sociopaths don't introspect and you do nothing but introspect. You're the queen of introspection."

"Why do you think I do that? Is it a defense mechanism or something?

"See? You're doing it again."

I wrote an article about my experience with Covid shamers,[20] which prompted people from all over the world to email their own stories to me. Many of them had it a lot worse than I did, their heterodox views having cost them jobs and friendships (and in one case, a marriage). Kulldorff tweeted a link to the article with an accompanying assertion that "shaming never is, never was, and never will be part of good public health practice."[21]

Also: it doesn't work. Calling someone a troglodyte for opposing a mask mandate does not bring about a change of heart. It just invites resistance—or drives people underground, as Harvard epidemiologist Julia Marcus points out[22]: "Shaming and blaming people is not the best way to get them to change their behavior and actually can be counterproductive because it makes people want to hide their behavior."

Amid all the shouting and shaming, some public health experts asked reasonable questions about how the GBD architects proposed to shield the vulnerable from a virus allowed to spread freely in society. Bhattacharya, Gupta and Kulldorff had answers to that, but the time for a fair hearing had come and gone. The window of opportunity to explore a focused protection strategy, pried open for a week or two by the Declaration, slammed shut again. It wasn't long before Facebook censored mentions of the document.[23]

This was not a healthy state of affairs. As Harry Truman remarked in 1950,[24] "once a government is committed to the principle of silencing the voice of opposition, it has only one way to go, and that is down the path of increasingly repressive measures." Likewise, the dismissal of the GBD as a "dangerous idea" would not have impressed Supreme Court Justice Louis Brandeis, who wrote that "the essential character of a political community is both revealed and defined by how it responds to the challenge of threatening ideas"[25] and that "fear of serious injury alone cannot justify oppression of free speech."[26] Is it just me, or were decision makers smarter back then?

With neither a Truman nor a Brandeis to defend them, the GBD creators no longer stood a chance in the public arena. Bhattacharya and Gupta turned their attention to Collateral Global, a UK charity devoted to documenting the harms of the lockdown policies, and Kulldorff joined the Brownstone Institute as a senior scholar. Which doesn't mean they forgot about what happened. In August 2022, Bhattacharya and Kulldorff, along with two other doctors, joined the State of Missouri's lawsuit against the federal government for quashing debate about Covid policies.[27] In the court document, which begins with George Washington's warnings against censorship, the plaintiffs accuse the US government of "open collusion with social-media companies to suppress disfavored speakers, viewpoints, and content." With any luck, the case will rattle some closet doors.

In the early months of the pandemic, scientists concerned about lockdowns feared "coming out" in public. The GBD partners took one for the B team and did the dirty work. They paid a heavy price for it, including the loss of some personal friendships, but they held their ground. In print, on air, and on social media, Bhattacharya continues to describe lockdowns as "the single worst public health mistake in the last 100 years," with catastrophic health and psychological harms that will play out for a generation.[28]

It's no longer unfashionable to agree with them. A *National Post* article written by four prominent Canadian doctors in late 2022[29] maintains that the "draconian Covid measures were a mistake." A retrospective analysis in *The Guardian* suggests that, instead of going full bore on the lockdown strategy, we "should have put far more effort into protecting the vulnerable."[30] Even the sober *Nature* admits[31] that lockdowns "exacerbate inequalities that already exist in society. Those already living in poverty and insecurity are hit hardest"—exactly the key takeaway from the Australian Fault Lines report released in October 2022.[32]

Kulldorff captures this sea change in one of his tweets[33]: "In 2020 I was a lonely voice in the Twitter wilderness, opposing lockdowns with a few scattered friends. [Now] I am preaching to the choir; a choir with a wonderful, beautiful voice." The landscape has also become more hospitable for Bhattacharya, who in September 2022 received Loyola Marymount University's Doshi Bridgebuilder Award, awarded annually to individuals or organizations dedicated to fostering understanding between cultures and disciplines.[34]

Perhaps the concept of focused protection simply arrived too early for a frightened public to metabolize it. But the idea never died down completely, and after the paroxysms of moral indignation ran their course, it slowly grew a second skin. By September 2022, the tally of GBD co-signatories had surpassed 932,000, with over 60,000 of them from doctors and medical/public health experts.[1] Not bad for a dangerous document by a trio of fringe epidemiologists. And would it be churlish to point out that the John Snow Memorandum maxed out at around 7,000 expert signatures?[10]

The GBD didn't get every detail right, of course. Nobody could have anticipated, back in the fall of 2020, all the surprises the virus had in store for us. While reasonable at the time, the Declaration's confidence in herd immunity proved overambitious. We now know that neither infection nor vaccination provides durable immunity against Covid,[35,36] leaving people vulnerable to second (and fifth) infections. And for all their effect on disease severity, the vaccines don't stop transmission,[37] pushing herd immunity still further from reach.

Be that as it may, the GBD creators wrote a crucial chapter in the pandemic story. They planted seeds of doubt in a locked-in narrative. After all the insults were thrown, the seeds took root in our collective consciousness and may well have shaped policy indirectly. And as research continues to document the dubious benefits and profound harms of the maximum-suppression strategy, yesterday's shamers and mockers are inching back toward the question: Could we have done it another way? Might focused protection have worked just as well, or better, and with considerably less damage?

UNMASKING UNREASON: VINAY PRASAD

V inay Prasad never shies away from a good Twitter tussle. And with over 200,000 Twitter followers and 30,000 tweets to his name, he's had a fair bit of practice.[1] A hematologist-oncologist and associate professor of Epidemiology and Biostatistics at the University of California San Francisco (UCSF), Prasad began his ascent to Twitter stardom several years before Covid, when he emerged as a vocal critic of the "precision medicine" trend in cancer treatment. He argued that the new cancer drugs target tiny populations, get approved far too easily, and carry absurdly high costs, while offering only peripheral clinical benefits.[2] "It is a crime to run a STUPID non-inferiority trial with margins that are INSANELY large!" he tweeted in August 2017,[3] referring to the clinical trials that elicit approval of these medications.

While his criticism of the medical-industrial complex has earned him some detractors, his nose for bullshit has made him a favorite among scientifically literate iconoclasts, and his trademark sass keeps his fans happy.

When Covid blew in, Prasad dove into the Twitter trenches and has hardly come up for air since then. "I find it fun," he says of the medium. "It's enjoyable, it's interactive, you get to hear from interesting people."[2] Happily for Prasad, Twitter serves as the perfect vehicle for his Covid zingers. Some nuggets from his feed[4-6]:

- "There should be a city just for people who still believe in COVID zero."
- "Once upon a time, medicine involved deep and spirited debates."
- "I am also one of the [Covid] Super Dodgers. Here is how I did it... 1. Luck. Sincerely, a true scientist."

When his thoughts don't fit into 280 characters, he records a video, snags an interview, or pops out an opinion piece. In one of his many op-eds for *Medpage Today*, he deconstructs the "follow the science" shibboleth that has followed us like a bad dream since the start of the pandemic.[7]

He explains it like this: science is *necessary* but never *sufficient* to create public health policy. Referring to the school closures that marked the first two years of the pandemic, Prasad argues that "science cannot tell you whether to open or close schools. Making the decision requires values, principles, a vision of the type of society we want to be. How much do we care about the kids that rely on public school? Is it enough to offset a theoretical (but unsubstantiated) risk of viral spread?"

Some people oppose the "follow the science" slogan on the grounds that science is a continually shifting landscape, not a church where people gather to follow a set of rules. Prasad's argument lies elsewhere. Even assuming a perfect pandemic science, a science that can predict with 100% accuracy which measures slow the spread and which ones don't, there's no such thing as following the science because "policy is a human endeavor that combines science with values and priorities."

Don't just take it from Prasad. Take it from Yuval Harari, the author of *Sapiens* and other mega-hit books that consider history and humanity through a wide-angle lens. "Science can explain what exists in the world, how things work, and what might be in the future," Harari writes in *Sapiens*.[8] "By definition, it has no pretensions to knowing what SHOULD be in the future. Only religions and ideologies seek to answer such questions."

Here's Harari again, reflecting on pandemic policy in his one-year Covid retrospective in the *Financial Times*[9]: "When we come to decide on policy, we have to take into account many interests and values, and since there is no scientific way to determine which interests and values are more important, there is no scientific way to decide what we should do."

There is no scientific way to decide what we should do. Even if we know exactly how many lives a policy will save, science can't tell us whether to go ahead with that policy, because science can't determine the value of what we're giving up in exchange. Is one life saved worth a hundred thousand missed foreign exchange trips? A thousand people depressed for a year? A hundred? Does it depend on how much longer the saved person gets to live? Science can't tell us any of that.

We're talking about the NOFI [No Ought From Is] principle here.[10] It's a legacy of 18th-century Scottish philosopher David Hume, who intuited that we can't hop from the material realm (what is) to the moral one (what we ought to do). Science gives us data—projections, cases, hospitalizations, and so on—but it cannot, by definition, tell us how to react to the data. It's beyond science's pay grade, if you will.

There is no direct line connecting a threshold of cases or hospitalizations to a decision to mask schoolchildren (or any other policy). Whatever the circumstances, we have choices—and these choices flow from our values. If we think nothing matters more than curbing transmission, we'll make one choice. If we think children's social development takes precedence, we'll make another choice. "Science cannot make value judgments," Prasad says again. Not just that, but "scientists have no special ability to speak about values on behalf of all citizens."[7]

Science is like a weathervane: it gives you information that you can use to make a decision, but it doesn't tell you what to do. The decision belongs to you, not to the swirling metal rooster. A weathervane can tell you there's a stiff wind coming in from the northwest, but it can't tell you how to react to it. One person may deem it insane to step outside on such a windy day, while another may see it as the perfect day for a bracing walk. Neither one is being unscientific: they're both following their internal compass—their values.

We must all act as one! No, we must have choices! Keep us safe! No, keep us free! Science can no more readily settle these ideological tussles than determine whether mountains are better than oceans. Two equally smart and knowledgeable people could pore over the same Covid data—the same facts, figures, variants of concern, and clinical trial results—and reach entirely different conclusions about how to proceed. Their decisions flow from their priorities, their visions of a well-functioning society, not from the shape of a curve or the RNA sequence in a variant. Science informs, but values decide.

Prasad brings the point home yet again in a September 2021 video:[11] "Science can delineate trade-offs, but it can't tell you which trade-offs are worth accepting and which are not worth accepting. And throughout this pandemic we have forgotten that." Indeed we have, and this collective amnesia has frozen the Covid discourse at a childish level. I'll say it again: there is no such thing as following the science. The slogan makes no sense—like, literally, in a two-plus-two-equals-five sort of way. We have Prasad to thank for bringing the misconception to our attention.

While an elite academic himself, Prasad shows a healthy skepticism toward the "expert class" and bristles at the intellectual conformity he often encounters in academic circles. "My colleagues all agree with me" doesn't impress him as a debating point, especially when it comes to Covid. Having observed how groupthink slammed the door on debate about lockdowns, masks, and early treatments, he worries that the professional classes "have devolved into tribal creatures lusting for blood when they see a view that falls outside their preferred platform."[12]

Equally frustrating to Prasad is the disconnect between expert advice and the needs of flesh-and-blood humans. In a post called "Memorial Day Travel: Experts vs. Americans,"[13] Prasad describes the public mood in the leadup to Memorial Day 2022: everyone ready to let loose, happily preparing to spend the long weekend with their loved ones despite expert warnings about the risks of traveling during a period of high transmission. So who is right, the "reckless" travelers or the professionals exhorting them to stay put? To Prasad it's a no-brainer: "Americans are correct and the experts are lost." Americans know that "after you get [vaccinated], plus or minus prior infection, optimize your home meds, and maybe drop some weight, there is literally nothing else you can do to lower your risk of bad COVID outcomes." If they stay home on this particular weekend, they may as well stay home forever—and that's a hard no for most people, expert warnings be damned.

"Americans aren't stupid," Prasad says. They have an intuitive sense of the lethality of the virus from having watched people around them catch it. "They don't want to get sick, but they know we have always risked getting sick to drink beers in someone's living room or bar, eat in a packed restaurant, and watch a movie." Experts who describe such behaviors as reckless or stupid forget that "we have always accepted some risk for fun, and we will do it again."

Before Covid, Prasad reminds us, we understood that zero risk doesn't exist. We didn't counsel immunocompromised people to avoid all contact with others, but encouraged them to "find a balance that is right for them. We have never embraced a philosophy of medicine that means avoid[ing] death to the point of giving up living."[14]

Prasad keeps returning to this point: Pandemic policy is not just about controlling an infectious disease. It's about balancing the need to protect life and to live it, to stay safe and stay sane, to risk a respiratory illness or a mental breakdown—trade-offs you don't need a PhD in viral load kinetics to have an opinion about. "Although we can't all be experts on epidemiology, we are all equally qualified—and, in a democracy, all obliged—to think through those questions ourselves," says Stephen John, a senior lecturer in the philosophy of public health at the University of Cambridge.[15] (Damn, what a cool-sounding title. I wish my high-school guidance counsellor had told me that philosophy of public health was a thing.)

Winston Churchill went a step further, asserting that the ordinary person has a leg up over the experts in assessing trade-offs[16]: "Expert knowledge is limited knowledge, and the unlimited ignorance of the plain man who knows where it hurts is a safer guide than any rigorous direction of a specialized character." That's it, exactly. The experts don't know where it hurts. They don't lose a hard-won business or a once-in-a-lifetime opportunity to trek across Asia. They just stay home and order DoorDash and nod off during Zoom meetings and wonder why people would risk traveling to see their loved ones during a pandemic.

I have to wonder what Churchill might say if he were alive and in charge during this pandemic. I suspect he would talk more about courage and freedom than about stopping the spread. But Churchill-style orations were nowhere to be found when politicians announced the lockdowns, with the notable exception of Angela Merkel's national speech of March 18, 2020, which acknowledged the moral complexity of the decision[17]: "Allow me to assure you that, for someone like me, for whom the freedom of travel and the freedom of movement were a hard-fought right, such restrictions can only be justified if they are absolutely imperative. These should never be put in place lightly in a democracy and should only be temporary." While time has weakened her "absolutely imperative" argument, she had the guts to say what other world leaders did not: we're making a trade-off, folks.

Sooner or later, Prasad and ZDogg—two Californians, both salty about Covid extremism, both willing to use cuss words on screen— were bound to find each other. In November 2021, the pair launched the VPZD show, which they describe as "two doctors, one podcast, alt-middle as heck." Think of it as a fireside chat about policy blunders. They have a bit of an Abbott and Costello vibe going, punctuating their rapid-fire repartee with eyerolls, headshakes, and full-throated guffaws. Here's a sample from a July 2022 episode[18]:

- Prasad: Do you sleep with an N95 or a full respirator?
- ZDogg: I sleep in a Darth Vader helmet.
- Prasad: Do I trust you? I've never shown my back to you, you know that.
- ZDogg: That's because we're both South Asian and we know that we're the most competitive—just like, dude, I'll kill you, I'll take your views.
- Prasad: You'll take, you'll pounce.

They do eventually get to the serious stuff, like the burden of proof before springing a restrictive policy on the public. "My view of policy is that the burden is on the people who want to [implement it]," Prasad says. "If you want millions of people to do something year after year"—say, wearing a mask indoors—"show me data that it works or shut the fuck up." (Hey, I'm just the messenger.) "Randomized [trial] or shut the fuck up."

Further along in the episode they move onto masks, one of Prasad's pet topics. He updates viewers on the return of mask mandates in San Diego and the new guidance for schoolchildren: if you don't want to wear a mask, you have the option to stay home. "There are a lot of troubled kids who are looking for reasons to not come to school," he says. "You're giving them the easiest one. Don't wear a mask, send me home. That's not good for them. They need school."

Prasad's bottom line[19]: "To justify continued masking of schoolkids—with no end date in sight—we have to prove that masks benefit kids." A trio of researchers led by infectious disease specialist Marjery Smelkinson has failed to find that proof, in part because children don't wear masks the way mannequins do.[20] I mean, they're kids, right?

Leaving mask mechanics aside, policies that mandate their use don't seem to have much benefit (not to mention pissing off a good portion of the population), as documented in Ian Miller's book *Unmasked: The Global Failure of COVID Mask Mandates*.[21] Even Monica Gandhi, Prasad's colleague at UCSF and a prominent mask advocate in the first year of the pandemic, was "able to reevaluate the data as we go along" and conclude that mask mandates don't make a significant difference in transmission.[22]

That's why Prasad looks upon mask mandates with a wary eye: in the real world, the only world that interests him, the math just doesn't work out. He likens the mandates to extreme weight loss plans[18]: "A diet that told you to eat just two carrots a day would theoretically result in dramatic weight loss. In practice, such a regimen could starve you of nutrients that your body requires." What's more, "overly strict diets often result in no weight loss at all, because nobody can stick to them." It's what public health types so often forget: the real world ain't the EPA laboratory in Chapel Hill.

Pragmatists like Prasad look beyond aerosol dynamics and mask filtration properties. They consider how mask mandates affect people, communities, and societies: the mask wars on Twitter, the showdowns in department stores, the flight attendants who kick families off planes because their two-year-old can't keep a mask on. All that sound and fury. And for what? At best, a modest decline or delay in transmission?

In Prasad's view, the CDC had the perfect opportunity to wean the public from masks after the vaccines arrived—especially the cloth masks advocated at the time: "It was the logical stopping point, and it could allow us to save face."[23] (Whether intended or not, the pun works brilliantly.) Having missed the moment, we may "find ourselves in mask wars for years to come."

Some people are fine with that. Just as we wear bras and underpants, they argue, we need to grow up and embrace masks as a fixture of the new normal. But there's a reason masks have become a flashpoint in free societies: they hinder our humanity in a way that bras and underpants do not. The human species has evolved to respond to faces and voices, and masks constrict these basic channels of communication. A simple smile at the cash register can brighten a day. An exchange of pleasantries at a coffee shop can jump-start a friendship or even a long-term romance—I've seen it happen more than once. Such interactions don't unfold organically in a masked world.

Likewise, many experts on pediatric development have warned that masking children for years on end impedes language acquisition, social and emotional engagement, learning, and mental health.[24] "Masks especially muffle high-frequency sounds in speech," says Lynda Gibbons, the director of Speech-Language and Audiology Canada.[25] For the one in 10 students with a language disorder and one in five with hearing loss, this muffling effect can stop communication in its tracks. "As usual with COVID, we are further disadvantaging high-risk children."

If carried forward indefinitely, masking hinders the full expression of our sociality. It conditions us to see other people as disease vectors, each fleeting interaction a loaded gun. As Prasad puts it, masking in perpetuity risks "turning us into a nation of panicked people constantly overreacting to cases, and constantly obsessed about one's Covid risk while ignoring all others."[26] It's what Prasad calls long pandemic—"taking excessive precautions that ultimately won't prevent the virus but will damage [people's] mental health and their societal interactions."[27]

Perhaps even our physical health. After all, humans and viruses have tangoed together for millions of years, and an obsession with avoiding infection could upset an evolutionary balance that runs deeper than we can currently fathom. "Our knowledge of immunology and the body is so primitive we should not conclude that avoiding [viral infection] is good for us," Prasad notes.[28] "If we got fewer infections, what would that mean for auto-immunity for cancer? We have no clue."

Remember the hygiene hypothesis? First proposed in 1989, the idea gained currency when scientists discovered that children raised in farms, where they got down and dirty with pigs and worms and black earth, had significantly lower rates of asthma and allergies.[29,30] The researchers postulated that too much sanitizing and germ avoidance, practices more common in the cities of developed nations, may rob children's immune systems of important training. While not conclusively proven, the hypothesis has earned the medical community's respect and continues to spur investigations. Prasad's takeaway: "We have no idea if we would actually live longer or healthier lives trying to dodge seasonal runny noses and coughs."

That's it: we don't know. In the meantime, Prasad is here to offer context, balance and perspective—precious commodities in an era of absolutes—with generous helpings of humor on the side. And I don't know about you, but a respected member of the medical community who dares use the F-word in a public forum has me on-side right off the bat.

DANGER, CAUTION AHEAD: ZEB JAMROZIK
AND MARK CHANGIZI

A bundance of caution. The expression dropped into the
zeitgeist in the spring of 2020 and became a grab-and-go
justification for Covid restrictions. "Out of an abundance
of caution," a Toronto school closed for a week after an itinerant
staff member tested positive.[1] "Out of an abundance of caution,"
the U.S. Department of Agriculture advised people with Covid to
keep a distance from their pets.[2] "Out of [an] abundance of caution,"
Singapore mandated a quarantine period for incoming travelers
who had antibodies after recovering from Covid, on the chance they
were harboring a new variant.[3] "Out of an abundance of caution,"
the Biden administration issued new travel bans in answer to the
Omicron variant.[4]

The phrase has a lofty ring to it, connoting wisdom and restraint.
*Fools rush in where angels fear to tread. Better safe than sorry.
An ounce of prevention.* It reflects the crisis-management approach
known as the precautionary principle, a.k.a. "just in case." In public
health, the precautionary principle asserts that, when a new threat has
the potential to cause serious harm, we must get a jump on prevention
even if considerable scientific uncertainty surrounds the threat.[5] In
a nutshell: when the stakes are high, you don't roll the dice.

The principle dates back to the 1970s, when politicians invoked the German concept of *Vorsorge*—literally "pre-concern"—to justify tougher environmental measures.[6] It found its way into the 1992 Rio declaration,[7] which states: "In order to protect the environment, the precautionary approach shall be widely applied by States according to their capabilities. Where there are threats of serious or irreversible damage, lack of full scientific certainty shall not be used as a reason for postponing cost-effective measures to prevent environmental degradation."

Over the years, the precautionary principle seeped into public health policy, and when Covid came along it seemed like just the right compass to follow. The virus was tearing through the world and our leaders didn't have time to debate the fine points, so they threw up a cloud of mitigation measures based on "just in case." Just in case plexiglass barriers help stop the spread. Just in case the park bench harbors the virus. Just in case Jane walks past Joe and gives it to him. It can't hurt, right?

It can, actually. The precautionary principle uses the worst-case scenario, rather than the most probable scenario, as a basis for creating policies. (And as we've seen with Covid, people often end up confusing the two.) Such policies are blunt and brutish. They require extreme societal disruptions that, over time, may cause more harm than they prevent.

With three years of hindsight behind us, we can ask ourselves: Did we take caution too far with Covid? Zeb Jamrozik, an infectious disease ethicist based in Melbourne, maintains that we did. "What happened was an *abuse* of the precautionary principle," he told me when we chatted on Zoom. "Our leaders used the principle to justify shutting down the world, without fully considering the dangers of doing that. They looked at the worst-case scenario for the virus, but not for the shutdowns. It's an irony of sorts."

Covid may be the most flagrant example of misapplied caution in a pandemic, but it isn't the first one. A post-mortem report on the strategies to contain the H5N1 and A(H1N1) viruses, published in the 2011 Bulletin of the WHO,[8] maintained that "worst-case thinking replaced balanced risk assessment. In both pandemics of fear, the exaggerated claims of a severe public health threat stemmed primarily from disease advocacy by influenza experts. [There is] no reason for believing that a proportional and balanced response would risk lives."

Historian Jesse Kauffman compares the global response to Covid to the advice generals gave President Kennedy during the Cuban missile crisis: "Nuke them first. Better safe than sorry. It's amazing how much misery and harm has been done by a 'better safe than sorry' mindset."[9]

The "precautionary" shutdowns left a trail of missed cancer surgeries,[10] lost livelihoods, and mental health struggles in their wake. Some of our youngest people, lacking the tools to navigate this strange new world, attempted to take their own lives.[11] As for the old people we were supposedly protecting, U.K. oral historian Tessa Dunlop, who talks to old women for a living, concluded that the restrictions dehumanized them "to the point that many no longer wanted to live."[12] Not only did we rob Peter to pay Paul, but in many cases Paul didn't even want our money.

Why did the policymakers not anticipate any of this? Should it not be obvious that shutting down society can lead to great harm? When I put the question to Jamrozik, he noted that "a pandemic doesn't encourage long-term thinking. There's a virus and people want to make it go away, so that's where they put their focus." And many believed, more or less, that flattening the curve would solve the problem. "They weren't prepared for the idea that a pandemic is a long game, so they didn't look far ahead enough."

In fact, the costs of abusing precaution may take years to come to light. As a case in point, the precautionary principle led the Japanese government to shut down most of its nuclear power plants after the Fukushima accident in 2011. In a paper called "Be Cautious with the Precautionary Principle,"[13] three economists made the case that the policy increased electricity costs, making heating less affordable to many people, which ultimately resulted in more excess deaths than those from the accident itself.

It's the law of unintended consequences, which John Ioannidis warned about on March 17, 2020[14]: "We don't know how long social distancing measures and lockdowns can be maintained without major consequences to the economy, society, and mental health. Unpredictable evolutions may ensue, including financial crisis, unrest, civil strife, war, and a meltdown of the social fabric."

Not to mention a widening of the equality gap. "I try to think at a global level," Jamrozik told me. "From an ethical standpoint, the worst types of decisions are those that widen social, educational and health inequalities across the world."

Which is exactly what happened. "The poorest of the poor have become poorer," Jamrozik says in a must-watch video interview with Vinay Prasad.[15] The list goes on: food insecurity in developing countries, major disruptions in TB, malaria and HIV programs, more child weddings... Some experts have also suggested that prolonged collective shielding from pathogens could make future epidemics more likely—a phenomenon known as "immunity debt."[16]

Jamrozik would like to see public health return to its roots of weighing benefits against harms. These harms include the loss of the freedoms we all took for granted before Covid—freedoms "so normal that nobody thought they needed protection." In our mad scramble toward safety, we forgot that "there are also benefits to freedom, not just for individuals but for society." That's why pandemic strategists have traditionally advised the least restrictive measures possible for the shortest possible time.

Covid turned that well-worn template on its head. "Least restrictive possible" wasn't going to fly when Twitter warriors were screaming that "people will die" if toddlers took off their masks at Chuck E. Cheez.

Jamrozik also objects to framing restrictions as emanations of the virus itself, rather than policy choices. I know just what he's talking about—all those media headlines announcing that "surging cases leads colleges to switch to remote" or "new variant pushes cities back to mask mandates." The wording always feels disingenuous to me: *Hey, don't blame us politicians, it's the virus making these decisions.*

Um, no. There is no gravitational force that causes a geography class to move to Zoom when cases reach a certain level. And I've never known a variant to strap a mask on someone's face. As Jamrozik points out, "we had choices about what to do. *People* decided to implement these things."[15] People, not viruses.

People likewise chose to "moralize the microbe," to use Jamrozik's inspired phrasing. In a paper called "Moralization and Mismoralization in Public Health,"[17] he and co-author Steven Kraaijeveld argue against turning the transmission of an airborne respiratory virus, especially an unusually transmissible one like SARS-Cov-2, into a moral failing: "Unless one is willing to dedicate one's life to the avoidance of Covid—and even then—there is no deeper sense in which one can realistically have control over getting infected with endemic respiratory viruses." As for people who engage in so-called higher-risk behaviors, like going to bars or concerts, can we justifiably heap moral blame on them when "everyone stands to be infected in the long run, including more cautious and risk-averse people?"

The world chose the precautionary principle to deal with Covid, but the choice didn't drop down from the sky. We could have made different choices, and people like Jamrozik believe they would have served us better. We could, for example, have treated young people more fairly. "How do you compensate children for missing two years of school? How do you compensate young people for missing out on pivotal milestones?" Jamrozik says he's "still waiting for that check from boomers to youth." (As a boomer myself, I'm happy to oblige. Just tell me where to send the check.)

Caution makes sense—except when it doesn't. When a threat becomes less acute, we need to set the precautionary principle aside and reach for a more balanced approach—like the principle of proportionality, which states that policies must be "proportional to the good that can be achieved and the harm that may be caused."[18] This principle pushes us to stretch our ethical muscles beyond the reflex to hide from a single threat. It insists we put the social costs of an intervention under a microscope.

Pandemics give us only bad choices. But if we keep a steady focus on proportionality, we can make them a little less bad. "We need to have a way of stopping those interventions eventually," Jamrozik says. "We need a way of saying, OK, it's over now. People can go back to being more free."

While the idea of trade-offs, of accepting *any* number of deaths, has made many people bristle during Covid, Jamrozik reminds us that "we can't optimize for everything. We need to have a conversation as a society about what we're willing to tolerate." It's a tough conversation. But then, he's an ethicist—tough is his playground.

* * *

The field of ethics has obvious relevance to pandemic management. But what about cognitive science? One of the most intriguing interdisciplinary fields to emerge in recent years, cog-sci brings together psychology, computer science, neuroscience, linguistics and philosophy. I don't know a single cognitive scientist that I dislike. (And I know a few, my son having majored in the field.)

What might a cognitive scientist have to say about Covid? If it's Mark Changizi, quite a lot. A theoretical cognitive scientist and assistant professor at the Rensselaer Polytechnic Institute in New York, Changizi is known for his hypotheses and theories about optical illusions, speech, music, red-green vision in primates, and—wait for it—pruney fingers.[19] A Renaissance man, to be sure.

When Covid hit, Changizi climbed down from his tower and dove into the Twitter trenches, where his witty jabs at the cognoscenti endeared him to me right off the bat. Like this one: "If you fancy yourself an intellectual, and yet showed no skepticism to the greatest suspension of civil rights in the West in a generation, then maybe you're not."[20]

In analyzing a complex situation, "we cognitive scientists tend to look at the social dynamics at play," Changizi told me when I caught him on the phone, adding that "pandemics are especially challenging because humans are wired to fear cooties, even more so than tornadoes or locusts. When there's a tornado, people naturally pull together to get through it. In a pandemic, people start treating each other as lepers."

As a big-picture thinker, Changizi approached the pandemic not just as an epidemiological puzzle, but as a complex social ecosystem with a bunch of moving parts pushing against each other. It baffled him that so many leaders focused on just one of these parts—the virus part—and presumed they could press pause on everything else[21]: "We learned that people actually believe that you can 'freeze' the economy, the economy has little relation to health, there's no large apocalyptic risks with stopping the economy, suspending civil rights en masse is no big deal, and stop fussing about 'freedom' like a kid."

Like Jamrozik, Changizi has deep reservations about the precautionary principle, at least the way it's been used during Covid. As he sees it, the Covid overlords not only abused the principle, but misunderstood it completely. "The precautionary principle is intended to protect us against new untested policies, medications, or technology," he explained to me. "We have a tendency to hurt ourselves with our hubris, and the precautionary principle acts as a braking mechanism."

This means the burden of proof should rest on the people introducing an untested policy, not on those opposing it. In the case of Covid, lockdown skeptics simply represent the status quo—the way societies have managed pandemics in the past—and should not have to defend their position. Ditto for mask mandates. If school administrators want mask mandates and parents don't, the burden of gathering evidence ought to fall on the administrators, not the parents. "I'm not slamming the restrictions themselves, just arguing about where the burden of evidence should lie."

The evidence to justify the lockdowns never materialized. The untested policy was simply declared scientific and inviolable, no questions allowed. Scientists and public health experts who presented alternatives, like the Great Barrington Declaration or the UK's Time For Recovery, were booed off the stage.

As expected from someone with a doctorate in applied mathematics and computer science, Changizi has a lot to say about risk. At the start of the pandemic, "all the publications were conflating case fatality rate with infection fatality rate, which is much lower," he told me. "So people were walking around thinking they had a five-percent risk of dying of Covid, regardless of heir age or health status. Once this gets embedded in people's minds, it's hard to get it out. So people kept overestimating the risks."

Several surveys bear out this claim. In July 2020, the Covid-19 Opinion Tracker survey asked a representative sample of adults in six countries: "How many people in your country have died of coronavirus?" US respondents estimated 9%, 220 times higher than the actual figure, while German respondents overshot by a factor of 300.[22] A Franklin-Templeton-Gallup (FTG) survey of 35,000 US adults found an equally dramatic gap between perception and reality: on average, respondents estimated the share of COVID-19 deaths from people under 25 at 8%—80 times higher than the actual figure of 0.1%.[23] (There's either something wrong with people's brains or the Covid risk communicators didn't do their job, and I know which way I'm voting.)

"It became a tribal thing, at least in the US," Changizi told me. "You signal your membership to a political tribe by your perceptions of Covid. If you're a Democrat, you *had* to think it was this very dangerous thing." This divide began early: in a nationally representative survey conducted in April-May 2020, Democrats guessed higher than Republicans on the risk of catching Covid, being hospitalized for it, and dying from it.[24]

Risk tolerance also went sideways. People who, before Covid, had cheerfully accepted the everyday risks of living—a nasty flu going around, a road trip across the country—now declared it irresponsible and unethical to accept any risk above zero. *How would you feel if you stepped out of the house and got Covid? Or worse, gave it to your aunt or your mailman?* Such cheap shots precluded a grownup discussion about risk.

Covid or no Covid, people's risk of dying goes up every year. It sucks, but it's baked into the pie of life, and before Covid we all understood this. As the BBC's Timandra Harkness points out in *UnHerd* magazine,[25] most people don't wake up on their birthday and ponder the statistical reality that they're 9% more likely to die than a year earlier. While acknowledging that willingness to accept risk varies widely in the population—she herself rides motorcycles—Harkness reminds us that living well entails risks for everyone. She would have liked to see Covid handled like motor vehicles—"as a risk that can't be eliminated altogether, but can be mitigated."

It bears noting that public health organizations lean heavily toward risk aversion. Take the CDC, an organization that instructs us never to cook meat without a thermometer and to avoid eating sushi. (That's a no from me, dawg.) Some people feel secure in that framework, while others find it stifling. During Covid, we were all asked to play in the safest sandbox: Reduce your risk by wearing two masks. Reduce your risk by talking softly. Whatever risk-reducing measure you *can* take, you *should* take.

Remember the war on drugs? Covid brought about a war on risk. As Michael Brendan Dougherty points out in the *National Review*,[26] "the war on mitigating risk is endless." You can always throw up a new policy to make it lower. Writing for *Reason* magazine, Robby Soave chafes at this blinkered focus on risk minimization—what he calls Faucism.[27] All that matters is "the calculus of the most risk-averse people: unelected public health experts."

When Jon Karl of ABC News asked Fauci if he thought we would ever reach the point of dropping masks on airplanes, Fauci responded[28]: "I don't think so. I think when you're dealing with a closed space, even though the filtration is good, that you want to go that extra step." This mindset presumes that nothing matters except reducing risk. Seeing faces doesn't matter. Smiling at a flight attendant doesn't matter. Cracking jokes with your seatmate (who could become your spouse, if you play your cards right) doesn't matter. From someone like Fauci, entrusted to oversee a country's well-being, I expected a more capacious world view. In any case, the joke's on him. Every day, more and more people are showing their faces on planes, on trains, on buses, evidently finding enough value in an N95-free life to justify an extra increment of risk.

Changizi says no to an indefinitely masked world for one simple reason, which he repeats nine times (with minor variations) in a short video clip[29]: "Masks cover our f***ing faces." (He bleeped out the first vowel to head off would-be censors.) "Our very identities are in that face, the socioemotional language that we use to communicate," he says. "If you're a normal human being, you know in your bones that how we live with other humans is using those emotional expressions." In the 2022 book *Expressly Human*,[30] Changizi and mathematician Tim Barber argue that the "emotional overtones" conveyed through facial expressions constitute our first and most important language. What we broadcast on our faces can dictate who gets the last slice of pizza or who clinches the multinational business deal (not to mention the poker tournament).

Judging from the global unmasking trend as Covid eases into endemicity, a good portion of the world agrees with Changizi's take on masks. His colleagues on Twitter, not so much: "I've lost all these people I used to follow, all far left, and some went out of their way to attack me," he told me. YouTube and Twitter also cut him off, "confusing opinion with misinformation." Not one to take the censors' verdict lying down, he joined Michael Senger and Daniel Kotzin in an April 2022 civil action suit against Ohio's Department of Health and Human Services.[31] The plaintiffs allege that criticizing government policies does not constitute misinformation and that, to their knowledge, nobody has had their account suspended for exaggerating the risks of Covid. It's a point many people miss: if downplaying a risk counts as misinformation, so too does inflating it, which can cause just as much societal damage.

On the personal front, Changizi has faced "Covid denier" accusations from several family members and friends—a rather curious word choice, when one considers that he began poring over Covid data while the Diamond Princess cruise ship was still idling off-shore. He carries on with enviable equanimity, which he attributes to having "the right kind of personality for this sort of thing. Like a duck, I let the droplets roll off."

Near the end of our phone chat, he tossed off one of his ideas for a future book: "Aloof: how not giving a damn maximizes your creativity." I suggested he start writing it, stat. A lot of us counter-narrative types could use some tips on growing thicker skins.

CHILDREN FIRST: LUCY MCBRIDE
AND JENNIFER SEY

I f there's one aspect of the Covid response that boils my blood, it's how we've treated our children. Using children as human shields to protect grownups? Really?

Was it necessary to pump them up with fear so they worried that one wrong move would kill their bubba or nonna? Was it necessary to separate them from their peers, both in and out of school? To keep them from the swings and monkey bars in the park? From playing their favorite team sports? Was it necessary to deprive them, for months that turned into years, of the irretrievable moments and milestones of childhood?

I'm familiar with the opposing argument: if we use children to protect their parents, the benefit circles back to the kids. But school is just one of myriad sources of transmission, and evidently not an especially potent one.[1] Parents and other household dwellers can just as easily catch the virus at the supermarket, the coffee shop, or Walmart. A strong rationale for keeping schools closed after commerce reopened never materialized. And after the vaccines arrived, using children as human shields lost its last shred of moral justification. If the vaccines worked even half as well as advertised, we could give children their lives back. We could certainly give them their schools back.

That's not what happened, though—at least not in North America. In Europe, many countries kept schools open after the first shutdown, leaning on evidence suggesting that closing schools wouldn't make a large difference in controlling the virus—but *would* set back children's learning.[2] Canada and the US took the opposite route, with a merry-go-round of open/shut/open/shut edicts that kept children and their parents guessing every morning.

Even when schools were operating, the arcane restrictions sucked the life out of the experience. Children were told not to talk during lunch[3] and to wear masks while playing their musical instruments— or in the case of wind instruments, to take it outside.[4] Some school districts advised them to limit the time spent in the bathroom.[5] (I cannot begin to understand the thinking behind that piece of advice, and I'm not sure I want to.) Schoolchildren returning to class in the Alaskan city of Anchorage were expected to mask up and kneel on the floor for hours, without any art, physical activity and recess to look forward to.[6]

None of this was OK with US doctor Lucy McBride, who began writing about the mental health impact of the Covid response early on in the pandemic. What started as emails to her own patients blossomed into a newsletter that wouldn't stop growing,[7] her trademark humor shining through in such post titles as "I'll have what she's having" and "Make nuance great again."

Princeton, Harvard Medical School, Cambridge, Johns Hopkins: McBride's CV makes garden-variety overachievers look like goof-offs, never mind career zig-zaggers like me. (My own brush with Harvard lasted just four months, leaving my poor mother to pivot from "she's in graduate school at Harvard" to "she's temping as a secretary in Montreal." It's a wonder she ever forgave me.)

McBride's philosophy of health—mental and physical health cannot be separated—drives her style of care, as captured in the self-introduction on her website[7]: "Hello, I am a physician who believes in treating the whole person." This holistic framework shouldn't just disappear during a pandemic, she says. On the contrary, "health comes from reducing total harms and balancing risks—not trying to eliminate something that we cannot eliminate."[8]

For all her passion and wit, McBride's message wasn't getting through to the decision makers. Even after life returned to near-normal for adults, schoolchildren labored under a mountain of restrictions. One positive case could send a whole classroom home,[9] a domino effect that left a quarter of a million UK children out of school in one particular week in 2021.[10]

The zeal to enforce the rules sometimes veered into outright cruelty. In Ontario's Peel District, if a child was "exposed" to a Covid-positive classmate, health authorities instructed parents to keep the child in a separate room from the rest of the household for two full weeks.[11] (In the Before Times, we called this solitary confinement.) On a cold day in November 2021, a four-year-old boy who developed cold symptoms at school was isolated in an outdoor shed and developed hypothermia.[12] "He couldn't talk, shivering like mad, hands red raw," his mother said. "They even made him eat his lunch outside, no toys, no games, nothing."

McBride had enough. At the beginning of 2022, she and a handful of other physicians and scientists launched The Urgency of Normal, an advocacy group to help school administrators, teachers, parents, and students make informed choices around Covid.[13] The group took the position, backed by studies on child learning loss and mental-health deterioration, that the kids were not all right. They argued that Covid posed a negligible risk to children, especially in the Omicron era. They urged school administrators to make childhood normal again—not the anemic new normal, but the exuberant, 2019-style normal. Their ask: unrestricted curricular and extra-curricular activities, masks optional, and pre-pandemic quarantine norms: if you're sick, stay home.[14]

Detractors countered that Covid *can* harm children and that suicide does *not* pose a greater risk to them. They accused the group of cherry-picking data to make their points. Well, sure. We all cherry-pick. Show me someone who claims she doesn't and you've shown me a liar. (Source: 28 years as a writer for the medical-industrial complex.) But that's almost beside the point. What often gets missed, in these battles of the cherries, is that the data don't capture everything important. A questionnaire may determine that a child is "not at risk of suicide" or "not clinically depressed," but it doesn't tell us how much happier the child would be in a world that didn't burden him with full-day masking and silent lunches.

The sacred experiences of childhood, like slumber parties and school plays are group tag games during recess, are no less important for evading our measurement tools. A bird in a cage may feel content if life behind bars is all it's ever known. But by keeping it in that cage, we're still cutting it off from a better life, still doing it an injustice.

That's why McBride felt dismayed when her 20-year-old son's university announced its decision to pivot to remote learning in early 2022. "I'm sad for my son," she told Vinay Prasad in a January 2022 interview.[15] "Kids need school like they need water, they need their peers, that's how they develop, that's how they grow." Even if the closure didn't threaten her son's mental equilibrium, they deprived him of the types of experiences that shape lives.

Nobody can accuse McBride of minimizing the pandemic. In every article she writes, every interview she gives, she acknowledges the pain caused by the virus itself. But this reality should not preclude a discussion about managing fear and risk. When fear takes over people's brains, we default to "primitive thought patterns including black-and-white thinking [and] catastrophizing," she writes in *The Atlantic*.[16] And when children see adults "processing endless loops of *what if* thinking, [they] become worried and depressed too."

Leaving fear aside, "fixating on a single threat to children's health can keep us from recognizing their broad human needs." Independence, for one. McBride recalls a rainy evening when her teenage son, a new driver, asked for her car keys so he could make it on time to his babysitting job. Couldn't he walk instead? Cue the adolescent eyeroll. "I let him use the car, but not before peppering him with reminders to be careful and to use the headlights and wipers. Shielding my kids from danger is a fundamental instinct; tolerating risk for them is hard emotional work."

And what about long Covid? As the mortality risk from the virus, already very low in children, continues to recede, some parents have pivoted to long Covid as a reason to keep restrictions going. Here again, context is everything: "Whenever I see posts about long Covid in kids, I wonder why we aren't talking about long depression. Long anxiety. Long addiction," says University of Michigan psychology professor Lilia Cortina.[17] "Many mental illnesses pose a greater threat to youth than Covid, and follow them throughout their lives." It's also hard to miss the irony in restricting one's life to avoid disease complications that could... restrict one's life.

If all you care about is slowing the spread, these arguments won't hold much sway. But if you believe, as McBride does, that health means more than absence of Covid and that children's well-being comes first, your heart may bleed along with hers.

* * *

Imagine getting offered a million-dollar severance package and saying, "nah, I'm good." If someone offered *me* a million dollars, I would immediately think of all the trips to Brazil I could take. Or the waterfront land I could buy in the Niagara region. But I digress.

Jennifer Sey got the offer in early 2022. It had a catch, though: she would need to keep quiet about her reason for leaving Levi Strauss, the company that had employed her for 23 years. "I made the decision to leave on my own, on my own accord and on my own terms so I could speak freely," Sey said to CBNC after refusing the offer.[18] "Accepting a package to stay silent would fly in the face of that."

An Olympic-track gymnast in adolescence, Sey joined Levi Strauss in 1999 as an assistant marketing manager and, over the next 11 years, worked her way up to Levi's brand president. With the 2008 publication of a memoir focusing on the dark side of elite gymnastics, she also found her voice as a children's advocate.[19]

When Covid hit, Sey's mama-bear instincts kicked in. "I felt—and still do—that the draconian policies would cause the most harm to those least at risk," she wrote in a guest post for independent journalist Bari Weiss.[20] Armed with a mountain of data on the harmful effects of school closures, she spoke out on legacy and social media, organized rallies, and even contacted her mayor. Like everyone who questioned the Covid orthodoxy, she was "called a racist—a strange accusation given that I have two black sons—a eugenicist, and a Q-Anon conspiracy theorist."

The drive to shut down schools came not just from governments, but from teachers. When the Chicago Teachers Union voted not to report to schools until a more robust testing policy was in place, the city's mayor, Lori Lightfoot, was left to beg teachers to return[21]: "I'm urging teachers. Show up to your schools. Your kids need you." To be fair, the public school teachers were only behaving as the institutional fear campaign had programmed them to behave. If you create a monster, don't blame it for doing monster things.

One thing kept bugging Sey: If Covid posed such a risk to children and their communities, if public schools *had* to shut down, why were private schools staying open? Given the demographics of private schools, Sey saw the double standard as "classist and racist."[20]

In fact, not all public schools bought into the panic. In one of my favorite Covid articles, published in *The Atlantic*, Carrie McKean describes how her West Texas community kept its schools open throughout 2021.[22] Not just school, but *normal* school: kids sitting where they want at lunch, playing with who they want at recess, acting in school plays and attending holiday parties, complete with pizza and sugar cookies.

First, you decide that kids belong in school. That's the title of McKean's article and the spirit that drove the local schools to stay open. "In my community, we understand that keeping kids in class is partly a matter of will," she writes. While letting children go about their lives risks increasing viral spread, "burdening children mostly for adults' sake is a moral judgment too—one that no community should make lightly, especially if adults can take other precautions."

It's a matter of priorities. *First, you decide.*

Sey made her own decision. After spending three decades of her life in California, she moved from San Francisco to Denver so her kindergartner could attend school. She wasn't alone: in the US, 1.5 million children left their existing schools in the 2020-21 school year, switching to private schools that stayed open or to home schooling.[23]

Sey continued to speak out. Her employer told her she could expect to become Levi's next CEO—if she stopped talking about the school stuff. Sorry, no deal. Tensions escalated when she appeared on Fox news. (If left-leaning news outlets won't give you a hearing, what's a liberal activist to do?) Social media warriors entered the fray, threatening to boycott the company if they didn't fire Sey, and the million-dollar severance package soon followed. In return for turning it down, "I get to keep my voice."[20]

Let us imagine an alternate universe in which Covid presents a real danger to children, like an airborne Ebola virus. In such a scenario, we can safely presume that both McBride and Sey would take a different tack. Neither one takes children's safety lightly, and McBride knows full well that "nobody wants their child to be sick and suffering."[15] But Covid isn't Ebola. The risk of serious harms from Covid is "really, really small in kids," she says.[24] Small, but not zero—and that's where so many people get stuck. "We can't take the risk down to zero, and nor should we, because taking it down to zero has enormous costs."

If a report from the National Center for Education Statistics is any indication,[25] the loss in learning was every bit as dramatic as people like Sey had feared. Between 2020 and 2022, 9-year-old children's standardized reading and math scores dropped by 5 and 7 points, respectively, representing the largest decline in reading since 1990 and the first-ever downturn in math. The greatest losses occurred among minorities and the poor. How could it be otherwise? When you don't have tutors or stay-at-home parents to help you through a long division problem, never mind food in your stomach, interruptions in your scholastic routine are bound to set you back more, impacting not only your earning potential but your future health. "There is nothing more fundamental to our good health than education," says Richard Schabas, formerly Ontario's Chief Medical Officer of Health. "And to educate children, schools have to be open."[26]

We can now add child abuse to the costs of the school closures. A September 2022 editorial in *BMJ Paediatrics Open* presented strong evidence that lockdowns significantly increased child abuse globally,[27] leading the authors to conclude that "it is ethically problematic to push children towards abuse in the name of public health." Well, yes. People like Sey were warning about such ethical breaches from the start.

In a letter to the *British Medical Journal*,[28] Aodnan Breathnach, a consultant medical microbiologist at St George's University Hospitals, frames up the moral calculus used to justify interrupting children's lives. The debate about Covid "has tended to overlook ethical questions about who benefits and who pays," he writes. "We would not compel a young person to donate a kidney to an elderly relative, or to have any medical procedure that was not in their own best interests, but public health interventions seem to be in a different moral category: we are happy to force our young to sacrifice their economic, social, and psychological freedoms so that the older generation can live a bit longer."

We have failed our young, but the "unfortunate but necessary" narrative has constrained people from calling the elephant by its name. Following is a short list of quotes (lightly edited for brevity) from some people who took the chance.

Adults, collectively, are supposed to protect children, and not the other way around. Sadly, coronavirus seems to have put paid even to this most basic moral certainty. It has become acceptable for adults to demand that children act to protect them. It is time to stop. Adults must once more assume responsibility for the next generation.

— JOANNA WILLIAMS,
author and journalist, writing for *The Telegraph*[29]

The treatment of children during the COVID era has been a moral stain on the profession... I believe that schools today are continuing to psychologically harm students by indoctrinating them into a lie—the lie that in school they are fundamentally unsafe and that only strict obedience to arbitrary authority can protect them.

— ALEX GUTENTAG,
writer and former public school teacher, writing for *Tablet*[30]

The young have undertaken enormous personal sacrifices to protect their elders [and] maybe it is time for the older generation to return the favour. Locking down society indefinitely to protect the fearful is not an option.

— STEPHEN COLLINS,
correspondent, writing for *The Irish Times*[31]

The decision to give young people the message that "you are not a priority, first we have to take care of older people" hurts everyone. A whole generation now believes, "our interests as a group, our wishes and needs, did not count."

— KLAUS HURRELMAN,
public health professor, in an interview with *The Guardian*[32]

Kids have been treated so unfairly it's hard to know where to begin. Pandemic policies harmed them by not only shuttering their schools, but also taking away the very things that brought them joy. This treatment of children as nothing more than vectors of disease is cruel.

— LILIA CORTINA,
psychology professor, in an interview with Vinay Prasad[33]

Hyperfocus on the avoidance of disease leaves less time for play, sports, music, art, togetherness and the outdoors, all of which can make childhood healthy if not magical. People count on us physicians to not forget what health actually is.

— TRACY HOEG,
epidemiologist, writing for Bari Weiss[34]

When we look at the Covid-19 pandemic through the lens of history, I believe it will be clear that we betrayed our children. The risks of this pandemic were never to them, but they were forced to carry the burden of it. It's enough.

— STACEY LANCE,
public school teacher, writing for Bari Weiss[35]

A PLEA FOR FREEDOM: MATTHEW CRAWFORD
AND LIONEL SHRIVER

Matthew Crawford likes fast cars, sharp turns, the feel of motor oil on his hands. Rounding a corner in a tricked-out Volkswagen. The pavement under his motorcycle, wind on his face. The blind faith of driving off-road, of "throwing oneself into the world with hope" when the way forward isn't clear.[1]

An American philosophy professor and writer who doubles as an electrician and mechanic, Crawford has little patience for people who can spout Foucault but don't know what to do with a wrench. His bestselling book *Shop Class as Soulcraft*, published in 2009, argues that the spirit grows on a diet of manual labor and that fixing a leaky faucet trumps Ivory Tower pontificating any day[2]: "The tradesman must reckon with the infallible judgment of reality, where one's failures or shortcomings cannot be interpreted away." Not one to take life with Zen-like resignation, he describes his spiritual trek as "the motherfucker process."

Crawford's book *Why We Drive: On Risk, Freedom, and Taking Back Control,*[1] which came out in the middle of 2020 but presumably took its shape before the pandemic broke out, celebrates the freedom of the open road and meditates on what we lose when we eliminate all risk from driving. He argues that sharing the risks of the road bonds people to each other and fears that self-driving cars will rob driving of its social component.

You kinda figure that a guy like that would grow restless during a pandemic that declares risk unacceptable and freedom expendable.

Right on cue, Crawford emerged from his tool shed in May 2020 to write an article on "The Dangers of Safetyism" for *UnHerd*.[3] "There appears to be a feedback loop wherein the safer we become, the more intolerable any remaining risk appears," he reflects in the piece. "At the level of bureaucratic grasping, we can note that emergency powers are seldom relinquished once the emergency has passed. Together, these dynamics make up a kind of ratchet mechanism that moves in only one direction, tightening against the human spirit."

Spurred by a moralizing media and a need for peer approval, with perhaps some genuine public-spiritedness mixed in, the laptop class threw itself into the safety net offered by the public health apparatus. Deference to expert authority, a habit inculcated in the knowledge economy, came naturally to what Crawford calls "the meritocrats who staff the managerial layer of society." They turned "trust the experts" into a slogan, branding anyone with the temerity to "do their own research" as a hillbilly.

Crawford casts a jaundiced eye on the safety-*uber-alles* culture that, already prevalent before the pandemic, "is having a triumphal moment just now because of the virus." Having experienced the deep rewards of taking calculated risks, he laments that public health "has claimed authority to sweep aside whole domains of human activity as reckless, and therefore illegitimate."

Among those who work in the "economy of *things*," on the other hand, Crawford finds greater skepticism toward what he calls the safety-industrial complex. "I am regularly in welding supply stores, auto parts stores and other light-industry venues," he reports in *UnHerd*.[3] "Nobody is wearing masks in these places. They are very small businesses: an environment largely free of the moral fashions and corresponding knowledge claims that set the tone in large organisations."

I've had the same experience. Without exception, the tradespeople who passed through my home during the height of the pandemic had a relaxed attitude toward the protocols. Nobody can convince me they "don't care" about their loved ones—the fierce pride in their voices when they talk about their children puts that idea to rest—but they brought a sense of perspective to the pandemic that I've rarely observed in the so-called knowledge class. (Apologies for the generalizations. Just calling it as I observed it.) Perhaps spending your workday lifting heavy things and measuring angles and fitting intricate parts together gives you a mathematical feel for life, for its risks and burdens and sheer unpredictability, that you don't get from Googling Worldometer stats or doomscrolling Eric Topol tweets.

"Covid is just nature doing its thing, trying to correct an imbalance in the world," our handyman, who keeps rescue ferrets in his home, told me while moving the hinges on my office door from the right to the left side. "There's only so much we can do about that."

Most people in mainstream Western society grew up with large doses of freedom. We understood the trade-off—more freedom, more risk—but wouldn't have it any other way. Then along comes the pandemic, and public sentiment does an about-face. As Crawford notes, to stand on the side of safety during Covid is to "don a bullet-proof halo of public-spiritedness." Safety becomes the all-consuming preoccupation and freedom gets branded as right-wing stupidity. Freedom to take a walk on the beach? Stop killing the vulnerable! Freedom to earn a living? The economy will recover! "Your right to get your hair streaked doesn't trump my grandfather's right to life," shout the Twitterati, turning freedom into a caricature.

"Muh freedumb," one of the earliest memes to surface during the pandemic, became code for a stock character—a tattooed man wearing camo gear and a baseball cap, spewing viral particles while yelling about his rights. The memes kept coming: "Warning, cliff ahead: keep driving, freedom fighter." "Personal freedom is the preoccupation of adult children." And after the Canadian truckers' convoy of January 2022: "Freedom is a two-way street—unless you're blocking it with your truck."

They may take our lives but they'll never take our freedom, the iconic battle cry that brought goosebumps to *Braveheart* audiences in 1995, got chewed to bits by the Covid narrative, which spat out the tiresome "stop whining about your freedoms, we're in a pandemic" as a rejoinder. Freedom, for centuries the crowning aspiration of democratic societies, was suddenly demoted to a laughingstock.

In truth, the world's tilt away from freedom began long before Covid. According to data from Freedom House, 2005 was the last year that saw a net increase in global democracy.[4] Every year after that, more countries lost than gained ground. The year 2020 had the worst track record by far, with 73 countries losing democracy points and only 28 raising their score. The Freedom in the World 2021 report[4] called out the pandemic policies as a key culprit: "As Covid-19 spread during the year, governments across the democratic spectrum repeatedly resorted to excessive surveillance, discriminatory restrictions on freedoms like movement and assembly, and arbitrary or violent enforcement of such restrictions by police and nonstate actors."

To Crawford, such tactics represent "a slow-motion desertion of liberal principles of government."[5] The word "liberal" has its roots in the Latin liber, which means free, but the past few decades have seen liberalism turn away from its origins. The object of modern liberalism—to remake man—requires "a highly illiberal form of government" and may explain why the "embrace of illiberal politics has met with so little resistance."

Some will argue that in a pandemic the usual rules don't apply. You confront the threat and worry about freedom later. You must also limit your freedom to protect others. Well, sure. It's something the great majority of people do naturally, without a government dictating their every step.

People have also stated that "you don't have the freedom to infect others." It's time to put that straw man under the knife. For one thing, no sane person seeks the "freedom to infect" any more than a vehicle driver seeks the freedom to slam into pedestrians. It's a disingenuous allegation that warps a simple desire for personal agency into a malevolent impulse. As Jeffrey Tucker says in his book *Liberty or Lockdown*,[6] "no one wants to be sick. No one wants to make others sick unnecessarily. If we understand these two truths, we have the basis for understanding how a free society can deal intelligently with the presence of disease."

Second, the injunction against infecting others loses its moral force when juxtaposed to the "assume everyone has Covid" messaging that prevailed throughout the pandemic. If anyone can be sick at any time, even when feeling perfectly fine, the only way to avoid infecting other people is to stay away from them indefinitely, an obviously unsustainable proposition.

Infecting others is neither a right nor an interdiction—it's simply a reality in a planet shared by humans and contagious microbes. People have always passed colds, flus and other bugs to each other, creating long ribbons of transmission that occasionally caused someone to die. Before Covid, we ascribed this to the victim's frailty. We grieved the loss, but didn't go hunting for a "killer" to blame. It's only since Covid that viral transmission has turned into a crime.

I'm talking about inadvertent transmission, of course. Willfully infecting someone is obviously not cool. Basic courtesy goes a long way here: don't cough on people and don't mingle if you're sick. At the height of a pandemic, you'll want take some extra precautions—and you'll do it quite naturally, for the simple reason that (this bears repeating) *nobody wants to get sick or make others sick unnecessarily*. But if you infect someone anyway, you haven't committed a crime. Sometimes shit just happens.

People also say that "with freedom comes responsibility," and I don't disagree. But a paternalistic government robs us of the opportunity to exercise that very responsibility. When a government takes over our private lives, Crawford argues, we become less kind and more hostile toward each other. Treating people like children also sets up a self-fulfilling prophecy, leading policymakers to conclude that a free society cannot deal with pandemics, despite ample evidence to the contrary from the past century.

As Crawford shrewdly observes, prosocial inclinations arise when we have some agency in managing a shared risk, not when policymakers give us long lists of thou-shalt-nots. Far from inducing a sense of shared purpose, such commandments "erode our readiness to extend to our fellow citizens a presumption of competence and good will."[1] In his book *Gone Viral,* Justin Hart boils the sentiment down to its essence[7]: "Altruism is not a government program."

* * *

If Crawford can be described as an old-fashioned sort of guy, there's nothing of the traditional woman in Lionel Shriver. The acclaimed novelist and journalist started her life as Margaret, a name that fit her about as well as a lace glove on a boxer. Not willing to wait until the age of majority, she swapped her given name for the muscular Lionel at age 15.[8]

An American who has lived in the UK for the better part of her life, Shriver shows none of the compulsion to please and placate ascribed to the feminine gender. Sugar and spice? Making nice? Not her jam. In fact, she loudly and proudly aligns herself with the not-so-nice. "I don't like little perfect people," she told podcaster Ben Domenech in a 2021 interview.[9] "I don't like virtuous people, especially show-off virtuous people. I like wickedness. I like mischief. I like people who break the rules. I like people who question the rules. Who are a little difficult and hard to control. I am a willful person and I admire other willful people."

A woman who likes wickedness? I'm in. And here I must pause to confess that I've been disappointed in my own gender during Covid. As a group, women have displayed markedly less "wickedness" than men, more inclination to comply with the rules without questioning the premises underpinning them. There are obviously lots of exceptions, but this statistical gender gap shows up in survey after survey.[10,11] Shriver serves as a model for women who yearn to make some mischief but may not know how to get started.

Blessed with the confidence to shrug off social disapproval, she lets her intellect roam far and wide. Happily for the rest of us, her intellect loves to roam in caves that few others have the guts to explore—and emerge with deliciously uncomfortable insights. Perhaps this is why *New York Times* reviewer Ruth Franklin has called Shriver the "Cassandra of American Letters," reminding readers that "the curse of Cassandra, after all, was that she told the truth."[12]

In 2003, Shriver wrote the chart-topping book *We Need to Talk about Kevin*, which peers into the minds of a high-school mass murderer and his mother. The description of Kevin soaking his younger sister's eye in acid is, hands down, the most chilling passage I have ever read. This is not a writer who turns away from the darkness.

In 2020, Shriver needed to talk about freedom—or more accurately, about its sudden exit from the world stage. "Across the western world, freedoms that citizens took for granted seven months ago have been revoked at a stroke," she wrote in an October 2020 piece for *The Spectator*.[13] "What we now take for granted is that we walk out of our own front doors only at the government's sufferance." In responding to Covid-19, "there's no aspect of our lives that we've not granted our betters total control over."

Six months later, Shriver was still trying to figure it all out, still shocked at how people "seemed to revel in being ordered about and being told what to do on an absolutely microscopic level"—like being informed they could now hold their mother's hand, but still couldn't hug her.[9] "I would never have thought them capable of such abdication of their civil liberties," she confessed to Domenech.

Ah, so I wasn't imagining it—the way some people *reveled* in this new normal, rather than simply tolerating it. "The old normal is never coming back," they intoned, with an undercurrent of glee that was difficult to miss. While I'm still trying to untangle the psychology behind this smugness, I suspect it has to do with wanting to stick it to the "selfish idiots" who chafed at the micromanagement.

The word "selfish" has been used as a weapon throughout the pandemic, a psychological tactic to get people to fall in line. That wasn't going to work on Shriver, who cheerfully appropriated the epithet in a 2017 article for *The Guardian*[14] called "No Children, Please. We're Selfish." She had no "reason" to opt out of motherhood—at least none that society condones, such as a health condition or heavy caretaking responsibilities. She just didn't want kids: "They would have siphoned too much time away from the writing of my precious books."

In counterpoint to the selfish rule breakers, the rule followers were cast as pandemic heroes. No matter how inhumane or impractical a restriction, those who supported it reaped praise for caring about the "common good," which is...what, exactly? Nobody ever comes forth with a definition. I suspect that Shriver would not define it in the same way as, say, Anthony Fauci or Justin Trudeau.

We would do well to remember that, in an earlier era, important people viewed the sterilization of "defectives" as a benefit to society. When Supreme Court Justice Oliver Wendell Holmes Jr. upheld a 1924 statute supporting the sterilization of "genetically unfit" people, he justified the decision with an appeal to the common good[15]: "It is better for all the world [if] society can prevent those who are manifestly unfit from breeding their kind... Three generations of imbeciles are enough."

Today, the common good has been rebranded as the safest possible world, with freedom positioned as a threat. As Shriver observes in an interview with *Spiked Online*,[16] "freedom is now becoming toxic." Free speech is *verboten* if it hurts others. The right to not feel upset trumps the right to say something upsetting. People are fragile and need their safe spaces.

Shriver has nothing against public health advice. It's public health absolutism she rejects. What concerns her above all is that the events of 2020 will become normalized and erode the liberal democratic values she holds dear. "It's been summarily demonstrated that civil liberties aren't worth the paper constitutions are printed on," she says.[13] "Rights may be rescinded with no warning and without even the fig leaf of parliamentary approval." To get people to comply, "all you have to do is tell them it's for the common good. That's how totalitarianism takes over."

Shriver is not the only luminary to observe that "when you give power away, it's really hard to get it back"—not only because government power seeks to perpetuate itself, but because the public comes to accept and even insist on government protection from "what might be out there." We've watched the Overton window shift in exactly this way over the past three years: both the leaders and the led ratcheting up the safety stakes, forgetting what they're losing in the balance.

That's why some observers of the Covid scene, like German political scientist Ulrike Guerot, view freedom as a non-negotiable right, even in a pandemic. "It is slowly becoming clear to many that freedom is not a fair-weather bonus for calm times, but a principle that must be defended, especially in crisis situations," says Guerot in an interview with the *Welt* newspaper.[17] "Freedom is an inalienable principle, not something that can be allocated and withdrawn depending on the situation."

Freedom desperately needs a comeback from its present incarnation as an indulgent frill. The clownish garments that have draped the word during the pandemic—the silly memes, the hillbilly overtones, the mantle of egoism—have made us lose sight of its essence. Placing a high value on freedom doesn't make us uncaring, any more than a love of mountains makes us indifferent to the sea.

Cherishing freedom doesn't mean we don't wish to protect other people. It simply means we want some agency in our life—and want the same for the people we love.

What people like Crawford and Shriver are trying to tell us is this: if we toss our freedoms into the river, the current will carry them away and may never return them to us. We'll forget they ever existed and will stop asking for them.

In fact, surrender of personal freedom carries the plot of many a dystopian novel. *The Handmaid's Tale, 1984, Fahrenheit 451, The Giver*... What these novels have in common are societies marked by inflexible rules, with extreme punishment for challenging the regime set up by the elite. Safe, lifeless societies. Prisons without bars.

In these novels, the loss of freedom goes unchallenged until an individual or group recognizes a different way to live and inspires others to rise up against the overlords. The rules and roles crumble, leaving the protagonists free to choose their own destinies.

Covid has flung the pendulum very far toward safety, and freedom fighters like Crawford and Shriver warn us that the world will be a smaller and sadder place if it remains stuck there. I am reminded of a magazine article I read many years ago, when the gay community was just finding its feet. The writer suggested that, far from being evolutionary misfires, gay people serve a highly adaptive function within a species that needs both procreators and creators to thrive. I think of people like Crawford and Shriver in the same way. They're here to remind us that we were put on earth not just to stay safe, but to roam free. That freedom gives life its pulse and, pandemic or not, needs a place under the sun.

SOUL SEARCHERS: PAUL KINGSNORTH, DANIEL HADAS, AND ANN BAUER

P aul Kingsnorth's three-part Vaccine Moment series burst onto the blog scene in late 2021. It broke loose from its local confines and circumnavigated the globe. Kingsnorth later compiled the three essays into a booklet, which he lets readers download free of charge on his website.

The series took my breath away, as much for its prose as its ideas. "We live in an apocalyptic time," Kingsnorth writes in part one.[1] "Beneath the arguments about whether or not to take a vaccine that may or may not work safely, glides something older, deeper, slower: something with all the time in the world. Some great spirit whose work is to use these fractured times to reveal to us all what we need to see: things hidden since the foundation of the modern world."

Something older, deeper, slower: something with all the time in the world. Can the guy write, or what?

While ostensibly about vaccines, the series ranges over much broader terrain. It travels across time and space, touching on Leo Tolstoy and Klaus Schwab and historian Christopher Dalton. Underneath the sweeping philosophical observations, we hear the cry of a bewildered soul who no longer sees the world as a welcoming place—certainly not to iconoclastic thinkers like him.

It's not the vaccines themselves that Kingsnorth takes to task, but the societal unrest they set in motion. "The divisions that have opened up in society about the covid vaccines are not really about the covid vaccines at all: they are about what vaccination symbolises in this moment," he reflects. "What it means to be 'vaxxed' or 'unvaxxed', safe or dangerous, clean or dirty, sensible or irresponsible, compliant or independent: these are questions about what it means to be a good member of society, and what society even is, and they are detonating like depth charges beneath the surface of the culture."

A former deputy-editor of *The Ecologist*, Kingsnorth lives in the West of Ireland. His multilayered fiction leans into myth, while his nonfiction covers big-picture themes like environmentalism, globalization, and macro trends that destabilize human societies.[2] His books have won many awards, and literary pundits place him among the British greats of all time. A wide-ranging traveler, Kingsnorth has also made the journey from atheism to Orthodox Christianity, with forays into Buddhism and witchcraft along the way.[3]

His writings lay bare a sensitive, ever-questioning soul, an organism that runs on spirit more than flesh. Like so many of the people featured in this book, he confronts difficult questions without flinching and pokes holes at received wisdom—like the "social contract," which he began questioning long before Covid. "No one ever asked me to sign the social contract," he wrote in *The Guardian* in 2008.[4] "Yet here I am, subject to the will of a state whose checks and balances are increasingly unchecked and unbalanced, and whose 'democratic' machinery is so clogged with patronage and power that my chances of influencing it are close to zero." He chafed at the version of life offered by his government, a life of consumption and conformity, and yearned for "the freedom, and the power, to say no to the Thing."

Then along came Covid culture, a culture more conformist and tribal than anything Kingsnorth had ever witnessed before. No surprise he had a problem with it.

The vaccination drive ramped up the tribalism still further. The new pandemic story had heroes (vaxxed) and villains (unvaxxed) and promised an epic battle that wouldn't end until the bad guys were either jabbed by force or kicked off the island. Ever the champion of liberty, Kingsnorth cried out against the authoritarian streak exposed by the campaign: "In the last month alone I have watched media commentators calling for censorship of their political opponents, philosophy professors justifying mass internment, and human rights lobby groups remaining silent about 'vaccine passports.' I have watched much of the political left transition openly into the authoritarian movement it probably always was, and countless 'liberals' campaigning against liberty. As freedom after freedom has been taken away, I have watched intellectual after intellectual justify it all."

And all this for an intervention that would not and could not end the pandemic. "Amongst the vast flock of contested facts that wheel around this virus like a murmuration of starlings, darkening the skies and addling the mind, one stands out. It is the single fact that blows a cathedral-shaped hole in the strategy being pursued by governments at present, and which offers a glimpse into the crypt. It is the fact that these vaccines, whatever their efficacy in other areas, do not prevent transmission of the virus."

Like a murmuration of starlings, darkening the skies and addling the mind. Just the language is worth the price of admission.

With such thoughts roiling inside him, Kingsnorth faced the personal decision: to vax or not to vax? He landed on no—not so much because of the product itself as the frenzied rhetoric surrounding it. Seb Thirlway, a philosophy researcher who lives in the UK, told me he has "never seen a propaganda campaign like it" in his lifetime. "It seemed to be less about actually vaccinating people than about getting them to perform an action and then insert it into their identity and everyday conversation."

Some people interpreted Kingsnorth's essay as an anti-vax screed, but they're missing the point: it's the vaccine evangelism he's rejecting. In broader terms, his refusal to get vaccinated flows from his rejection of the whole pandemic world view—a world view that erases personal agency and traffics in fear. David French, quoted here in a *Dispatch* article,[5] understands this perfectly: "[For skeptics], excessive fear of COVID is the primary cause of public-health restrictions, and their refusal to take the vaccine is, in some small way, an attempt to model a life unruled by this fear."

My daughter, Tara, drew a similar line when Canada's vaccine campaign ramped up in early 2021. Twenty-four years old at the time, she refused to get vaxxed for several months. While I had no interest in changing her mind, I did want to understand what she was going through. Was she afraid of side effects? *No.* Long-term safety? Fertility issues? *No.*

Finally, on an afternoon in mid-July, Tara informed me that she had received her first Moderna shot that morning.

I texted back: "How are you feeling? Any symptoms?"

"My only symptom is regret."

I didn't have to ask why.

Covid came at an especially bad time for Tara: she was just finishing university and about to enter the world of work. She was also coming into her own as a singer-songwriter. When I attended her last live performance before the pandemic, in a poky bar in Toronto's Kensington Market district, her alt-pop songs crackled with spirit and her voice rang with a newfound confidence.

And then it all ended for her. Her passion, writing and performing music, became "non-essential." She could accept the loss for two weeks, two months, even six months. But a year later, with live music still under lock and key, she began to question what it was all about. At what point did canceling life's greatest joys stop making sense? At what point would policymakers broaden their focus beyond curves, spikes and variants?

Refusing the vax was a way for Tara to draw a line in the sand, to let the universe know she was not OK with a world that so readily cast artistic expression aside. But Tara has a pragmatic side, and the media's screeching exhortations to "do your part" were also beginning to weigh on her. So she went ahead and got the first shot—and then then regretted the self-betrayal. (She eventually got the second shot, too. As fate would have it, she got Covid a few months later and had to step away from a concert tour with a new band.)

I myself didn't give much thought to the shots. It is not in my nature to fret over such things. But I wanted nothing to do with the disgorgement of hatred toward the unvaxxed—that was my own line in the sand. I could live with a background risk of Covid in the air, but not with the risk of alienating my unvaccinated friends and adding bricks to the fortress of vitriol closing in on them, on full display in a front-page *Toronto Star* layout splashed with such sentiments as "I honestly don't care if they die from COVID. Not even a little bit."[6] Besides, I was far more interested in learning if they were dating someone new or if *The Walrus* had accepted their pitch than in discussing their vaccination status.

In Part 2 of his series, Kingsnorth explores the two competing Covid stories that flow beneath all the shouting about science and public health. Reflecting that human history can be seen as "a never-ending series of battles over stories," Kingsnorth draws on philosopher Peter Limberg's analysis of the pandemic to articulate the two Covid stories.[7] Like ZDogg, whom we met in Chapter 4, Kingsnorth calls them the Thesis and Antithesis, their respective plots now updated for the vaccine passport era.

The Thesis postulates that only lockdowns can contain the virus, that mask mandates are necessary, that people need to take the vaccine to protect themselves and others, and that vaccine passports will help dislodge vaccine hesitancy, allowing the world to open up more quickly and completely.

The Antithesis questions the necessity of lockdowns and views the vaccine as an oversold commodity. Far from hastening the end of the pandemic, vaccine passports just erode social cohesion and lay the groundwork for increasingly draconian control measures that will persist long after the pandemic is over.

Most of the scientific, political, and media community took shelter under the Thesis. The Antithesis story belonged to what Kingsnorth describes as a "ragtag of political dissidents of all stripes." (That's not quite true: the B team included prominent scientists and doctors from the get-go—John Ioannidis and Marty Makary come to mind—and kept growing as the harms of the Thesis policies came to light.)

In Kingsworth's view, the team you choose depends not so much on "the science" as on your personal experience. If someone close to you has died, for instance, you may have little patience with people who question the restrictions or mandates. If, on the other hand, the pandemic policies have cost you a job or a business or a reputation, you likely won't "trust the authorities to play nicely with your civil liberties." People forced to delay a cancer diagnosis past the point of effective treatment may also look on the Thesis with suspicion. As the pandemic wears on, the positions become "increasingly impossible to reconcile."

What sometimes gets lost in this tug-of-war is that both teams have always wanted the same thing: the end of the pandemic. They just disagree on how to get there. The Thesis people believe that complying with restrictions will hasten the end, while the Antis maintain the end will only come about when people stop complying, a perspective nailed down by Michael Brendan Dougherty in the *National Review*[8]: "Public-health authorities don't know how to stop giving you extra-restrictive advice. And they can't learn how to stop giving it if we don't learn how to stop asking for it."

In the final instalment of his series,[9] Kingsnorth zooms out and considers the Covid story as "a testing-ground for new ways of being human in an increasingly post-human world." He explores the blurred boundary between counternarrative and conspiracy, noting how "conspiracy theorist" has been used as "a term of dismissal that can be applied to any and all who question the Narrative, no matter how reasonable their questions might be." While skeptical of the more fanciful takes on Klaus Schwab's Great Reset agenda, he does see a new world order emerging from the rubble of the pandemic—a high-tech, homogenous world with global actors pulling the strings. To a guy like Kingsnorth, with his Thoreau-esque self-reliance and reflexive mistrust of Big Tech, this does not bode well for Western civilization.

Kingsnorth has "learnt more about human nature in the last two years than in my preceding forty-seven." I can confirm: as a learning experience, there's nothing like a global crisis. It blasts open people's insides, leaving all of us bewildered at what we find in other people's hearts, and sometimes in our own.

* * *

This bewilderment infuses the Covid essays of Daniel Hadas, a lecturer in ancient Greek and Latin literature at King's College London and one of the most eloquent Covid commentators I have come across. His incredulity at the "dehumanizing" pandemic restrictions embraced by the mainstream.[10] His consternation that "the public voices whom we trusted...have almost uniformly embraced this brave new Covid world." The surreality of suddenly finding common ground with "libertarians, Marxists, and 'unaffiliated oddballs'." (Ditto: I barely knew what a libertarian was before Covid. Now? I can quote Ludwig von Mises, and my disillusionment with the left-right axis has thrust me firmly into the unaffiliated-oddball camp.) Above all, the shock of learning that his concerns about the Covid narrative, which seem so *reasonable* to him, do not resonate with many of his peers. (I feel this one hard.)

Some people support measures like masks and social distancing on the grounds that they help curb transmission. To Hadas, that's beside the point. In an article called "The Agony of the Lockdown Centrists,"[10] he argues that "the proposed new normal of indefinite intrusions on our freedom and our flourishing is unacceptable *regardless of these policies' effectiveness against Covid.*" [Italics his.] The version of life offered up by the Covid bureaucrats "threatens the death of society, to be replaced by a grotesque ballet of the masked and vaxxed, interacting only at the whim of governments and experts." The shift in our way of life "is taking place not just in science, but in this wider world of moral and social norms," and it is "first and foremost these moral and social changes that have horrified us anti-lockdown centrists."

A grotesque ballet of the masked and vaxxed, interacting only at the whim of governments and experts. It's the *cri de coeur* from the dissenting soul, from those of us who cannot muster any enthusiasm at the triumph of "public health" over everything else in life.

"It's an impoverished idea of health," Hadas told me in a phone call. "Health is communal and being in a community is part of health. Isolation is not." When we consider health through this wide-angle lens, "we're actually making people ill by keeping them 'safe' from each other." He spoke of how science "colonized ethics and politics" and "silenced other human dimensions" during Covid. While scientific expertise has obvious value, "it is not a scientist's place to say you can't be with your parent on their deathbed."

Like Kingsnorth, Hadas sees the vaccine as the lead actor in a story, one that took shape long before the product became available for public consumption[11]: "The world would lock down and stay safe, while brave scientists hammered away at a vaccine. Then we would all get vaccinated, and come back out into the sunlight." The storytellers created several subplots to support this dramatic arc: Covid is deadly to everyone, distrust in the vaccine means distrust in science, and refusing to get vaccinated is immoral. "The veracity of these claims didn't matter: they were in the script, and it was too late to deviate." Looking back, we can argue about "who acted in good faith, who was outright lying, who thought the lies were noble," but Hadas does not presume any grand plan. It just happened, because creating stories is what humans do. The story came before the science and remained largely impervious to it during the vaccine rollout, even as the hope of sterilizing immunity faded away.

Many fellow dissenters have told me that they sensed, right from the start, that the virus wasn't going anywhere. Hadas is no exception. He remembers thinking, on one of his innumerable solo walks in the spring of 2020, that "there would be no 'after Covid'." The virus would never, as Boris Johnson had promised, "be sent packing."

My thoughts flowed along similar lines as I trudged through Toronto's snowy streets during that silent spring: the virus was here to stay. I'm not sure why I reached this conclusion so early on. People whose knowledge of viruses and pandemics vastly exceeds my own believed that if we just worked hard enough, we could stamp this one out. With the benefit of hindsight, Hadas gives a shoutout to those of us who suspected that "once Covid has a toehold, non-pharmaceutical interventions do vast harm and have little or no effect."

Unlike me, Hadas started his pandemic journey with some alarm about the virus itself. "I read things by experts, I got scared," he recalls. "But I had a sense that the model was not sustainable, and the ethical horror was there from the start. That's what ultimately pulled me to the 'no' position."

He continues to roam the streets of his UK town, his thoughts now turning to what comes next in the story. It would be "easy to conclude that the war is indeed over," he writes in a retrospective article for *City Journal*.[12] "Apart from the occasional masked passer-by and unused hand sanitizer station, the regime's symbols have vanished from view."

And yet. The very failure of the mitigation measures is why he predicts the 2019 version of normal will not return. "For governments to abandon the measures outright would be to suggest the unsayable: that they should never have been undertaken in the first place"—and governments don't do such things. Instead, they will save face by maintaining the measures at a low ebb. Recommendations to "distance." Masks off, masks on again. A closure here, a mandate there. The same grotesque ballet, but off to the side somewhere, entering and exiting our peripheral vision.

The ballet could not have been contemplated, much less

choreographed, "without the foundational assumption that the imperatives of disease control set the proper limits to personal and political freedom," Hadas says. In this sense, the Covid response was "a political, even spiritual, project." It was about what people were willing to give up to feel safe. It was about what they considered essential and disposable in life. Although Hadas calls himself an optimist, he sees no swift resolution to "the crisis in political legitimacy and the gnawing anomie that made the Covid response palatable to governors and governed alike."

* * *

Ann Bauer has written three novels, a cookbook memoir, and numerous essays for such publications as *Salon*, *Slate*, and the *New York Times*.[13] When Covid hit, the global response to the virus put Bauer on high alert. She had been through this before: the claims of scientific certainty, the morality play, the mockery and suppression of dissent, the institutional hubris that brought tragedy to her life. Her sense of helplessness and rage came rushing back.

She poured it all into an essay for *Tablet*,[14] a Jewish publication that has put out consistently fresh and thought-provoking pieces about the pandemic. The article chronicles the life and death of her oldest son, Andrew, one of the saddest stories I have ever read. It starts in the 1950s, when psychology professor Bruno Bettelheim, originally from Austria, won a grant to start a program for autistic children. Parents from across the country hung onto his advice, which he consolidated into the "refrigerator mother" theory of autism. The belief that cold mothers caused autism became gospel. As Bauer notes, it "turned a mysterious and heartbreaking condition into a simple problem of who was to blame." Even mothers embraced the theory, hoping they could fix themselves and thereby fix their child.

Bauer was 23 years old when Bettelheim died by suicide at age 86. The following year her toddler son lost his language, almost from one day to the next. An older relative steeped in the Bettelheim mythology accused Bauer of ruining the child.

Bettelheim's rages and abusive behavior eventually came to light and his theories fell off the pedestal, to be replaced with the new psychobiological model. As Bauer puts it, "nature was in, nurture was out. Brain chemistry became the only thing that mattered." Each new theory claimed to have finally unlocked the mysteries of autism, the earlier theories now derided as prescientific mumbo jumbo.

In his teenage years, the autism now compounded with mood disorders, Andrew rotated through a series of antidepressants and antipsychotics, with little to show for it. When Bauer wrote an article questioning the cavalier use of antipsychotics, a psychiatrist fired off a rebuttal calling her an "anti-science nut."

At age 28, Andrew was found dead on the floor of his living room, not long after telling his mother there was no happiness for him in this world. Bauer suspects that "he was tired of being controlled by the fickle czars of autism and he was just done."

After four years of crippling grief, Bauer began to function again. And then Covid rolled in, and along with the virus came "a cadre of pandemic experts who recommended—then quickly required—extreme and unprecedented things." People who questioned these strange new policies were "muffled, derided, sidelined."

Sensitized from a lifetime of having blame heaped on her, Bauer immediately saw the parallels between her experience and the response to the pandemic. "Doctors and officials blamed their audience of 3 billion for the disease. The more the cures failed, the greater the fault of the public. The flaw was never in the remedy, but in those who failed to 'behave' and thereby brought the plague upon themselves." It was the autism experts all over again: their smug certainty, their sneers at those who opposed them, their propulsion into "an evidence-free atmosphere where every passing theory became both law and truth."

Bauer lay awake at night, "imagining all the children like my son who were mute, sensitive, bound to routine, friendless, in desperate need of services and incapable of learning on Zoom." She began advocating for the reopening of schools, a stance that cost her half her friends and many of her colleagues.

Before interviewing Bauer, I read her *Tablet* article again—and cried again. When I told her how much her article meant to me, I cried a third time. Tearing up during interviews is not my usual MO as a journalist, but sometimes you just go with the flow. As it turns out, I'm not the only person moved by Bauer's essay. Tablet put it on their "best of 2021" list, and she's currently in negotiations with a producer hoping to turn her piece into a TV special.

The first thing we talked about was hubris—the hubris of the early autism experts and the hubris of the expert class during Covid. "The autism experts of the past were terribly certain about their ideas," she told me. "Theirs was the correct method, the right way to go about it—and 50 years later we realize they were dead wrong." And remember lobotomy? "Same deal, experts declared it 'the science,' and we know how that worked out." In the same way, there's every chance that "people will look back on Covid in 50 years and say we didn't know what we were doing."

Next up was blame—the human need to look for a culprit. "We still don't understand autism," she said. "There's no pill. There's no reason. There's no real intervention. When people face something so mysterious, they look to blame." With Covid, people blamed other people for not being "careful enough." "This false morality play that governments sold us, that careful people are the heroes and less careful ones are the villains, has nothing to do with what we knew about infectious disease or about people."

Bauer's gut response to the Covid policies mirrors my own. In the first few months of the pandemic, she walked around "feeling like a crazy person" while her friends cheered the lockdowns and jeered at renegades who stepped out of the house without a mask on. (She lives in a "progressive central" enclave of the progressive city of St. Paul, Minnesota.) She despaired at the policies' disregard for young people: "I can't think of another time in history where we've asked the young to stand in front of a bus for the *potential* to help elderly people." Me too, I kept telling her. Me too me too me too. It's been like this throughout the pandemic: we put out feelers, sniff around, and when we find a kindred spirit our hearts swell in gratitude and relief.

Like Kingsnorth, Bauer admits she doesn't know the end of the Covid story. She can't be sure that she's right. But one thing she does know: the experts aren't always right, either. They often aren't. Anyone who became a parent before the last decade remembers doctors' confident pronouncements about peanut exposure: avoid it in the first three years of life. In 2017, the National Institute of Allergy and Infectious Diseases turned the advice on its head[15]: go ahead and give your baby a lick of peanut butter—it won't raise their risk of developing an allergy and may actually decrease it.

We should not forget John Ioannidis's meta-science essay of 2005, which explained why most published research claims are false and may simply reflect the prevailing bias.[16] The paper has been cited more than 11,000 times, suggesting that millions of scientists have read it. It gets worse: a 2022 analysis of 1,567 well-studied medical interventions, reported in the *Journal of Clinical Epidemiology*, found that 94% of these therapies didn't have high-quality evidence to back them up.[17] Claiming certainty is no longer a good look.

Future generations may look back on the Covid lockdowns as the crazy thing that unenlightened, prescientific people tried out—the lobotomy of the early 21st century. In the meantime, as the harms of lockdowns continue to come to light, it wouldn't hurt to remember Bettelheim's fall from grace. A little less hubris, yes?

PANDEMIC PHILOSOPHERS: GIORGIO AGAMBEN AND ANGIE HOBBS

I always wished that governments had sought guidance on Covid-19 strategy not just from medical experts, but from philosophers. Epidemiologists can estimate the spread of the virus. Virologists can track mutations. Public health specialists can suggest interventions. But these experts can't—or won't—answer the questions that matter most: How much quality of life and opportunity should people sacrifice to save a life? Which matters more, living longer or living better? Do human rights have a role even in a pandemic? Philosophers grapple with exactly such questions.

When I was around 16, as tall and awkward as they come, I mentioned to my Hungarian-born mother that philosophy sounded like a cool thing to study. She answered, "yes, but vat do you *do* viz it? Just sit on a mountain and tink? Who's going to pay you for dat?" I ended up studying biochemistry, and later music composition, but philosophy never lost its pull on me. Sitting on a mountain and thinking? Surely the best job in the world (and yes, mom, all the better if you find a way to get paid for it).

Giorgio Agamben, one of the world's best-known philosophers, found a way. Like many people who make philosophy their life's work, Agamben anchored his career in the halls of academe, rotating through full-time and visiting appointments in various universities. He published widely, achieving international acclaim for his series of works titled *Homo Sacer: Sovereign Power and Bare Life*, which builds on Hanna Arendt's and Michel Foucault's studies of totalitarianism and biopolitics.[1] His trenchant essay writing earned him the Prix Européen de l'Essai Charles Veillon in 2006. All told, a pretty solid CV.

Not surprisingly, given his interest in biopolitics, Agamben had a lot to say when the pandemic blew in. Demographically he brought a unique vantage point to the table: He lived in Italy, the country that set lockdowns in motion in the Western world. He was about to turn 78, an age when he might reasonably want some protection from a virus that was killing so many of his countrymen. But he didn't want protection. He didn't want the preoccupation with a virus to rule his remaining years. When asked by a Swedish interviewer if, as a person in a high-risk age bracket, he feared encountering other people,[2] he responded with a quote from Montaigne: "It is not certain when death awaits us, so let us await it everywhere. Knowing how to die frees us from all subjection and constraint."

Agamben expressed his dismay at his country's response to the pandemic in a series of short essays and interviews, which he later compiled into a slim volume called *Where Are We Now?*[2] He made some missteps in his assertions, notably the political blunder of drawing parallels between Covid and the flu. He called Covid a manufactured epidemic, earning him the label of Covid denier. Some of his erstwhile fans proclaimed him a crotchety old guy whose best ideas were behind him and who deserved to be ignored.

We shouldn't ignore him. He may have gotten some of the epidemiology wrong, but he knows his philosophy, and his analysis of the response to Covid raises important questions about the experience of living and the body politic.

In an early critique of the pandemic response,[3] Agamben decried the unilateral concern with what he calls "bare life," the willingness to give up everything that makes life worth living—relationships, work, study, religion, political rights—for the sake of protecting our physical bodies. As he saw it, this preoccupation with staying alive at all costs came from a harmful separation of life from living.

What we were witnessing, he suggested in an interview, was a rupture between body and spirit. "People have broken the unity of their vital experience—which is always (and inseparably) corporeal *and* spiritual—into a purely biological entity on the one hand, and a social, cultural and political experience on the other."[2] Agamben attributed this schism to the growing medicalization of bodies, which was deeply transforming people's experience of their own lives. He did not see this as healthy.

Some of his critics maintained that he had it all wrong, that the fervor to keep people alive at all costs revealed what was noblest and most caring in humankind. A fair point, but a grossly incomplete one. We were not being very noble and caring to young people, who had the most to lose from "staying home" for months on end. We were not being noble and caring to people who had devoted the past decade of their lives to building a restaurant or music career. We expected these people—people with their lives ahead of them or awash in family responsibilities—to bear profound losses they might never recuperate. To some of us, this seemed neither right nor fair.

The exaltation of bare life also devalues the experience of living. I found myself agreeing with Aleksandr Solzhenitsyn, who wrote, in *The Gulag Archipelago*[4]: "But I had begun to sense a truth inside myself; if in order to live it is necessary not to live, then what's it all for?" Yascha Mounk, a journalist who earned my respect during Covid, put forth a similar sentiment in *The Atlantic*[5]: "Like our ancestors, we should prioritize the living of life over the minimizing of mortality."

The obvious counter to such statements is: chill out, this is all temporary and normality will soon return. But nothing suggested to Agamben that the preoccupation with bare life, the single-minded focus on preserving the physical body, would go away. It certainly didn't go away after the initial two weeks to slow the spread. Public health experts and politicians declared it selfish to celebrate US Independence Day. Thanksgiving? Not this year. Christmas? Not possible. Zooming instead of hugging, watching Netflix instead of traveling, forgoing new experiences and new friendships for... two more weeks? Two more years? Two more decades? To Agamben, this perspective revealed what Jesse Kauffman calls a "strangely shallow conception of the human condition."[6] It was all about *whether* we live, not *how* we live.

In in an op-ed for *The Telegraph*,[7] Janet Daley, the cantankerous UK journalist with the don't-mess-with-me face, argues that our technical success in prolonging life may be driving our attitudes in the wrong direction: "We appear now to believe that death and ill-health can and should be preventable indefinitely" and expect that "governments should be directly responsible for the permanent welfare of everyone." US lawyer Mark Oshinskie concurs. "Medicine has become the new American religion," he writes in an article about the explosion in medical expenditures,[8] adding that this religious fervor has ramped up people's "sense of entitlement regarding medical treatments."

As Daley notes in her piece, scientists are developing drugs that keep the sickest people alive, which for the most part she considers a good thing. I myself have witnessed the power of these new medicines: after one of my cousins battled treatment-resistant lymphoma for two years, losing as much ground as she was gaining, CAR-T technology came along and blasted the cancer out of her body. But some of these next-gen treatments only marginally extend life. In clinical trials of the metastatic breast cancer drug Enhertu, the medication gave patients six extra months of life compared to chemotherapy,[9] which an expert pronounced "stunningly successful."[10] As a feat of scientific prowess, sure. But is throwing the full weight of medical interventionism at a dying patient the best use of our health dollars and our humanity? Might the patient have a richer end-of-life experience holding loved ones' hands and watching sunsets and reflecting on what it all meant, rather than racing to doctors' appointments and infusion clinics? Whatever one's personal feelings on the matter, these questions are worth asking.

Another theme running through Agamben's writings, even before the pandemic, is the political impulse to extend a state of emergency beyond its natural conclusion. Left unchecked, this penchant culminates in what he calls a "permanent state of exception." In his view, Covid led us exactly to this place: a "biosecurity state" that transforms our whole life into a health requirement. "People have accepted, as if it were obvious, renouncing their own freedom of movement, work, friendships, loves, social relations, their own religious and political convictions, producing a sort of superlative good citizenship in which imposed obligations are presented as evidence of altruism and the citizen no longer has a right to health (health safety) but becomes juridically obliged to health (biosecurity)."[11]

As if it were obvious. That's the crux here: the assumption that all of this was obvious, necessary, inevitable. *Of course* we give up our freedom of movement if it keeps us safer. *Of course* we give up hugging and singing and sex with a new love if it slows the virus's trajectory. *Of course* we stay home and turn our computers on and keep tweeting. Why of course? Samantha Godwin, a specialist in legal and political philosophy at Yale University, has wondered the same thing[12]: "For the past 14 months we have collectively accepted, without meaningful debate, the ideological belief that the greater good can be equated with maximum COVID mitigation, without concern for or recognition of the collateral harms caused by these mitigation efforts."

Once set in motion, the biosecurity state fortifies itself with rules and norms that ensure its perpetuation, one of them being a recalibration of risk. "Instead of adapting the protection to the actual level of risk, [the biosecurity state] tends to adapt the perception of risk to the growing need for protection," says Robert Esposito, another Italian thinker with a watchful eye on the Covid policies.[13] Under normal conditions, people are presumed healthy unless they show or tell you otherwise. In the Covid biosecurity state, everyone is presumed sick. This is in fact what our leaders told us the early days: assume that you and everyone else you encounter carry the virus.

Agamben recoils against the term "social distancing," which he sees as an oxymoron: distancing is inherently antisocial. As others have observed, the term "physical distancing" might have served us better: neutral, clinical, limited in scope. If you're physically distanced, you can still be socially close. But "social distancing" clearly communicates "a new paradigm of social organization."[2]

"Asking young people to 'social distance' is asking them to stop being young." That's how Dr. Zoom put it to me when we discussed the Trinity Bellwoods affair—the crowds of young people who flocked to the Toronto park on a resplendent Saturday afternoon in May 2020 and made a big honking mess. He called it the life force asserting itself. "Many of these people have spent the last two months cooped up in tiny apartments, with no access to green spaces," he told me. "They're young, they're lonely, they're confused. Of course they're going to crack." (That's why I stuck with the good doctor throughout the lockdowns: while less troubled by the Covid policies than I was, he had the spiritual breadth to look beyond "safety first" and he never went in for shaming.) To his mind, the Twitter warriors who cried "selfish idiot" lacked a fundamental understanding of human nature, as did our political leaders. Instead of insisting that everyone stay home, they could have encouraged young people to socialize outside and avoid getting into each other's faces: to go hiking and cycling together, to enjoy the sun and the wind on their faces.

Mathematician Wes Pedgen, whose pandemic musings on Twitter never fail to intrigue and delight, reached a similar conclusion[14]: "We should question public health approaches which expect various regulations to halt socialization among young adults, as we would a sailor whose plan to reach his destination involves getting the wind to blow the way he wants."

And what about old people? Is social distancing what they truly wanted? Few people bothered to ask. It was simply assumed that the elderly wanted more years rather than more quality, a mindset that behavioral scientist Paul Dolan calls middle-aged privilege. Writing for the LSE School of Public Policy, he argues that the Covid policies were designed by and for mid-lifers and do not serve older people's interests[15]: "Not only are older people often more strongly in favor of prioritising [the young] in resource allocation decisions in healthcare, but they are also more willing to trade off life expectancy for better life experiences."

UK pensioner Maureen Eames would no doubt agree. "I'm 83, I don't give a sod," she said in a October 2020 video interview for the BBC[16] after learning that new restrictions would take effect in South Yorkshire. "I've not got that many years left of me and I'm not going to be fastened in a house... By the end of this year there's going to be millions of people unemployed and do you know who's going to pay for it? All the young ones." The news clip went viral.

In a Greeley, Colorado nursing home, residents staged an anti-lockdown protest, waving signs that read "I'd rather die of Covid than loneliness" and chanting "freedom, freedom, freedom."[17] In Toronto, a 90-year-old retirement home resident chose medically assisted death over another lockdown.[18] The woman, described as "intensely social," died surrounded by family and friends who played a song she had selected.

Do these news-making cases reflect a more general view among people nearing the end of their lives? We don't know, because we never bothered to find out. We do know what Agamben thinks about death in a socially distanced and masked world[19]: "If the living lose their face, the dead become only numbers, who, in so far as they had been reduced to their pure biological life, must die alone."

* * *

I discovered Angie Hobbs in October 2020, while doing research for an essay, and quickly recognized her as my kind of philosopher: she regularly climbs down from her mountain at Sheffield University, where she holds the ultra-cool title of Professor of the Public Understanding of Philosophy, to translate her thoughts into practical ideas for living. The consulting group Jericho Chambers calls her "one of the UK's most sparkling and life-enhancing academics" and "as far removed from a dusty university garett [sic] as possible."[20] She asks the types of questions that change not only how we think about life, but what we may choose to have for breakfast tomorrow.

While everyone else was talking about reproductive numbers and the area under the transmission curve, Hobbs was exploring the types of ethical dilemmas that buzzed in my own mind: rights versus responsibilities, prioritizing present or future generations, the outer limits of safety and freedom. Her article in *Prospect* magazine[21] tackles what she calls the question behind all the other questions: "Should the overarching aim of governments, and indeed of other bodies and individuals, be to protect life or quality of life?" And how do we find the right balance?

Even people who insist that saving lives trumps all other considerations may not actually feel that way, Hobbs argues. To make her point, she invokes a what-if scenario that I myself have considered many times: What if a government were to tell us to stay home forever and offered to bring food, clothing, and other necessities to everyone's door? Although this strategy would undoubtedly keep everyone as safe as possible and save many lives, Hobbs suspects that most people wouldn't agree to the deal, because "we do not just want life but a life worth living." It's a theme that we lockdown dissenters keep coming back to: At what point does the erosion of quality of life in the name of safety stop serving the greater good?

Which begs the question: What exactly is quality of life? For Hobbs, it's not just physical or even mental health. Her notion of quality invokes the concept of "flourishing," which Plato (her favorite philosopher) and Aristotle conceived as the realization of one's physical intellectual, emotional, and imaginative potential.

Flourishing includes care and compassion, but also puts a premium on "activities that bring delight." For many, this includes eating out, dancing, travel, live music, theater, worshipping, attending lectures and seminars, and a hundred other things that give life its texture and shine. Advising artists and performers to just "retrain or consider cyber" doesn't cut it, she says. We need to honor the value of these enriching activities, just as we honor life itself, and put them on the weigh scale when considering how to manage a pandemic.

Some critics of this view retort that you can't have quality of life without having life itself, so survival *should* trump all other considerations. Such sentiments cropped up online all the time in 2020: You can't see your friends if you're dead. You can't go to the movies if you're dead. You can't travel to Spain if you're dead. But these arguments don't stand up to logical scrutiny: they set off a fact (can't see friends under lockdown) against a low-probability hypothetical (death if the lockdown is lifted). One way or another, the vast majority of people do not end up dead from the virus. Lockdown or no lockdown, mandate or no mandate, they get to keep their lives. The honest, apples-to-apples trade-off is this one: when we loosen restrictions, quality of life goes up for just about everyone and serious risk may go up for a few. That's the *quid pro quo* we need to look in the eye.

Hobbs hastens to add that putting flourishing first doesn't mean letting the virus rip. She takes duty of care seriously and supports strong government action to help control a pandemic in its first stages. But the government "also needs to have a clear direction toward a thriving society in mind, and to clearly communicate that direction." The goal of a thriving society means that "some people may die of Covid-19 who might otherwise have lived—although other lives will be saved from diseases of poverty or from suicide."

The painful reality is that pandemics incur losses—loss of life, but also loss of dreams and opportunities. Some of these dreams may never come back. If a 39-year-old woman misses her chance to have a child because her IVF got canceled repeatedly during Covid (I know of at least two such women), can we confidently appraise this loss as less tragic than the Covid death of an elderly, frail person whose body was already giving out? People like Hobbs, who don't hide from such questions, deserve our respect. Bare life matters, but so does a free and unrestricted life, with all its surprises and opportunities and "activities that bring delight." Ideally, government policies should make room for both.

That's what many of us felt was missing in the political discourse about Covid: an acknowledgement of what was being traded away and the political will to restore it. If anything, decision makers took the opposite tack. When we timidly asked them when they planned to phase out this or that restriction, they responded with a knee-jerk "too soon." In Hobbs' ideal world, our leaders would have assured us—and shown us—that they were working toward restoring a full, flourishing society, not just a safer one.

ETHICAL WARRIORS: JULIE PONESSE
AND AARON KHERIATY

Two academics, both living the quiet life: one in Eastern Canada, the other in Southern California. Both fulfilled in their careers, loved by their students, respected by their peers. Never imagining it would all come crashing down in 2021.

That was the year the institutions that employed them gave them an ultimatum: get vaxxed or get out.

Julie Ponesse, who lectured about classical philosophy and medical ethics at the University of Western Ontario (UWO), and Aaron Kheriaty, who taught psychiatry and directed the medical ethics program at the University of California Irvine (UCI), drew the same line in the sand, a line that cost them their careers.

They both refused the Covid vaccine, arguing that their immunity from prior infection with the virus should exempt them from the requirement. Ponesse wrote an explanatory note to her university and Kheriaty sued his institution. They both got fired.

What troubled the pair was not so much the products themselves as the discourse that grew around them—the overblown claims, the suppression of data and debate, the intense social pressure accompanying the vaccination campaign. Safe and effective, safe and effective, do it for your neighbor, do it for your immunocompromised uncle, do it because you're a normal person who cares about others, do it or else.

Most governments started gently: Will you please, pretty-please get vaxxed? When vaccine uptake plateaued, they piled on the incentives, from Krispy Kreme doughnuts to crisp $100 bills.[1] Free eggs in China, hummus in Israel, blenders in India. Then came the warnings: get the vax or pay a fine, get the vax or lose your job. And finally, the full weight of social opprobrium. Do it or you're a bad person. Do it or you're a science-denying troglodyte. Do it or you deserve to die. The venom and the vitriol, the runaway train of coercion—Ponesse and Kheriaty wanted no part of it.

The particular hill they chose to die on, mandating vaccination in people with prior immunity from Covid, rested on the following train of thought: We've had Covid. We have antibodies that protect us from serious disease, just as vaccinated people do. If we get vaccinated, we bear the risks without the commensurate benefits. Ergo, we shouldn't be forced to do it.

In support of their position, Jeffrey Klausner, a clinical professor of population and public health sciences at the University of Southern California, co-authored an analysis showing that infection with Covid generally confers protection for 10 months or more.[2] Ten months isn't forever, but then neither is the protection offered by vaccines. "From the public health perspective, denying jobs and access and travel to people who have recovered from infection doesn't make sense," Klausner maintained. Others countered that vaccination offers extra protection even to those who have had Covid and that we can't go looking for antibodies in everyone who claims prior infection, making vaccine mandates the only practical solution.

For the record, the battle that cost Ponesse and Kheriaty their jobs is not my personal battle. I felt no pride when I got the shots (and cringed at the displays of jabbed arms on Facebook) but no pressure, either. The vax passes did disturb me: the show-your-papers vibe, the clannishness, as though we had paid our way into a secret club for the virtuous. I had no interest in belonging to a virtue club, and whipping out my vax papers at a pub left a bad taste in my mouth. (If I had to do it over again, I would skip those beers.) Even so, my discomfort with the mandates didn't rise to the level of outrage. My deeper misgivings bubbled up later, after I came to understand how vaccine absolutism grew out of Covid absolutism and an unhealthy tree cannot grow healthy branches.

A little digression: about 15 years ago, I got a three-month gig writing materials for an adolescent program run by Toronto's Hospital for Sick Children. Everyone hired by the hospital, whether full-time or on contract, had to get a slew of vaccines as well as a police check. Even though I would be working in an off-site building that did not admit any children—basically a Dilbert-style office with industrial carpeting and a sea of cubicles—policy was policy, so I had to get the shots. I grumbled about it, more at the inanity of the rule than the inoculations, but didn't think to fight the requirement. As for the police check, by the time the results came back (not a criminal, yay!) I had already wrapped up the gig. Ah, bureaucracy.

All of which is to say: I have no personal skin in the Ponesse & Kheriaty fight. But some of my friends and colleagues do—people who chose not to get vaxxed and lost their jobs, friends, and social standing along the way. People who had ethical concerns about mandating a product we still knew very little about. People who opposed the vaccine mandates for the same reason they opposed lockdowns: it was all too hasty and heavy-handed.

I've given Ponesse and Kheriaty a chapter of their own so they can speak for the millions of people who've traveled this path. Also, theirs is a story about exploring complex issues, about taking a stand, about speaking out amid intense pressure to shut up, which is more or less the point of this book.

Although they both lost the battle with their respective employers, they continue to fight the war: bringing the ethical issues surrounding vaccine mandates to a wide audience and restoring respectful debate to science and ethics. Ponesse even wrote a book about it, *My Choice*, published by The Democracy Fund in 2021.[3]

The book lays out all her arguments against the vax mandates, starting with the premise that vaccines that don't stop transmission "must be seen more as a treatment and less as a public health measure. And if the vaccines are not about public health, then what justifies the mandates?"

While "a person's autonomy is typically regarded as the highest priority" in Western bioethics, Ponesse allows that public safety imperatives may override this principle in some crises. But the precedent everyone loves to cite, the smallpox vaccine mandate, doesn't apply to Covid because "the viruses and vaccines are vastly different in kind." Not only does smallpox pose a much graver danger, but the vaccine stops transmission in its tracks. Also pertinent is the level of coercion used to enforce a mandate. In some US jurisdictions, refusal to comply with the smallpox vaccine mandate carried a penalty of $5 (about $150 in today's dollars)— hardly the same coercive force as losing your livelihood.[4]

Invoking the principle of "disproportionate harms," Ponesse argues that young people face a disproportionate risk from the vaccines, for the simple reason that they have more years ahead in which adverse events can develop. She also notes how risk tolerance varies widely among individuals. "Some will opt to take a chance and others will not," and a rule that "forces us all to behave in the same way...is an affront to personal autonomy."

When UWO first announced its mandate policy, Ponesse responded with a long email outlining these arguments, supported with 24 references. She got no response from the university, not even a "we value your input" blandishment. Not a word from her colleagues, either. UWO further tightened the screws, removing the option of twice-weekly Covid tests in lieu of vaccination, and Ponesse confirmed she would not comply with the mandate. After teaching at the university for two decades, she was let go. "I was a professor of ethics, questioning what I view as an unethical demand," she says. "You don't have to look hard to see the irony."

After leaving UWO, Ponesse joined the Democracy Fund, a

Canadian charity devoted to advancing civil liberties, where she holds the position of Ethics Scholar. In a November 2021 video presentation for the Fund,[5] which garnered more than 160,000 views, Ponesse addresses the titular question: "Why are so many people choosing life in a cage?" She has no answers, just more questions: How can you rally a people to stand up for their rights when they don't think their rights are slipping away? Have we decided that a life of comfort, security and conformity—if that is even possible—is worth the price of freedom? What if you're blind to the cage that has been erected around you? What if you helped to build it?

On the last day of March 2022, I went to see Ponesse chat with Robert F. Kennedy Jr. (beamed in from his home in Los Angeles) about Covid policies and democratic values. The event took place in a high school auditorium in a small city near Toronto, with about 500 people in attendance. Ponesse spoke with a natural fluency, words tumbling over words like polished stones, and commanded the stage with her proud bearing and stylish garb. It was hard to see her as the type of person who makes enemies.

In the mix-and-mingle portion of the event, people formed a long queue to get signed copies of Ponesse's book. I grabbed two copies, one for me and one for a friend and fellow writer I would be meeting the next day. I hadn't talked to her in many months, but had heard she had refused the vaccine, so I thought she would appreciate the book.

I met my friend at the entrance of the Leslie Spit, a long and skinny peninsula that juts out into Lake Ontario. With the wind whipping at our hair and faces, I gave her a hug. She burst into tears.

We started walking, the churn of the waves muffling her sobs. "I'm so *relieved,*" she said finally. "I kept thinking you wouldn't want to hang out with me, and certainly not to hug me. Being unvaxxed and all. I worried you would want to go for coffee and I would have to say no, because I don't have a vax pass. I spent all last night worrying about it. I hardly slept at all." She took a breath. "And you know what's really nuts? I even worried that you were playing an April Fool's joke on me and wouldn't show up. That's how crazy the vax wars have made me."

This is why we need people like Ponesse, I thought as we continued to walk. The vaccine policies had sliced through the social fabric, leaving blood and guts in their wake. People were calling off longstanding friendships and calling each other unprintable names. Any putative benefits from the mandates paled in comparison to this social carnage. We needed the Ponesses of the world to tell us: stop this train and do it now.

I thought of what my brother, a cardiologist, often told me: "One thing I've learned is that not all patients will do what I ask them to do, and I've come to accept that. If I keep pushing beyond a certain point, I'm just shooting myself and my patients in the foot."

The perfect is the enemy of the good. Governments took a wrong turn when they decided that everyone needed to do their bidding. As most pandemic strategists understood before Covid, coercion does more harm than a virus. Besides, a product that delivers on its promise should sell itself without force, especially if it costs nothing. That's just market economics.

* * *

Aaron Kheriaty began throwing his ethics at the real world long before Covid. His 2015 letter to the American Medical Association (AMA) urged the group to maintain its stance against medically assisted suicide, arguing that the bid to end one's life "is a distress signal indicating that something in the patient's situation (medical, psychological, or social) is not adequately being attended to."[6] He lost that battle in 2019, when the AMA enshrined physicians' right to help people die "according to the dictates of their conscience without violating their professional obligations." But his standing with his peers remained solid. During the early months of the pandemic, he co-authored UCI's pandemic ventilator triage guidelines and advised the California Department of Public Health on the state's triage plan for allocating scarce medical resources.[7]

I first met Kheriaty on a Zoom call. He was holding a Q&A session for a Reddit group, shortly after taking legal action against UCI, and I was one of the moderators.[8] The "silence of mainstream bioethics as these policies were rolled out" left him deeply troubled, he told us. That, and the lack of dialogue about preventive health. Diet and exercise to strengthen the immune system? Dropping a bit of weight? Nobody talked about it. "We know that that exercise improves immunity; we know that obesity is a major risk factor for bad outcomes with Covid. So this messaging should have been present from the beginning."

But Kheriaty's objection to the mandates goes beyond health and immune function. In *The Wall Street Journal*, he and co-author Gerald Bradley argue that university vaccine mandates violate basic principles of medical ethics[9]: "We don't immunize [healthy young people] against diseases that primarily harm the elderly in hope of reducing transmission risks for the elderly... That would use the recipients as a means to another end, which is unethical." Of all the arguments against the vaccine mandates, this one resonates most strongly with me, especially when applied to young children who don't have the capacity to make their own health decisions. Using society's youngest members to prop up older people's health seems, well, icky. I wish I had a more scholarly term for it.

Curious to learn how Kheriaty might address the opposing argument—that using children to mitigate community transmission can benefit them directly if it keeps their own parents safer—I put the question to him in a personal interview. "That's a theoretical piled on a theoretical," he told me. "We don't actually have any data showing this. Give me the facts." Even if we did have data pointing in this direction, Kheriaty views the whole thing as deeply unethical. "Using kids as a shield is exactly what a healthy society doesn't do. In a healthy society, adults take risks to protect children." What's more, saddling children with the responsibility to protect adults "is deeply harmful, psychologically. Don't lay that on a child."

As a practicing physician, Kheriaty takes the mandate to heal and do no harm to heart. At the same time, he respects his patients as autonomous beings with agency over their own health: "If I think an intervention will benefit a patient but it doesn't accord with their values, I can make some effort to persuade them, but it's not OK for me to violate their integrity as a separate person."

Kheriaty's arguments take us back to the principle of bodily autonomy, which posits that each of us owns our body and can decide what goes in it. If I want to eat doughnuts all day, it's my business. The state can require the doughnut manufacturer to list calories and place upper limits on the use of trans fats, but it can't tell me not to buy the products. By the same token, the state can't force-feed me if I decide to go on a hunger strike to protest the imprisonment of a political dissident.

If we let go of bodily autonomy as a governing principle and lean too hard into our "collective duty," we enter precarious ethical territory. One can imagine making the case that, for example, donating a kidney constitutes a moral obligation because the benefit to the recipient (living without dialysis) exceeds the harm to the donor (living with just one kidney, which most people can manage quite well). Is this the direction we want to take? As ethical norms mutate—and they always do—we need to keep talking about what we lose when we throw bodily autonomy overboard.

Shortly after Kheriaty was fired, the U.S. Supreme Court nixed the Biden administration's vaccine mandate for large private companies, which Kheriaty sees as a win. "By putting a stay on the OSHA [Occupational Safety and Health Administration] mandate, the court indicated, in principle, that there are limits to... what institutions can do to mandate vaccines," he says.[7] "That's all positive." Even so, he doesn't expect the ruling to reopen his own case, which "has to do with whether the University of California has authority to mandate vaccines for its employees."

Not that he lacks for things to do. His numerous appointments include chief of psychiatry and ethics at Doc1Health, chief of medical ethics at The Unity Project, director of the Zephyr Institute's Health and Human Flourishing Program, and member of the advisory board for the Simone Weil Center for Political Philosophy.[10] He has written a book, *The New Abnormal*,[11] which focuses on the biosecurity state and the militarization of public health. "It's about our overreliance on the state of exception, on jumping from one emergency to the next, and on recasting problems such as climate change as public health issues." And the private practice he started "is doing just fine. The vast majority of my patients have followed me to my practice."

While he misses his students, he points out that teaching young people can take many forms: "We can teach with our words, [but] we can also teach with our actions."[7] In the summer of 2021, when he pictured himself facing his fall students on the podium, he "couldn't imagine teaching about integrity and moral courage if... my actions didn't back up what I taught in the classroom." So, instead of preparing lectures on depression or assisted suicide, he gave his students a model for speaking out. "Several students have told me, 'Your sacrifice has encouraged me or inspired me to take a stand myself.' "

Lawsuits like Kheriaty's pave the way for more lawsuits, and sooner or later the plaintiffs start to win. In mid-2022, for example, 500 healthcare workers in Illinois won a $10.3 million victory against their employer, NorthShore University Health System, which had fired them for refusing the vaccine.[12] In this case, the complaint revolved around religious conscience, but the argument matters less than the message.

Later in the same year, a judge reinstated 16 sanitation workers who were fired for refusing to comply with the New York City vaccination mandate issued a year earlier—and ruled they should get back pay.[13] "There is nothing in the record to support the rationality of keeping a vaccination mandate for public employees, while vacating the mandate for private sector employees or creating a carveout for certain professions, like athletes, artists and performers," the ruling stated, exposing the capriciousness of the mandate. In the judge's estimation, "the mandate was not just about safety and public health; it was about compliance."[14] (The city is appealing the decision, but the ruling paves the way for the next court challenge.)

As momentum from such lawsuits builds, employers may think twice before tethering people's livelihoods to a vaccine that prevents neither contracting nor transmitting a contagious disease. Best case scenario, the dominos start to fall and we can subject the hot-potato question—did the Covid vaccine mandates have an ethical leg to stand on?—to an uncensored public debate.

13

ALERT TO OVERREACH: ROBERT FREUDENTHAL AND FATHER RAYMOND DE SOUZA

What constitutes overreach in a pandemic? It depends who you ask, of course. What one person experiences as reassuring protection feels like intrusive overreach to another. It's not a question you can settle with a yardstick, like "is your fence encroaching on my property?"

Even so, it's a useful question to ask. Not just useful, but necessary. Governments wielded an extraordinary amount of power during the pandemic, with knock-on effects that will reverberate for decades. If we don't talk about it, we're giving political leaders *carte blanche* to do it again, and handing over a blank check is never a good idea.

Governments throughout the world used the "can't hurt" argument to enact measures that had little basis in evidence, like masking toddlers or not taking Yappy for a walk past 8 pm. Roped-off housewares sections, social bubbles, chalk circles on the grass, masks on the beach. The famous "glory holes" for safer sex. Can't hurt, right? (Of course it can hurt, but we weren't allowed to say that.)

Liberal democracies have built-in safeguards to hold government power in check—legislative and judicial processes that jam the gears of executive overreach before the train loses control—but these mechanisms went AWOL during Covid. Want people to stay home? Easy, declare a state of emergency. Emergency about to expire? Extend it for another month. Or six. Want a mask mandate in the schools? Consult the experts (always public health experts, of course, never experts in child development). The lack of due process, of an avenue to interrogate the restrictions, created the perfect storm for overreach.

To Robert Freudenthal, a psychiatrist with London NHS mental health services, government overreach is *the* pandemic story. When government bureaucrats hold sway over people's every movement, when they see fit to divide life's messy reality into essential and non-essential activities, when "almost every aspect of civil society, including religious and political activity, has been criminalized"[1]— well, yes, Sherlock, that's overreach.

It's a "legislative and criminal justice response" to a public health crisis, which Freudenthal says doesn't work. Not in the long run, anyway. "It only destroys trust, especially in marginalized communities," he told me in a private conversation. "The forced closure of services that people rely on to live their lives is just cruel." Instead, he would have liked to see governments "invest in community infrastructure to enable people to keep functioning."

When Freudenthal cast his lot with psychiatry, he got a crash course in government strong-arm tactics. By definition, psychiatry has the power to detain a patient against their will if they meet certain criteria—a power that society has bestowed on the profession. Involuntary detention does have an upside, namely "trying to provide healthcare to people who need it."[1] But Freudenthal says it can also "act as a way of perpetrating various injustices in society," citing the "disproportionate detention of young black men" by the Mental Health Act as an example. And if you detain someone in a way they disagree with, "it's expected there will be some pushback."[2]

The parallels with Covid policy could not be more obvious. Taking the charitable view, countries that locked down were simply trying to protect the public. But their heavy-handed policies ignored the simple fact that no two people are alike. A lockdown may cause barely a ripple in the life of a financial analyst with a paid-up home and a family, but for a single young man looking for his place in the world it represents a life-altering setback.

It's these young and restless types who aroused my greatest sympathies during lockdown, no doubt because my two children belonged to this group. Both completed their final stretch of university online and both got their degrees in late 2020, joining the glut of "pandemic graduates" competing for rapidly disappearing jobs. Freudenthal, meanwhile, felt most protective of his own flock: the mentally fragile people who struggled with life at the best of times and were now struggling a hundred times more.

Like just about all the people featured in this book, Freudenthal had a "sense of abject horror" at the thought of police roaming the streets, watching people's movements and controlling how often they left the house. He thought of all the people who did not have the skills to navigate this alien new world: the mentally ill, the homeless, the undocumented... None of this seemed public-spirited or harmless to him.

Drawing on the work of Austrian philosopher Ivan Illich, Freudenthal divides medical harm into three types: direct harms from a medical intervention, like the side effects from a medication; social harms, such as the separation of family members resulting from a border closure; and cultural harms, meaning the loss of the activities and rituals that keep us grounded. "This third type of harm rarely gets acknowledged or talked about," he told me. For example, "some people live for things like live theater or music. The Covid policies summarily cast these things aside, as if they had no importance at all, which seemed extraordinarily blinkered to me." During lockdown, Freudenthal had the sense that "something was being ripped from society, but nobody was talking about it."

Could we not find more humane ways to stop the spread? Could we at least talk about it? Apparently not. As Robert Jackman points out in a 2021 essay for *Reason*, lockdown became the default, with the burden of proof placed on dissenters.[3] The zeitgeist had spoken: "This is necessary. There is no alternative. And don't you dare speak about trade-offs—we're talking life and death here."

Freudenthal spoke anyway. "Too frequently the public health response to Covid-19 is framed as a struggle between health versus the economy," he wrote in the *Labour Hub*.[4] In fact, lockdowns involve "much broader tensions and trade-offs," including "concerns about mental health, safeguarding, wider health implications of a society living under various degrees of lockdown, civil liberties, concerns about authoritarian policy, issues of over-policing, and impacts on existing inequalities."

Freudenthal returned to the theme of inequality in an October 2020 article for *The Lancet*, co-written with three other psychiatrists.[5] Noting the safeguards against indiscriminate detention of psychiatric patients who *could* pose a risk to others, the authors carried the argument to Covid-related detentions: "It is essential that that appropriate legal safeguards are put in place to make sure such detentions are appropriately scrutinised." Considering the outsized impact of Covid restrictions on marginalized and over-policed groups, "these powers should not be left for the government and police to exercise unchecked."

Sounds like democracy 101 to me, but governments evidently thought otherwise. They continued to impose restrictions without nuance, leaving people on life's margins in despair. Predictably, psychiatric care stepped forward as the only acceptable response to this distress. Hospital chaplaincy services? Withdrawn. Peer support sessions at the local community center? Expendable. To Freudenthal's dismay, "only psychiatrists were able to continue seeing their patients in person, including doing home visits."[6]

Governments were also quick to suggest a "greater investment in mental health"—an irony not lost on Freudenthal, who points out that the cause can't be the cure. People don't need "mental health services" to deal with inhumane rules—they need more humane rules.

Politicians had no time for such subtleties. They filtered all their decisions through an epidemiologic lens, assessing all human activities on the basis of viral transmission risk and disregarding the wider meaning or context of those activities. Toxic home environment? Abusive spouse? Fear not, you're keeping the virus away. The "psychosocial determinants of health" that Freudenthal sees as a bedrock of public policy got swept aside.

That's why he bristles at the facile suggestion, reinforced by a parade of memes, that good people support lockdowns and only selfish jerks oppose them. "There continues to be a refusal to consider any criticisms of the lockdown approach as [anything but] uncaring selfishness," he reflects in a letter to the *British Medical Journal*.[7] But does the path not taken—a policy approach rooted in "decisions being made with people rather than imposed upon them" and "a profound respect for civil liberties"—sound anything less than humane?

Why do governments grab power? Some people say it's just what they do. Horses run, governments seek control. But government actions also reflect the will of the people, and we saw this play out with Covid. Government overreach happened because people let it happen. They looked to their leaders to make it all better—to stop every "preventable death" from Covid—and the leaders feared an angry mob if they didn't deliver. When people blame their leaders for every death, when they regard a risk-free environment as their birthright and insist their government provide it, politicians will naturally seek to protect themselves from liability. Viewed through this lens, the institutional response to Covid was nothing more than a giant cover-your-ass operation.

In a video chat with Vinay Prasad,[2] Freudenthal unpacks this newfangled idea that we're entitled to avoid all risk. Right to life? Sure. Right to a *risk-free* life? Not so much. Drawing another parallel with psychiatry, he explains that "if I detained every patient who could possibly harm themselves or someone else, I would be detaining everybody." When making such decisions, he considers the *probability* that a patient will put others at risk. It has to be fairly low, but it's never zero. Ditto for viral transmission, he says. "I'm not going to be exposed to any risk at all" is not a reasonable expectation, and we can't expect our governments to fulfill it. Life's not like that.

Society was already leaning hard into safetyism before the pandemic, and Covid just pushed the timeline forward. Greg Lukianoff and Jonathan Haidt, authors of the 2018 bestselling book *The Coddling of the American Mind*, define safetyism as "a culture or belief system in which safety has become a sacred value, which means that people become unwilling to make trade-offs demanded by other practical and moral concerns."[8] The ever-increasing appetite for safety prompts a call for more and more rules, and who better than government to supply them? Safetyism also brings forth a preoccupation with the biological, medical side of life. The medical establishment obliges with (often pill-shaped) solutions, leading to what Freudenthal calls a "system of viewing people as objects for medical intervention."[9]

Some people welcome the cultural shift—after all, they helped bring it about—but others recoil at an ethos that views them as mere "units of safety," to use a bull's-eye locution I encountered in 2020. They reject this reductive view of their personhood: safe or unsafe, healthy or diseased, A-grade sirloin or inferior rump steak. To Freudenthal, this explains a lot of the pushback on mask wearing. Aside from its public health function (of hotly debated benefit, but that's another story), the mask serves as "a signifier that we are willing to consider ourselves primarily as a medical object, which can be monitored, tracked, traced, and injected."[9] Not much wonder, then, that wearing a mask leaves many people "feeling manipulated and used." They want their personhood back.

It's what many restriction enthusiasts fail to grasp and why Freudenthal ultimately lands on the "no" side of coercive pandemic measures: they work against, rather than with, human nature.

But Asians have been wearing masks for years, some Westerners say. *Why can't we entitled brats do the same?* Here's a fun little reality test: search for "Tokyo trains 2019" on YouTube and watch the video clips that pop up. You may see a mask or two, but you'll see a hundred times more bare faces, even on the jam-packed commuter trains. Having lived in Japan for 13 months and visited several other cities in the region, I can confirm: pre-Covid, masking in Asia never came close to the norm.

But it's no different from motor vehicle laws, others say. Actually, it is. Human interaction is a need, driving unsafely is not. Craving a hug or a smile from your mother after a year apart is not like wanting to get plastered behind the wheel. "The idea that the government has the power to legislate restrictions on innate human behaviour, such as social contact, is false," Freudenthal says.[10] When government legislation departs too sharply from people's realities and needs, we're left with "a fractured society," and sooner or later people push back.

Even if governments confiscate people's tools of resistance—say, by making protests illegal—they can only stem the tide for so long. With each passing day, another person decides they would rather work up a sweat in a dance club than watch their life roll by in stillborn safety. When enough people reach this point, it's game over for government.

* * *

A psychiatrist and a priest walk into a bar... Is there a joke that begins like this? If not, there should be. Both in the business of compassion and forgiveness, psychiatrists and priests make a natural pairing. Both listen to people confess their most troubling thoughts and behaviors—the psychiatrist from an upholstered armchair, the priest from behind a curtain in a confession booth. Both grant absolution: the psychiatrist through analysis and the priest through divine grace.

They both know a thing or two about what makes people tick, so they'll likely have a lot to talk about in that bar. If the psychiatrist is Freudenthal and the priest is Father Raymond de Souza, they'll eventually get to the topic of Covid policies, and they'll both agree that their governments made a serious miscalculation in ignoring human nature and human needs.

Father de Souza is a priest for the Sacred Heart of Mary Parish on Wolfe Island in Ontario and a chaplain at nearby Queen's University, where he also teaches in the department of economics.[11] A prolific essayist, he writes a column in the *National Post* and serves as editor-in-chief of *Convivium* magazine. Like Freudenthal, de Souza ministers to people who need a refuge from life's slings and arrows. To help them get through the day, he offers his ear—and assures them they have God's ear, too.

For the record, religion has never called to me. I'm more likely to seek comfort on a lake or in a forest (or once in a while, in a gram or two of mushrooms) than in a place of worship. But Covid helped me understand that some people *need* religious communion. To de Souza's flock, there's nothing "non-essential" about what he offers: it's basically IV therapy.

As a religious leader, de Souza has an obvious stake in the question: Does the state have the right to interfere in freedom of religious expression? And if so, to what extent? He delivered his verdict on October 23 in the *National Post*[12]: the Canadian government crossed the line. Under the pretext of containing a pandemic, they betrayed a "naked urge to extend the reach of the state."

As Exhibit A, he presented the six-month ban on in-person worship in British Columbia, orchestrated by provincial health officer Bonnie Henry. "Her edict permitted people to meet for an Alcoholics Anonymous meeting in the church basement, but that same number of people could not meet in the much larger church to pray," he said. "It wasn't about regulating meetings, but banning worship"—a power play masquerading as public health.

His Exhibit B brought the power dynamics even closer to the

surface. When an Alberta Justice sentenced Artur Pawlowski, a protestant pastor in Calgary, for violating public health orders, he not only gave the pastor a large fine, but a script about "expert opinion" to read before discussing Covid with his congregants. "Forcing people to say what they do not wish to say—and do not believe—violates all the fundamental freedoms of the Charter," de Souza maintained. "It's what tyrants do."

He revisited the topic a couple of months later, after learning that vaccination would be required to attend a place of worship in Quebec—a ruling he saw as "moving into new territory" for the government.[13] In addition to dictating the number and configuration (six feet!) of congregants, government officials were now deciding "who can enter the house of God at all." Churches were supposed to welcome everyone. But now Quebec wanted pastors "to become a vaccine gendarmerie, demanding not a public confession of sins, but rather a display of vaccinated virtue." To de Souza, this represented an "intolerable affront to religious freedom."

While Canadian courts have ruled that the restrictions do not contravene the country's religious freedom guarantee, state lawmakers in Ohio have taken de Souza's side. In June 2022, they passed a resolution urging the US government to put Canada on a religious-freedom watchlist, which includes Azerbaijan and Cuba, judged guilty of severe violations of religious liberties.[14] (At press time, Canada does not appear on the list.)

So which is it? Violation or no violation? After everyone has spoken (or shouted), we find ourselves at the same fork in the road, with irreconcilable values on either side. Take the left path if you believe we must shield as many people as possible against a novel virus, full stop. Take the right path if you see people as hurting souls and places of worship as welcoming arms that heal them—even in a pandemic.

While I don't share Father de Souza's religious impulses, I can't help but sympathize with a world view that looks beyond the need for protection from a virus. I also understand, more than ever before, why people of faith sometimes get frustrated with nonbelievers like me. The writer Robertson Davies once stated that he doesn't understand atheists. I can't locate the essay where he wrote it (even Google ain't God, sad to say), but I remember he used the word "numinous." He said, more or less, that life has a numinous quality that atheists just don't see. He likened the atheist perspective to living without an arm. We live-with-Covid types keep telling the forever-restrictionists the same thing: "There's something about the experience of living that you're not seeing—something capacious and numinous and vital. Look here. Look over there. Can you see it, off in the distance?" They tell us there's nothing to see.

I would love to join de Souza and Freudenthal in that bar, talking about safetyism, freedom of conscience, power, overreach, and the numinous shimmer under the surface of things. I have a feeling we would get along famously.

HOPPING MAD: CHARLES WALKER
AND EHUD QIMRON

Charles Walker was one of my best buddies during the early months of the pandemic. I'll admit it was a one-way-relationship—he had no idea I exist—but I felt certain we would be great friends if we met.

A member of the UK's conservative party since 2005, Sir Charles Ashley Rupert Walker became an Officer of the Order of the British Empire in 2015 and a Knight Commander of the Order of the British Empire in 2019.[1] I'm not exactly sure what it takes to become a knight, but I'm told the bar is pretty high.

When the UK locked down, Walker reacted much the same way Laura Dodsworth did: with incredulity and outrage. Like Dodsworth, he accused the government of ramping up fear of the disease. When police officers arrested a 72-year-old woman protesting the regulations, he called them a "disgrace."[2]

Week after week he would stand up in the mostly empty House of Commons chamber and, turning to face the Speaker of the House, put words to his anger. He described lockdowns as a strategy that would "unleash a tidal wave of misery," citing the four million UK residents suffering from mental health problems and those who had to put their cancer treatment on hold.[3] "We need to have a frank, open and honest debate about the ethics of trading lives tomorrow to save lives today," he said.

In a later speech, he acknowledged the lockdowns had been brutally effective—"so brutal that we now have children too frightened to go outdoors lest they kill their parents, adolescents isolated at home suffering from anxiety, eating disorders and self-harm, parents battling with depression, desperation and suicidal thoughts and many old people fading away from loneliness."[4]

I couldn't get enough of his speeches: the diamond-cut British syllables, the precise hand movements, the passion and pain in his face. His erudition seemed to spring directly from the heart, no doubt helped by his London private-school education. I mean, who uses "lest" in their spoken language? Certainly not any North American politician I know.

When Walker said something especially brilliant, I would raise my fist in solidarity. "Yes, yes! Go for it, Charlie!"

"What's that?" Drew would call out from the next room. "Did you say something?"

"Never mind, I'm just swooning over a British guy." (It's one of the things I love about my marriage: we can say things like that without anyone walking off in a huff.)

In one speech, which apparently "sparked fury," Walker pushed back against his government's insistence that all Covid deaths were both tragic and preventable. "No government can abolish death," he said, reminding his listeners that 615,000 people die in the UK every year.[5] "A tragedy is when a child dies. A tragedy is when some young woman or young man dies." When a 90-year-old meets their mortality and we call it tragic, "we diminish that life so well lived."

Before Covid, most people understood this. Anyone who has ever attended the funeral of a 90-year-old and a 10-year-old would agree they're not the same thing. When 90-year-old grandpa dies, people may shed tears, but their hearts aren't too heavy for celebration. They share stories about his antics, reminiscing about the day he fell out of his canoe or sprinkled salt on his ice cream. They smile and may even laugh a little. When a 10-year-old dies, it's an affront to the life cycle. Angels weep.

But Covid turned death into a crime. If you dared suggest, as Walker did, that not all deaths are equally tragic, a thousand people blocked you on Facebook—the same people who showed no sympathy for the locked-down people suffering from isolation, depression, and hopelessness.

Deaths from Covid were given special status as preventable (and therefore unacceptable), but we can extrapolate the "preventable" label to just about all deaths. People don't die of old age, they die of something. An extra echocardiogram might have detected the atherosclerosis in time. A more frequent mammography schedule could have caught that breast cancer tumor before it spread. If a different dressing had been used, the wound might have healed. And so on. Even so, death comes for all of us. And once you've settled into a nursing home, just about any virus can do it: long before Covid, an outbreak of respiratory disease in a Canadian nursing home killed 8.5% of affected residents.[6]

This is not to say we just "let old people die." Of course we don't. We shield them, we protect them, and if they fall ill, we lovingly tend to them. But maybe we don't make young people pay such a high price? Maybe we think twice before bringing civilization to its knees? That's what Walker was arguing with such passion: if your policies flow from a refusal to accept any Covid deaths, you end up causing a lot of human misery.

In a personal email, Walker shared his thoughts about how the UK might have dealt with Covid after May 2020, when the disease's risk gradient became clear. "At this point, there could have been a debate about how we could protect [higher-risk] groups without closing down our economy and curtailing almost all aspects of day-to-day life," he suggested. For example, "we could have paid pensioners to stay at home, perhaps doubling their state pension as a reward and recognition of their sacrifice. We could have encouraged those with underlying health conditions to work at home if they could, topping up their salary by 50 percent as a thank you." Would it have saved every life? "Absolutely not. But the plan we followed didn't save every life either and it did untold long-term damage to the health and psyche of our nation."

It's not by chance that Walker keeps returning to the mental health effects of lockdowns: he himself lives with obsessive compulsive disorder (OCD), including a compulsion to do things in multiples of four.[7] He has gone public with his affliction and helped convince his government to support a bill to reduce the stigma of mental illness.[8] The mental demons that, to some degree, persecute us all clearly matter to Walker—a lot.

Walker's second passion, freedom of expression, infused his speeches long before Covid. In 2016, he asked his government "what legal protections are in place to protect people's freedom of expression with regard to religious satire," in reference to an athlete subjected to a "manhunt and vilification on social media" after posting a video making fun of Islam.[9] "Freedom of speech and religion are core values that make our country great. They are, indeed, protected in law. What is or is not a joke, or what constitutes satire, is, I believe, in the eye or ear of the beholder and is not, perhaps, for Government to opine on."

When the government banned peaceful protests during Covid, Walker saw it as an affront to democracy and called for an immediate reversal of the legislation. "Let us get people back on the streets and allow them to get things off their chest again," he said. "Not tomorrow, not next week, but this afternoon."[10]

In March 2021, following a debate on the six-month extension of emergency powers, he announced his intent to stage a protest of his own. "For the next few days, I will walk around London with a pint of milk on my person because that pint will represent my protest," he said, inviting other people to join him.[11] "Perhaps they will be protesting the roaring back of a mental health demon brought on by lockdown, perhaps it will be protesting a renewed battle with anorexia, with depression, with anxiety, with addiction."

Reporting for *The Guardian*, John Grace described the oration as "the most surreal Commons speech" he had ever heard.[12] "*Why milk?* We never got to find out." Unable to decide if the speech was "genius or madness," Grace opted to give Walker the benefit of the doubt. Although I didn't understand the milk thing any better than Grace, anyone who risks ridicule for what he believes in has my respect.

OK, truth time: I went to a pandemic protest myself. This was not in character for me. I had never waved placards at Queen's Park or Parliament Hill before and knew nothing about protests. Was there a dress code, or what?

I tried to talk myself out of it, but something pushed me to go. It wasn't this or that rule I wanted to protest, but the *gestalt* of it: the nonstop panic, the moralizing, the intolerance, the push for a new and asocial normal. I wanted the universe to register my complaint.

And so it was that, on May 15, 2021, I joined a crowd of people gathered around the horseman statue on the grounds of Queen's Park, Ontario's Legislative Building, in an official protest against the ongoing Covid measures. Called the World Freedom Rally, the event was being held in major cities across the globe. A few people from my Q-LIT posse were also here: my strange new tribe.

I looked around, afraid of what I might see. OK, not so bad. Fathers with toddlers on their shoulders, young women with interesting hair, smiling seniors... It was a bright and balmy day, the type of day that feels especially magical after a Canadian winter, and the park was filling up quickly. A row of police officers stood off to one side, looking bored. Evidently they didn't intend to ask people to stay six feet apart.

Uh, oh, just what I feared: a woman with a wooden cross in one hand and a sign saying "God doesn't wear a mask" in the other, smiling and nodding. Moments later a bearded dude walked by, dragging a long pennant behind him. "Question everything," it said. These were clearly not my people. Should I leave?

A man in combat gear, his face concealed under what looked like a goalie mask spray-painted in bronze, walked up to me. He was holding onto a leash that had a rather large dog at the other end, a pit bull by the looks of it. I took a quick step back.

"Aw, she won't bite," the man said, patting her head. "She's a sweetheart."

"Cool mask," I mumbled.

"I'm only wearing it to stay incognito. There's gotta be some moles around here. I sure as hell ain't wearing it 'cause of the 'rona."

In truth, I also worried about being identified—not by moles, but by people who knew me. What if one of my clients spotted me? What if my friend Ruth, who still wore a face shield and wiped down her groceries, showed up? Would she block me on Facebook?

All of a sudden everyone was marching: up University Avenue, a short stretch on Bloor Street, then back along Yonge toward the downtown core. Pedestrians lined both sides of the road, some cheering and others shaking their heads. I found my Q-LIT companions and fell into step with them.

When my group reached Adelaide Street we ducked into the Craft Beer Market, where we got to taste such items as Mascot Gold Rush Sour and Beyond the Pale Pink Fuzzy Grapefruit Pale Ale. As I relaxed into my beer, I reflected on the protest: a little too brassy for my taste, a little uncomfortable, not an experience I would likely repeat. Still, it felt good to have shown up.

I wondered if Walker went ahead with his protest. Did he strap his pint of milk to his chest? Did he give a speech in Hyde Park and did anyone listen? When I watched him hold forth in the House of Commons, I sometimes felt sorry for him. So much anger, so much passion, and none of it moving the needle. He spoke to a near-empty room, his peers betraying no emotion at his words. They just swirled in the air, a current of anger with no place to go. "Almost all of my colleagues were working from home, dialing remotely to take part," he explained in his note to me. "I felt obliged to turn up, given that so many of my constituents were still going to work and felt underrepresented."

If 90 percent of life is showing up, as Woody Allen has suggested, Walker certainly did his part. And words have a way of escaping the place where they are spoken, traveling in directions nobody can predict. A whisper here, a tweet there. Occasionally the words land in the right ears and the needle moves. That's how change happens, one conversation at a time.

* * *

Ehud Qimron has none of Walker's political priors. One of Israel's leading epidemiologists, Qimron runs a sophisticated research lab at Tel Aviv University, studying the adaptive immune system of bacteria in the hope of outsmarting antibiotic-resistant pathogens. But when lockdowns and panic took over his country, science became political for him.

On September 6, 2020, he added his name to an open letter, signed by dozens of other Israeli scientists and doctors, urging the government not to impose a new countrywide lockdown in the midst of rising coronavirus cases.[13] The signatories recommended protecting vulnerable groups, above all the elderly, and avoiding one-size-fits-all collective measures—essentially the Swedish model. "A lockdown does not stop the pandemic, it merely slows its spread slightly and temporarily," the letter stated. "When the restrictions are lifted, the virus continues its spread, and this after the country's citizens have been weakened emotionally, economically and above all in terms of their health. A lockdown does not prevent deaths. On the contrary, it extends the period of time during which populations at risk are exposed to the virus…thus paradoxically causing excess mortality."

The government disagreed, at least on paper. In a private interview, Qimron told me that "someone high up in government supported my recommendations and said he would spread the word." So why didn't it happen? "Politicians knew the media would tear them apart if they went against the orthodoxy. And being scrutinized by the media is a politician's greatest fear." I pressed further: *Why* had the media become such a Covid monolith? "Part of it is ratings, part of it is key opinion leaders trying to make a name for themselves. And part of it is simply not understanding that you can't suppress a virus like this."

Qimron and his allies upped the ante with a lawsuit to the High Court of Justice, alleging the state was basing its assumptions on erroneous data.[14] The plaintiffs also took issue with the imposition of a new lockdown during the High Holy Day period. The suit went nowhere.

While most Israelis went along with the new lockdown, the Haredi (ultra-Orthodox) community, which accounts for 12 percent of the Israeli population, wasn't having any of it. Moshe Gafni of the United Torah Judaism party told then-prime minister Netanyahu that his constituents would take their guidance from their spiritual leader, Rabbi Chaim Kanievsky, who insisted that schools must stay open throughout the crisis.[15] Mainstream Israelis were furious: the Haredi were brazenly flouting the rules and allowing the virus to spread—not to mention breaching the church-state divide.

While I don't generally vibe with the Haredi world view, despite my mother's Orthodox roots, a part of me understood their position perfectly: they were putting their children first. "It is normal and natural for parents to sacrifice for their children—not the other way around," my mother used to say. She told me the fable of a Jewish man who plants a carob tree, which bears fruit only after seventy years. When asked why he would plant a tree he would never use, the man replies, "Just as my ancestors planted for their children, I am planting for my sons."

In defending the Haredi response to the pandemic, Mendy Moskowits, a member of the Belz Hasidic sect in Jerusalem, argued that mainstream Israelis just didn't understand the Haredi way of life. "We can't have a generation go bust," he said to the Associated Press.[16] "We are still sending our boys to school because we have rabbis who say Torah study saves and protects." Ah, yes. The next generation. The one my mother and I most cared about. I didn't want them to go to bust, either. (Also: if the virus posed a real threat to young people, I have no doubt the Haredi leaders would have recalibrated their thinking. The Jewish religion places a high value on preserving life.)

Israel got through the fall lockdown and, like just about every other country, saw Covid transmission go up in winter 2021 again. Up and down, up and down. Wave after wave after wave. March, June, September, December. The government seemed stuck in the same reactive mode: cases up, more restrictions. Cases down, let people breathe a little. On and on and on. Where was this all going? What was the end-game?

Qimron had enough. On January 10, 2022, he wrote an open letter to the Israeli minister of health. You won't find any polite preliminaries in the letter, reproduced below in abbreviated form below.[17] It's gloves off and game on.

Ministry of Health, it's time to admit failure. Two years late, you finally realize that a respiratory virus cannot be defeated and that any such attempt is doomed to fail. You refused to admit that the infection comes in waves that fade by themselves, despite years of observations and scientific knowledge. You insisted on attributing every decline of a wave solely to your actions, and so through false propaganda "you overcame the plague." And again you defeated it, and again and again and again. You insisted on ignoring the fact that the disease is dozens of times more dangerous for risk groups and older adults, despite the knowledge that came from China as early as 2020.

From the heights of your hubris, you have also ignored the fact that in the end the truth will be revealed. And it begins to be revealed. The truth is that you have brought the public's trust in you to an unprecedented low. The truth is that you have burned hundreds of billions of shekels to no avail. You made children feel guilty, scared, smoke, drink, get addicted, drop out, and quarrel, as school principals around the country attest. You have harmed livelihoods, the economy, human rights, mental health and physical health. You slandered colleagues who did not surrender to you, you turned the people against each other, divided society and polarized the discourse.

There is currently no medical emergency. The only emergency now is that you still set policies and hold huge budgets for propaganda instead of directing them to strengthen the health care system. This emergency must stop!

It looks like Qimron got his wish. As of late 2022, all that remains of Israel's former Covid mandates is a set of recommendations, "which the public is largely ignoring." And what if cases go up again? Could the whole apparatus come roaring back again? "I doubt it will happen with Covid. But we've set the precedent and I worry it will happen with a different crisis. So many lines were crossed—things that are not supposed to happen in a democracy. Until those in charge are held accountable, I will not sleep well."

15

IMMUNE TO THE HERD: ANDERS TEGNELL AND MARK WOOLHOUSE

The land of ABBA, Ikea, H&M, Spotify, Volvo, and...freedom? In March 2020, while the rest of the world locked down and imposed strict social distancing policies, Sweden rolled out largely voluntary containment measures.[1] It *advised* older people to limit social contact, *recommended* that people work from home, and *suggested* they avoid non-essential travel. It didn't close businesses or in-person classes for students under 16. It kept its borders open.

I think of Sweden of a well-ordered country with a history of staying out of trouble and not a drop of libertarianism in its national blood—not the sort of place I would expect to make waves. So why did Sweden, of all places, go zag when the rest of the world went zig?

A little digging turns up one clue. A consulting firm called Hofstede Insights has rated countries across the world along six cultural dimensions, one of them being "uncertainty intolerance." (Their website[2] makes it easy: enter a country and out come the six results. It's a lot of fun.) Countries that score high in this dimension seek certainty and control. France and Spain have extremely high scores, putting a new spin on all the *gendarmes* and *policiales* they deployed during the first lockdown. Sweden scores uncommonly low—well below the United States, Canada, Germany, and its own Nordic neighbors. This peculiarity could, in part, explain the country's ability to tolerate a "wait and see" period.

But perhaps the "Swedish solution" has less to do with the national psyche than with a single Swede, Anders Tegnell. A physician specializing in infectious disease, Tegnell was Sweden's state epidemiologist between 2013 and 2022 and the architect of the country's Covid strategy.[3] In his bestselling pandemic book *The Herd*,[4] Johan Anderberg describes Tegnell as "prudent, controlled, and unaffected by pressure and stress"—just the qualities needed to withstand the pressure from a frightened mob. Upon meeting Tegnell for the first time, Johann Giesecke, an earlier state epidemiologist, read his future protégé as "completely apolitical"—to Giesecke, the highest compliment one could pay a colleague.

Above all, Tegnell is a realist. "This is not a disease that can be stopped or eradicated, at least until a working vaccine is produced," he told *Nature* in an April 2020 interview.[1] "We have to find long-term solutions that keeps the distribution of infections at a decent level." Rather than locking down, he promised to steer his country through the storm with a minimum of disruption.

To some extent, Tegnell's hands were tied: the Swedish constitution forbids peacetime emergency measures, so there was "not much legal possibility to close down cities in Sweden using the present laws." The constitution also enshrines freedom of movement, charmingly described as "freedom to roam" in some texts, as an inherent right.[5]

These constraints don't fully explain Sweden's choices, though. As the past three years have made abundantly clear, decision makers who want to enact a measure can find a loophole (state of emergency, anyone?) and forge ahead. If Tegnell had wanted Sweden to lock down, he could have made it happen.

Tegnell wasn't looking for a loophole, though. While locking down sounded plausible at face value—keep people apart so they can't pass a virus around— "sounds good" didn't meet his standard of evidence. When people questioned his approach, he pointed out that none of the lockdown measures had a scientific basis.[1] Schools?

"The science shows that closing schools at this stage does not make sense. You have to shut down schools fairly early in the epidemic to get an effect." Closing borders? It's "ridiculous, because COVID-19 is in every European country now." Face masks? "Evidence for an effect of face covering to limit the spread from asymptomatic persons is not clear."[6]

Wobbly science aside, Tegnell understood that once set in motion, lockdowns would be difficult to wind down. He also trusted the Swedish public to follow recommendations. Swedish infectious disease laws rest on the premise that citizens have a responsibility to avoid spreading disease, and "this is the core we started from."[1]

Besides, Tegnell was only doing what the world had always done before Covid. In its 2019 guidance document on nonpharmaceutical interventions to manage pandemic influenza, the WHO recommends *not* quarantining exposed individuals, tracing contacts, or closing borders, even for the most severe pandemics.[7] The UK's 2011 pandemic guidance document also cautions against closing borders, citing evidence that a 90% restriction on air travel only delays a wave by one to two weeks.[8] The CDC's 2017 pandemic mitigation guidelines state that reactive school closures are "unlikely to affect virus transmission" and advises "carefully considering and justifying any restrictions on individual freedom."[9]

He wasn't the guy going off-script—the rest of the world was. It seemed to Tegnell that other countries were "trying to swap out their jet-engines midflight," Anderberg writes in *The Herd*. "To understand it, you needed a doctoral degree, not in epidemiology, but in sociology."

Nonetheless, the world elected to paint Tegnell as a reckless outlier. (Everyone needs a scapegoat during a crisis.) Suddenly on the spot and in the spotlight, he responded to interviewers' probing questions with unflappable calm, his blue eyes holding steady behind his specs. (If I sound a bit star-struck, it's not just me: Tegnell's face became a tattoo request in April 2020, and you can still find Tegnell merch all over the Internet.) Online warriors took delight in pointing out that Sweden had a higher Covid death rate than its Nordic neighbors, conveniently failing to mention the disproportionate impact of the early nursing-home outbreaks or the country's quiet regression to the European mean.

One got the sense that the world *wanted* Sweden to fail. But there was every reason to root for Sweden's success: If a more moderate policy could steer a country through the pandemic, wasn't this great news for the rest of the world?

I had never thought to visit Sweden before, but it now became my top travel destination. I wanted to roam freely in a country that had chosen proportionality over panic, to assure myself that such a thing still existed. Plus my mental health was circling the drain and I needed to GTFO for a while. Even Dr. Zoom thought so. Taking advantage of the EU's hiatus in travel restrictions for "low risk" countries, I booked a seven-day trip in August 2020. Three days in Amsterdam, four days in Stockholm, fourteen days of quarantine back in Toronto: on paper it sounded preposterous. I went anyway.

A wall of heat slammed into me when I landed in Amsterdam, and for the next three days the temperature never fell below 90°F. I spent most of the time walking up and down the streets, sweat running down my back and blisters sprouting on my feet. The old city hummed with life, with much of the action taking place in the cafés and pubs lining the canals. When I needed a break I would grab a seat at a patio, order a Heineken, and strike up a conversation. In near-perfect English, my interlocutors told me they were ready to face the virus as a long-term lodger they would need to make peace with, rather than wrestle to the ground. COVID-19 had not been forgotten, but the impulse to live life was reasserting itself in a way I had yet to experience in Canada.

On one occasion I struck up a conversation with a sex worker and asked her how COVID-19 had affected the business, which had resumed in July.

"Why would it affect anything?"

"I thought there might be rules against getting too close to your clients' faces. Hugging, kissing, stuff like that."

She laughed. "My clients don't come to me for hugging and kissing. They come to get the job done, know what I mean? The virus hasn't changed that."

I arrived in Stockholm as the sun was setting, marveling at my luck in landing a room with a killer view at half the price I had paid in Amsterdam. Over the next three days I fell in love with the city, thanks in part to the dazzling weather that brought the residents out en masse to the flea markets, parks, and beaches.

Not that the Swedes had ignored the virus—they had kept a distance from each other throughout the spring—but they were now ready to squeeze the juice out of the summer's final stretch. It was easy to forget the pandemic as I ducked into old churches and oversized H&M stores, grabbing a box of lingonberries at the outdoor market along the way. While having lunch at a floating restaurant, a sudden urge to dive into the surrounding water superseded my embarrassment at making an ungainly splash in front of strangers. Yes, it was dorky.

I had hoped to meet Tegnell in person and interview him for an essay I was writing (and maybe get his autograph). A public health department official invited me to attend one of Tegnell's weekly briefings, but the dates didn't line up, so I didn't get a chance to play fangirl. Even so, the short trip lifted a weight from my chest. I had seen, with my own eyes, how a city could live through a pandemic without losing its head.

The more time passes, the saner Sweden's Covid policy starts to look. We can quibble about the fine points, but the tsunami of death predicted by the simulations never materialized. Within a year, Sweden's all-cause excess deaths were back at zero.[10] A study concluded that Sweden's decision to keep primary schools open prevented the learning loss observed in comparable nations.[11] And here's one for the history books: a Pew Research study includes Sweden in a very short list of countries that have become *more* socially united since the pandemic's inception.[12] Erna Solberg, prime minister of Norway—the neighboring country praised for its un-Swedish approach—concluded that her strategy had been overly cautious. "I probably took many of the decisions out of fear," she said in a television interview.[13] "Worst case scenarios became controlling."

People still wonder why Sweden didn't follow the herd, but that's not the question we should be asking. Considering how well Sweden has fared, we should be asking why other countries didn't take more of an interest in the Swedish approach. If political leaders across the world had hopped on Zoom to pick Tegnell's brain, we might be living in a saner world today.

* * *

An epidemiologist who believes epidemiologists have too much influence in a pandemic? Mark Woolhouse is just that guy. A professor of infectious disease epidemiology at the University of Edinburgh for over 20 years, Woolhouse played a role in both the UK's and Scotland's response to Covid.[14] His 2022 pandemic memoir, *The Year The World Went Mad*,[15] chronicles his experience as a Covid policy insider attempting to dial back the insanity.

"The novel coronavirus response is being driven too much by the epidemiology," Woolhouse stated at an advisory meeting in June 2020, echoing one of my own concerns since day one. Where was the psychological perspective? The sociological one? The educational one? "We epidemiologists were repeatedly told it was someone else's job" to worry about these things, he said. But "whose? Nothing was ever made public."

Teams of epidemiologists were churning out projections of Covid cases, hospitalizations, and deaths under different scenarios, but nobody was modeling the impact of the lockdown strategy. "Where was the formal impact assessment—a standard government planning tool—on the effect of lockdown?"

This single-minded focus on viral containment represents a stark inversion of earlier pandemic responses, which sought to balance mitigation with societal functioning. As Woolhouse has noted, schools stayed open during the Swine flu of 2009-10, even though more UK children died of it than of Covid in 2020.[15]

Some of us also remember Woodstock, the 1969 music festival that took place during the Hong Kong flu pandemic of 1968-70.[16] (My best friend and I wanted to go, but I was twelve. "Vat is dis Voodstock?" my mother asked me. "Don't be silly, of course you're not going. Now help me peel some potatoes.") Patty Mulhearn Lydon, who did make the trek to the festival, told the *New York Post* that "there was no food or water, but one of our guys cut an apple into twenty-seven slices and we all shared it."[17] None of the revelers wore masks and no government officials suggested they stay apart from each other.

Some people will counter that nobody at the time wore seatbelts either, and it's a good thing we've smartened up since then. I don't disagree: I've often wondered how we boomers survived the family road trips of our youth, with screaming children bouncing up and down in the rear of a station wagon. But let's not compare seatbelts to closing schools and businesses and keeping loved ones from each other, shall we?

Woolhouse endorses the model of harm reduction, initially developed to manage problematic drug use. Rather than chasing perfection, harm reduction seeks "better" or "less bad" as a policy goal. Safer sex, rather than no sex or risk-free sex. Safer human contacts, rather than no human contacts. "There is precedent for slowing the spread of an infectious disease by making contacts safe," he says. For example, most AIDS campaigns focus on "knowing your HIV status...not on banning sex altogether."

In the realm of drug use, harm reduction rests on several core principles, which include[18]: 1) Accept that drug use exists in our world; 2) Recognize the social determinants of drug use; 3) Establish quality of life, rather than cessation of drug use, as an outcome; 4)

Give drug users a voice in the programs created to serve them, and 5) Provide services without judgment.

Now imagine these principles transposed to the pandemic: 1) Accept the presence of the virus in our midst; 2) Recognize that everyone faces different social and economic challenges; 3) Establish human flourishing, rather than viral elimination, as a policy objective; 4) Give people a voice in the mitigation measures deployed to protect them, and 5) Don't shame or blame.

Such principles would have steered us toward more humane and sustainable measures and away from the chimera of elimination. Not that lockdowns promised elimination in the first place. In fact, had the vaccines arrived any later, the lockdowns could have made the pandemic a lot worse. Neil Ferguson, whose mathematical projections laid the groundwork for the UK shutdowns, admitted as much in an early briefing[19]: "The more successful a strategy is at temporary suppression, the larger the later epidemic is predicted to be in the absence of vaccination, due to lesser build-up of herd immunity."

The lockdowns only went ahead because of worst-case models like Ferguson's. As an epidemiologist, Woolhouse has the training to distinguish sky-is-falling warnings from likely scenarios and holds that the public was misled to conflate the two. When a model presented at an October 2020 news conference forecast 4,000 deaths per day, he noted that other calculations "gave much lower numbers" than this projection.[20] But this was the projection shown to millions of viewers—and the one that triggered UK's second lockdown.

While Chicken Little predictions continued to pop up in news headlines, Woolhouse stuck to his message of overall harm reduction. He devotes a chapter of his book to the topic, beginning with the idea that good public health seeks a balance: if you start with the premise that "no death from coronavirus is acceptable, [it becomes] impossible to tackle [the pandemic] in a rational manner"—a sentiment echoed by many others in this book.

In retrospect, Woolhouse maintains that the lockdowns and their aftermath caused too much misery and social disruption to defend the strategy. Other approaches could have also saved lives, but with less collateral damage. He has apologized to his daughter, on behalf of his generation, for the harms inflicted on the young and for the "morally wrong" decision to close schools.[20] In his ideal world, mandatory social distancing would have shifted very quickly to voluntary measures. Above all, "we should have done far more to protect those most vulnerable."[15]

Near the end of his book, he delivers his final verdict: "I'm a lockdown sceptic." For a policy insider like Woolhouse, who has faced continuous pressure to move with the herd, it's an astonishing declaration. Like Tegnell, he zigged when the rest of the world zagged. Unlike Tegnell, he couldn't get his country to listen, but his strategic insights live on in his book, ready for future policymakers to ponder.

16

MEETING IN THE MIDDLE: FRANÇOIS BALLOUX, STEFAN BARAL, AND DAVID LEONHARDT

've heard the term "centrist" defined as "living in uneasy acquiescence to the existing order." Centrists don't love the way thing are, but they don't hate it enough to go live in the woods. They vote for the major political parties, without particularly identifying with them. They send their children to normal schools, while worrying that the schools are doing more testing than teaching. They use Amazon, vaguely concerned about the hulking megalith but not concerned enough to forgo the convenience. They grumble about big government, but also believe it serves a purpose.

Centrists have a bit of a bad rap as flip-floppers who can't put a stake in the ground. I admit I find some of them a little boring (show me some fire, dammit!), but they're probably right about a lot of things. They're less wedded to their narrative than the flashy folks, more comfortable changing their minds. They see both sides of a complex issue and don't hate you if you're on the other team. Best of all, they can talk to people of different political persuasions without starting a fight.

François Balloux ticks all the centrist boxes except the "boring" one. A professor of computational biology and director of the University College London Genetics Institute, Balloux uses genomic data to help reconstruct epidemic patterns and, with his colleague Lucy van Dorp, led the first large-scale sequencing of the Sars-COV2 genome.[1] He calls himself a "militant corona centrist"—a contradiction he manages to pull off rather brilliantly. "I wanted to just create my mini-movement, a bit tongue-in-cheek, to place myself outside of the very borderline dogmatic groups," he says. (Given his 150,000 Twitter followers,[2] we can safely say his movement has gone past the "mini" stage.)

Balloux's gentle absurdism comes as a breath of fresh air in a pandemic that has largely kept humor under lock and key. "It was probably a major mistake to stage a pandemic in a US election year," he quips in an interview for *Perspective* magazine.[3] Or how about this one?[4] "I, for one, look forward to the moment when there will be so many variants, characterised by such long series of numbers, that hardly anyone will be able to keep track of them, and even fewer, besides the scientists in charge of their surveillance, give a toss about them."

Balloux supports some pandemic measures, some of the time, but he also thinks the world has lost its marbles. He sees both sides, but he's not a "both-sidesist." When he thinks one side has gone off the rails, he's not afraid to call it out. School closures get him especially riled up—like the closures in Uganda that shut children out of school for well over a year, many of them unlikely to return.

What troubles Balloux above all is the ideological obstinacy that has turned the Covid discourse into a giant tug-of-war. At one end of the rope you find the eradicationalists, who want Covid gone at all costs, and at the other end the Anders Tegnell and Great Barrington Declaration (GBD) groupies. The tug-of-war makes no room for nuance: Killers! Delusional puritans! You don't value life! You relish the drama of restrictions! The rope frays, leaving both teams exhausted.

A strong proponent of free speech, Balloux welcomes forceful statements, and for a six-month stretch during the Covid wars he took pains not to block his Twitter opponents. In the end he gave in, because "you cannot be under a constant avalanche of insults and abuse."[3] In late October 2022, Balloux abruptly deactivated his account, leading to speculation that he had displeased the Twitter gods, though he assured me in an email that he simply "needed a break from the toxicity of the discourse...and I need to get some things done in real life." Two days later his account was up and running again. Someone once described Twitter to me as an abusive partner you know you should leave, but can't, and Balloux's relationship with the platform serves as the perfect case study.

While he falls short of aligning with the GBD, his exasperation with the eradication solution, which he calls "some kind of borderline religious belief," comes through loud and clear in his tweets and interviews. He insists the only way forward is endemicity. And how does this happen? "We essentially get there, I'm afraid, by everyone having been infected."[3]

Balloux's scientific training has schooled him in the biases of scientific inquiry, like the well-known fact that studies with positive results (masks work!) are more likely to get published than studies with negative outcomes (boh-ring).[5] There's also the "winner's curse" effect, whereby the first study to get media traction gets ingrained in people's minds, even if later studies refute it. "Our brains work in a Bayesian way," he explains. "We have priors that influence how we regard new information."[6]

But his beef with the follow-the-science imperative runs deeper than concerns about human biases. Echoing Yuval Harari and Vinay Prasad, he notes that science can inform policy decisions, but cannot dictate them. "What's the value of, say, the life of an 80-year-old in a care home versus the education of a child?"[3] There's no scientific way to answer the question because "different people will put so much different value on different things," he says. That's why "decisions should be taken by elected representatives of the population, and not by scientists. Really not."

And another thing: most scientists' predictions are wrong. Most of *any* expert predictions are wrong, as psychologist Philip Tetlock discovered in one of the world's longest experiments.[7] Over a period of 20 years, Tetlock collected forecasts from 284 highly educated experts, for a whopping total of over 80,000 probability estimates about the future. His conclusion: the experts did little better than a die toss.

Not much has changed since then: people still love to pontificate about the future, but you don't hear their *mea culpas* when they're wiping egg off their face. That's why Balloux takes all predictions with a grain of salt and maintains that it's impossible to predict which variant will emerge next and how its turn on the world stage will play out.[8] The only thing we can reasonably anticipate is that "mutations will continue to appear and the virus will progressively drift."

Whether the drift makes the disease milder or more severe is anybody's guess, but Balloux has noted a tendency, among both academics and the public, to assume the worst. We've certainly seen this bias in the media. News headlines like "variant that could kill one in three infected people a realistic possibility" or "viral mutations may cause another 'very, very bad' COVID-19 wave" assault us from all sides, while good-news clips remain conspicuous in their absence.

What's missing in the doom-and-gloom discourse is probability, Balloux says. Terms like *could, may,* and *possibly* don't tell you much. I *could* find a baby elephant under my bed tomorrow. I *could* get a seven-figure publishing deal with Knopf. Anything is possible. The key question is, how probable is it?

Ever the centrist, Balloux underlines the importance of balancing "the scariness of predictions with their likelihood."[7] Referring to the killer variant prognostication, he notes that "a lineage emerging that is 50 times more lethal is extraordinarily implausible. We've never seen that kind of sudden change in mortality. I'm not saying it's impossible, but you may have a better chance of winning the lottery jackpot many times over." This means we should either stop worrying about the variant that will strike us all dead or start buying lottery tickets. Either way it's a win.

People have been making a sport of doomsaying since long before Covid. Starting in 1947, a group of scientists, politicians, and journalists have been gathering every January at the National Press Club in Washington, DC to unveil the Doomsday Clock, a symbolic timepiece intended to alert us to the impending apocalypse.[9] In 2019 the clock was set at two minutes to midnight, suggesting the apocalypse was breathing down our necks. The pundits in attendance enhanced the mood with pronouncements like "frightening reality" and "catastrophe of historic proportions."

The inclination to hop on the doom train exists in just about all of us. In a 2018 community survey led by Harvard psychologist Howard Gilbert, subjects consistently stated that the world was getting worse, despite data showing improvements in life across almost all domains.[10] Gilbert speculated that, as humans solve certain problems, they keep inventing new ones in a process called "concept creep." For example, definitions of abuse, bullying and trauma keep getting broader and broader, covering scenarios previously deemed relatively benign. Yesterday's "deal with it" becomes today's "you need treatment for PTSD."

The psychology of doom also feeds on itself. When people get their doom on, they tend to retreat from the world and to "actively look for signs of doom to validate their position of hiding behind a rock," says consultant and author Alan Weiss.[11] Seek, and ye shall find.

If humans are indeed wired for doom, Covid injected a bolt of lightning into the circuitry. Those with the greatest propensity to catastrophize (dubbed "doomers" by more skeptical types) seemed to revel in predicting the worst of the worst outcomes. Eric Feigl-Ding led the charge with such portents of doom, starting with his famous (and now-deleted) "it's thermonuclear pandemic level bad" tweet of January 28, 2020.[12]

Centrists escape this trap. Something pulls them away from the black crystal ball, allowing them to look at a situation with less emotion and more clarity. In the Babel of Covid discourse, they keep the more fiery types from killing each other.

* * *

Stefan Baral exemplifies this sober perspective. A Toronto physician-epidemiologist, Baral has provided clinical care and public-health support to unhoused people in his city throughout the pandemic. The people in his care fall outside the tidy systems invented by the laptop class, like flashing vax passes on iPhone 14s. Insisting that the most disadvantaged members of society plug into a system that has no place for them is simply not fair, he says. As he explains in an interview for *Healthy Debate*,[13] during Canada's vax pass era, "we've never had a vaccine mandate for activities of daily living." Communities already on the margins "risk being further excluded from indoor spaces, which is particularly concerning as winter arrives." If they can't access bathrooms—well, that's a problem.

The Covid vaccine mandates trouble Baral on a more fundamental level: Once we go down that path, what's to stop us from mandating flu shots? After all, they *could* make life safer. As an interesting historical note, in 2015 the Ontario Nurses Association (ONA) won a legal challenge to a "flu shot or mask" policy implemented in about 30 Ontario hospitals.[14] According to Linda Haslam-Stroud, then-president of the ONA, enforcers of the policy "were basically coercing and shaming nurses into getting the influenza vaccine if they individually chose not to take it. They made them all wear masks and they had little stickers on their name tag that everyone knew meant 'I don't have my vaccine'." Even in a hospital setting, this level of coercion didn't make it past legal scrutiny in 2015.

Covid changed all that: new virus, new rules—at least that's how the decision makers justified their heavy-handed policies. Baral doesn't buy it. "I'm confused about COVID exceptionalism," he says.[13] "Safety in the way that we've defined it here has taken some sort of absolute form." The real world Baral lives in has no place for one-size-fits-all rules: "In public health, if you try and develop an intervention that serves everyone, you end up serving no one."[15]

He also calls out the Covid absolutists for making assumptions about the vulnerable groups they allegedly seek to protect. "Has there been a single study of what residents in long term care facilities want in terms of masking rules?" he asks the Twitterverse.[16] "Or should Twitter just keep telling these folks what is best for them..."

Baral's pandemic management philosophy flows from the idea that most people are reasonable, even people on the "other team," but not everyone has the same capacity to navigate the world. What's more, on a planet of almost 8 billion people, it should surprise exactly nobody that different individuals and communities will disagree on how to balance costs and benefits.

His message to policymakers: Don't bury the individual under an amorphous "collective." Don't throw mandates around like confetti. Coercion may temporarily stall a virus, but it does irrevocable harm to public morale and trust. And above all, don't expect perfection, because you're not going to get it.

I've gathered a few items from Baral's list of "public health truths"—a string of policy pearls that, if I had my way, every public health expert would be required to say out loud before having breakfast[17]:

- Given a choice between clean and dirty needle, someone will always want to inject with a clean one.
- If you ask someone to do something that you wouldn't be willing or able to do if in their shoes, the program is doomed.
- Except in the most extreme examples, no one wants to infect anyone else with an infectious disease.
- In public health programs, try and show people why you think something is beneficial rather than just telling them to do it.

- People often will not do what you think is in their best
interest to do and shaming them for this will only make
meaningful engagement that much harder.
- If public health is relying on police to help them implement an intervention strategy, something has already
gone very wrong.
- Public health programs never work just as they were envi-
sioned to. That's ok.
- If you ask someone to do the impossible, don't be surprised
with the outcome.

Speaking of impossible, Baral has a few words to say about erad-
icating the virus[18]: "No one likes #Covid19, but it is time to accept
that this virus is now part of this world. Forever." According to
philosopher Jonathan Chait, an all-or-nothing approach to Covid
(which he calls Zeroism) betrays an inability to conceive of public-health measures in cost-benefit terms.[19] "The pandemic becomes
an enemy that must be destroyed at all costs. Any wavering around
this goal could lead to death and is therefore unacceptable."

Three years in, some people continue to give oxygen to the Zero
Covid idea. Invoking the "no true Scotsman" principle, they maintain
that we never instituted a *real* lockdown—that if we all stayed home
for a few weeks, no cheating, we could get rid of Covid once and for
all. Um, really? And how would we deal with people in warzones?
Refugees? Kids starving to death in Syria and Yemen? Poor people in
the global South? Would they just agree to stay home until the Twitter
intelligentsia declared it safe? Even if we could somehow create these
miraculous conditions, Covid has shown us how quickly and effectively
it can adapt to new circumstances, evading its human pursuers at every
turn. Continuing to chase after a moving target, week after week and
year after year, just leaves people sweaty and breathless.

On a more fundamental level, the Zero Covid ethos betrays
a desire to scrub life of all risk, which has exasperated Covid
centrists from the get-go. Baral's Feb. 21, 2021 tweet[20] says it all:

"Risk assessment? Absolutely! Risk mitigation? Absolutely! Risk management? Absolutely! Risk communication? Absolutely! Risk elimination? Impossible."

Some people call this attitude defeatist. I call it realistic. There's nothing wrong with pursuing a dream, but if you're a fiftysomething recreational skater hell-bent on becoming a figure-skating champion, you're chasing not a dream, but a delusion.

* * *

I began subscribing to *The Morning* in 2020, joining about five million other people who have their breakfast with a side of David Leonhardt.[21] While the newsletter, published by the *New York Times* (NYT), doesn't confine itself to Covid, the topic got top billing throughout the first two years of the pandemic.

On the NYT payroll since 1999, Leonhardt has served the paper as an economics columnist, Washington bureau chief, and Sunday reviewer, and won a Pulitzer prize in 2011 for his "graceful penetration of America's complicated economic questions.[22] He began writing *The Morning* in April 2020, when the pandemic was just gathering steam, and soon positioned himself as a counterweight to what he called "Covid alarmism." Picture a soothing uncle saying, "hey, kiddo, it's not as bad as you fear. Have a look at this graph. Have a look at this chart. See? It's not an apocalyptic event. We know who's at risk and we can take steps to protect them, and you don't need to stop living your life."

I often got the sense that he wanted to push his readers a little harder, but as a NYT writer, addressing a left-wing audience with a reflexively cautious response to the virus, he could only go so far. He spoke to his readers as a therapist might talk to a patient, aiming to gently, ever so gently, steer them away from the ledge and toward level ground.

This trademark "gentle nudging" suffused his Dec. 10, 2021 installment,[23] in which he tackled the subject of risk: "Maximizing

health and well-being is not the same thing as minimizing Covid. If
that sounds strange, remember that society would cease to function
if it tried to minimize every medical risk. Schools and offices don't
close each winter because of the flu. Families travel in cars even
though crashes harm vastly more children than Covid does. People
jog, play sports and ride bicycles even though thousands end up
in emergency rooms... The economic and social costs of our Covid
precautions are real."

His tone ("If that sounds strange...") sometimes bordered on
paternalism, but Leonhardt knew what he was doing: just as a
therapist needs to tread softly to gain a patient's trust, he understood
that his audience wouldn't hear him if he used stronger language. His
readers had their feet firmly planted on one side of the tug-of-war—
the side that demanded more and more government action—and
the only way to move the rope was to play the avuncular card.

As it turned out, even this mild-mannered style didn't protect
Leonhardt from hostility. A group of prominent pandemic experts
wrote a letter to the NYT calling his reporting "irresponsible
and dangerous."[22] An emergency physician called it "bonkers."
Upping the ante, public health scholar Cecilia Tomori tweeted that
"Leonhardt paints caution (in the middle of an enormous surge)
due to caring for others as irrational and unnecessary."[24]

Such backlash is all too familiar to Covid realists like Leonhardt.
If they dare suggest easing back into normal life, out come the
accusations of "eugenics" and "being willing to accept deaths" and
the whole rattling toolbox of guilt screws. Such invective cuts off
any meaningful dialogue about managing a virus that isn't going
away, which no doubt is the point.

Leonhardt defends himself by invoking the centrist's mantra:
every intervention has a cost, which needs to be weighed up against
its benefits. "Many liberals have [thought] of Covid mitigations as
responsible, necessary, even patriotic," he told *Intelligencer* writer
Sam Adler-Bell,[25] but the "mental-health problems, anger, frustration, isolation, drug overdoses, vehicle crashes, violent crime,

learning loss, [and] student misbehavior" flowing from this liberal caution can no longer be ignored. In a January 2022 appearance on the NYT's *The Daily* podcast,[26] he called the persistent fear of Covid among younger Democrats "overcautious," especially after the virus shifted "to something that looks more like things that we deal with all the time without shutting down daily life, like the flu."

Leonhardt's position enraged some of his readers, but many others greeted his words as the balanced perspective they had been craving: finally, someone dared to put words to their thoughts. As it happens, Leonhardt's supporters include Joe Biden, who reportedly applauded the journalist for saying what Americans stuck in extreme caution mode needed to hear.[22]

The White House's policy began shifting within a few weeks of the podcast, signaling what New Jersey governor Phil Murphy called "a huge step toward normalcy."[25] Nobody knows how much influence Leonhardt had on the policy change, but having the president's attention every morning surely didn't hurt.

My taste for strong opinions will probably always draw me to the firebrands, but centrists like Balloux, Baral and Leonhardt have a distinct advantage in making change: when you're standing in the middle of the road, the people lined up on either side can hear you.

17

COOL-HEADED ANALYSTS: SANJEEV
SABHLOK AND PAUL FRIJTERS

conomists think differently from most other people. While
many of us lean into the idea of "more"—more money, more
healthcare, more environmental regulation—economists work
with the premise that the pie has a finite size. If you put more apples
into one slice, you're taking them away from another.

An *American University* article called "What It Takes to Think
Like an Economist"[1] explains it perfectly: "Economic theory is
fundamentally about the idea of scarcity, the idea that everyone—
individuals, corporations and governments—only have limited
resources and must decide how and where those resources will be
allocated. Economists evaluate the 'cost' of individual and social
choices to determine the best choices for themselves or others in
the face of this scarcity."

Sanjeev Sabhlok, an economist living in Melbourne, also views
economics as a branch of moral philosophy[2]—a lovely pairing that
makes more sense than apparent at first blush. Unlike science,
which merely seeks to understand reality, economics and morality
both deal with decisions—what people ought to do. In the case of
morality, the decision point revolves around good and evil, while
economics weighs up social benefits against costs to achieve what

Sabhlok calls the "greatest happiness of the greatest number." (And if you look deeply enough, the two weigh scales begin to converge.)

Costs and benefits. It's what the critics of the "health experts" have been screaming from the rooftops all along. As Nate Hochman writes in the *National Review*,[3] "assessing trade-offs, which is essential to sound public policy, is not what these experts are good at." During Covid, public health advisors consistently argued for draconian restrictions because "they monomaniacally viewed the goal of public policy as reducing Covid infection rates at all costs. They recognized no other inputs—mental health, drug addiction, education outcomes, basic constitutional freedoms, and so on—in their evaluation of any given policy."

Public health officials and politicians may protest that yes, they did consider all these inputs, but their concern never went beyond lip service. Nobody dared suggest that "a healthy society needs to balance public safety with basic freedoms." Nobody had the courage to say, "We will keep schools open, even if it increases transmission. Keeping schools open has so many benefits that the trade-off is worth it."

Even if it increases transmission. This is where everyone got stuck. Not economists, though. They live in a world of finitude, of hard limits, so they're used to looking trade-offs in the eye.

Originally from India, Sabhlok is a citizen of Australia and has held public service positions in both countries. Throughout the pandemic, he warned both his native and adopted land about the knock-on effects of the Covid policies, and compiled his thoughts into a book called *The Great Hysteria and the Broken State*.[4]

Sabhlok's warnings started early. On March 6, 2020, writing for his *Times of India* blog, he acknowledged that the virus required a serious response but strongly advised against locking down entire societies.[5] "Instead, we need a risk-based, data-driven approach that will minimise the spread of disease while facilitating economic activity." Masks, social distancing, he was fine with all that—just no lockdowns, please.

His warnings intensified in a follow-up article called "Lockdowns Won't Defeat the Virus but Will Definitely Destroy Us All."[6] He argued that the potential 2% fatality rate of the virus, used as a justification for lockdowns, represented an improbable upper limit. With the high transmissibility of the virus making containment an unviable option, he recommended that India "go full-blast into age-based prevention, with isolation of the elderly, and big gatherings stopped (but not necessarily schools)."

With his economist hat firmly in place, he reminded decision makers that "a good policy process must not only recognise all trade-offs, opportunity costs and unintended consequences, it must ensure that people's freedoms (of movement, and economic freedom) are not diminished unless they are causing significant harm." Lockdowns didn't tick any of these boxes.

Lockdown harms aside, the strategy's effectiveness depended on a vaccine. At the time, nobody knew if vaccines would arrive in a year, five years, or never. Neither society nor individuals could survive years of lockdown, so Sabhlok urged the Indian government not to start what it couldn't finish.

Week after week, month after month, he kept beating the same drum, arguing for a "risk-based analysis and preliminary analysis of costs and benefits."[7] Quoting Nobel laureate Vernon Smith, he pointed out that "there is no such thing as a minimum risk policy defined only in terms of unweighted outcomes." Take away one risk and another one pops up, and we have to consider them all. His warnings went unheeded. In September 2020, he resigned from his post as economist for the state of Victoria as a protest against the "violations of human rights and the Police State created by the Daniel Andrews government."[8]

He filled me in on the details in a Zoom call, periodically pulling out a well-thumbed volume from the bookshelf next to his desk to make a point. "My boss and HR called me into an online meeting and asked me to take down my posts and tweets criticizing the policies," he recalled. "I got off the call and told my wife I can't continue in this situation. Ten minutes later I quit." Was it a hard decision, after 15 years of service? "Not really. I had resigned from a top post in India because of corruption, so I wasn't going to let this intimidate me. And when I resigned I got a mass of support."

Introduced by Ronald Reagan in 1981 as a requirement for US regulatory policy,[9] cost-benefit analyses (CBAs) underpin government policymaking in Western nations—and were summarily forgotten when Covid rolled in. "Not a single government has published a cost-benefit analysis to justify lockdown policies—something policy makers are often required to do while making far less consequential decisions," Philip Lemoine wrote in the *Wall Street Journal* in March 2021.[10] To be fair, such analyses would present significant challenges, if only because not all costs have a value we can all agree on. How much does infringement on liberty cost? How many lost businesses or years of depression do we trade for a life?

To Sabhlok, these uncertainties don't let policymakers off the hook. Having lived and breathed CBAs throughout his career, he maintains that all countries and international organizations must use CBAs as a safeguard against big policy mistakes. "Even a bad CBA is better than no CBA," he explained to me, citing the CBA justifying the ban on plastic bags in his jurisdiction as an example. "It was very obvious they didn't include all costs and benefits. But it's out there for people to pick apart. Journalists can look at it, economists can look at it, which means we can argue for fixing it. That's why it's so important to conduct CBAs: it's an exercise in transparency that forces people to prop up their claims. Someone says the virus will kill X number of people? A CBA forces them to provide the data."

None of this happened with Covid. Within days of the pandemic's inception, "a group of Australian economists published a piece arguing against CBAs in this case," Sabhlok told me. Covid was the delicate flower, the exceptional child exempt from family rules. As Sabhlok sees it, "most economists lost their heads. They forfeited their fundamental role, which is to look deeper and tease out unforeseen consequences." Others stayed silent. "Several government economists privately agreed with me, but the pressure to conform was just too intense."

In the rare instances that CBAs were proffered, like the Dutch analysis estimating that lockdowns would cause more than three times as much health damage as they averted,[11] governments didn't listen. Instead, they latched onto the "stay home, save lives" slogan and threw it at the public, human costs be damned.

In March 2020, to justify the statewide shutdown, New York's then-governor Andrew Cuomo declared that "if everything we do saves just one life, I'll be happy."[12] I hoped Cuomo said this to score political points: if he truly believed it, he had no business running a state. At least two young people understood this when they wrote, in an April 2020 article for the Intercollegiate Studies Institute,[13] that "when politicians say, 'if it saves just one life,'" they can appear to care deeply while simultaneously absolving themselves of the responsibility of crafting a rational response to a difficult issue." Two years later, *Bloomberg* opinion columnist Stephen Carter knocked the slogan down an extra peg[14]: "Early in the pandemic, I heard one public health 'expert' proclaim on television that no measure is too extreme if it saves a single life," he reported. "Such an assertion does not even constitute a serious argument, still less the teaching of an academic discipline. But the host treated the claim like Holy Writ."

A cost-benefit mindset strikes some people as cold and calculating, devoid of human feeling. They recoil from the idea of putting a value on life. Not economists, though: they do it every day. While they may quibble about the exact figure, many estimates converge around $10 million. The Environmental Protection Agency uses $7.4 million, while the Federal Aviation Administration lands on $9.6 million.[15] Setting limits on public expenditures to protect life helps governments allocate resources fairly, as their constituents rightfully expect. "'You can't put a value on human life' is a good slogan, but a bad policy," Dan Hannan writes in *The Spectator*.[16] "The one thing worse than putting a value on life is refusing to do so."

Perhaps I should have become an economist, because it doesn't offend me in the slightest to have a number attached to my life. Am I worth $9,357,644? Or maybe $7,224,968? If it helps allocate resources, I'm down. By the same token, I'll be the last to object if a government puts a higher price on my children's lives than my own. They have a lot of living ahead of them, so it makes sense to put them first. It's not that my life has any less inherent value, but I've already had a good run: school, travel, romance, trying out different careers, family life, writing, more travel, more writing. Failures that knocked me flat out and moments of triumph that picked me up again. I want my kids to have all that, too (and your kids, if you have them).

None of this was controversial before 2020. Health economists routinely used Quality Adjusted Life Years (QALY) to guide government decisions about whether to fund a new medication. If a drug cost $500,000 and gave a person 10 extra years of life? Great, full speed ahead. If it extended life by a month? Maybe not. The savings could be funneled to little Lucy, who needed a kidney or a cochlear implant.

All that went out the window with Covid. Anyone who brought up QALY risked accusations of "wanting people to die," leading governments to shy away from a well-established metric that could have helped them create more balanced and humane policies. "QALYs haven't been used much by the UK government during the pandemic response," says Brunel University health economics professor Subhash Pokhrel, who estimates that each QALY saved through lockdowns may have cost hundreds of thousands or even millions of pounds—far more than governments normally spend on one good year of life.[17] It's money they can't pour into other life-giving programs, like early education support or subsidized housing.

Sabhlok warned against lockdowns because they didn't pass his cost-benefit test, even if they saved some lives early on. But even that article of faith—lockdowns save lives—crumbled in the face of subsequent research. Canadian economist Douglas Allen analyzed over 100 studies to produce a report on the cost-benefit of lockdowns, which was published in the *International Journal of the Economics of Business* in 2022.[18] Allen's conclusion: "Lockdowns have had, at best, a marginal effect on the number of Covid-19 deaths," in part because people in less restricted jurisdictions followed public health recommendations of their own accord. "It is possible that lockdown will go down as one of the greatest peacetime policy failures in Canada's history."

A Johns Hopkins School of Applied Economics study yielded equally damning results: lockdowns only reduced Covid mortality by 0.2%—and in some cases backfired altogether.[19] "Often, lockdowns have limited peoples' access to safe (outdoor) places such as beaches, parks, and zoos...pushing people to meet at less safe (indoor) places," the three study investigators explain in their report. "Indeed, we do find some evidence that limiting gatherings was counterproductive and increased COVID-19 mortality." What's more, the 0.2% figure only applies to Covid deaths. The analysis didn't consider the people who may have died from lockdown effects such as delayed cancer treatment.

The Johns Hopkins report generated enough buzz to spark a global conversation. Policymakers had presented lockdowns as the only alternative to a global graveyard, but the study cracked open the door of doubt. A few months later, Sabhlok pushed the door wider open with an analysis showing that countries with harsher lockdowns witnessed *more* Covid deaths than their more lenient counterparts.[20] Lockdown dissenters could finally state their case without triggering the histrionic retort that shut off all reasonable discourse in the first year of the pandemic: *Do you want people to die?*

* * *

Like Sabhlok, Paul Frijters is all about cost-benefit analysis—but it has to be the right kind. A top-cited UK economist and author of 150 papers and 6 books, including a 2021 volume called *The Great Covid Panic* (written with two co-authors),[21] Frijters maintains that CBA must include not only readily measurable parameters like hospitalization or death, but less tangible outcomes like well-being. Frijters wrote his doctoral thesis on well-being in Russia and currently advises governments on implementing well-being policies, so he knows a thing or two about the subject.

Dominant cost-benefit analyses "undervalue social life and mental health," he explains in a video presentation for the Pandemic Data & Analytics group.[22] Lacking the metrics to measure these variables, analysts end up "presuming these elements have no value." To capture costs and benefits in a more holistic way, Frijters uses a metric called Wellbeing Years (WELLBY), which he helped develop. Designed to evaluate complex policies that impact multiple dimensions of life, WELLBY quantifies how much a policy adds to—or detracts from—a population's overall satisfaction. Viewed through the WELLBY lens, the government's job is not simply to save lives, but to "maximize the number of satisfied years its population lives."

To gauge well-being, "you ask people one of the most studied questions known to mankind: Overall, how satisfied have you been with your life over the past year?" If they answer 8 (out of 10), they're happy campers. A score of 2 or less means they don't much care if they live or die. The difference between the two figures—6 WELLBY units—translates to a year of satisfied living. Just as governments use QALY to make drug-funding decisions, they can use WELLBY to make decisions about which public health programs to subsidize.

Listening to Frijters' presentation helped bring my frustration with the "save lives" mantra into greater focus: none of the Covid policymakers had ever bothered to look at well-being, either individually or on a population level. I had some follow-up questions, which Frijters was gracious enough to answer on a Zoom call from

Saudia Arabia. (He also made me laugh at least six times and told me that he and Sabhlok became friends during the pandemic, which didn't surprise me one bit.)

First question: Why hasn't WELLBY supplanted QALY as the thing to measure? "People are still stuck on physical health as the key to a good life," Frijters told me. "But that's not what the research shows. You can be physically unhealthy and very happy, and vice versa." Statistically, "physical health only accounts for 30 to 40 percent of our well-being." And the rest? "Hands down, social relationships are what give people the greatest satisfaction," he said, corroborating what many lockdown skeptics intuited from the start: human connection isn't a frill. For a social animal like *homo sapiens*, it's life itself.

Next question: Why do people get so hostile if you bring up the costs of a policy? "People don't like to be reminded that the pie has a finite size," he explained. "If they get a slice, it means somebody else is doing without. It makes them uncomfortable." That's where economists come in: "We earn our living by being the nasty person in the room. We pull out the figures to show that there's no such thing as a free lunch: if you close down 'non-essential operations' in a hospital, a year later people are going to die."

In fact, when Frijters heard about the lockdown plan, he immediately thought: "Globally, ten million people may die from this. And a lot more will suffer." He wasn't alone. "In the well-being research community, we had a pretty unanimous consensus that lockdowns were a bad idea." But the panic train had left the station, and it would take more than a handful of WELLBY geeks to stop it.

Frijters started doing the math back in March 2020. By January 2021, the average well-being in the UK's population of 60 million had plunged by 0.8 WELLBY units—"the biggest drop ever seen." Not everyone was miserable during lockdown, of course. Some people found comfort in its quiet rhythms. (Having a cozy home and a steady paycheck didn't hurt.) On the flip side, many of those who suffered *really* suffered.

Of course, even if the UK hadn't locked down, the pandemic itself would have decreased people's well-being—but not to the same degree. Sweden, which avoided lockdown, saw its average WELLBY go down by no more than 0.3 units. Frijters' conclusion held firm: even if lockdowns saved some lives, they caused a helluva lot more suffering. In health-economic terms, their costs exceeded their benefits.

In theory, WELLBY can measure all the losses incurred by lockdowns, from loneliness and frightened children to missed chances for in-vitro fertilization or missed funerals. The lost fun in life—the parties and graduations and summer internships abroad—also enter into the calculations. According to Frijters, "that's exactly what is almost impossible to capture with classic CBA, but is relatively easy with WELLBY."

You may wonder: Why on earth would we include parties and graduations in a cost-benefit analysis? Aren't these things a little, um, frivolous? On the contrary, says Frijters: "it's exactly such events that fill our cup of well-being." Janet Daley, *The Telegraph*'s grouch in residence, expresses the same sentiment with a tad less good humor[23]: "What was deliberately, and quite carelessly, sacrificed was the dimension of human experience which gives meaning and value to private life. That was unquantifiable, and so apparently it did not count. It may never be possible to calculate the full extent of the damage."

Frijters also beams his economist lens on the morality of pandemic management, likening the dilemmas facing policymakers to the famous trolley problem—the one you may have discussed in philosophy class or at the beach while sharing a joint with friends. For those who missed these formative events, the problem goes like this: You are operating a trolley, headed toward a switch in the tracks. On the current track stand five people, who will all be killed if you let the train continue on its course. Your sin, in this case, would be doing nothing—a sin of omission. You have access to a lever that will switch the trolley to the other track, but another person is standing there. If you pull the lever, that person will die—a sin of commission, which for many people weighs more heavily than just standing by and watching something bad happen.

To connect this dilemma to the pandemic, Frijters asks you to picture yourself as the operator of the trolley.[24] Ahead of you on the tracks is John, an elderly man suffering from many diseases. You know him personally, and all his family and friends are watching you. "Divert the damn trolley," one of them shouts, insisting it's the only moral thing to do. If you don't do it, your friends will shun you and you may lose your position in society—so you pull the lever and send the train to the other track. You don't know it yet, but the train will run into over 50 people on the new track, maiming or killing them all. Multiply this by millions of people and you get the "corona dilemma"—either keeping society open and risking more deaths from the virus or locking down and putting billions of people at risk of job loss, depression, or death from other causes.

No sane person wants to watch a train run over someone they love. The very thought may offend us. But when we consider a dilemma through an economist's eyes, we realize that knee-jerk emotions do not reliably guide us to the most humane choices. Economists, with their dispassionate and analytical minds, may ultimately lead us to a kinder place.

SHARP NOTES: ZUBY, DAVE MUSTAINE, AND VAN MORRISON

For two weeks.
Once hospitals have extra capacity.
Once cases come down.
Once all adults have access to vaccines.
Once all adults have access to boosters.
Once we get past this variant.
Once schoolchildren have access to vaccines.
Once we have effective treatments.
Once children under five can get vaccinated.
Once death rates go down to flu levels.
Once N95 masks and at-home tests are available to every household.
Once we have more data about long Covid.

Do you hear the scrape of metal on ice as the goalposts move away? Zuby does. From one of his Twitter threads[1]: "The goalposts have been moved 100 times... People are saying and doing things that don't even make basic, logical sense." And a couple of months later[2]: "The goalposts have moved so far since 'flatten the curve' that they are no longer on planet Earth."

As Zuby sees it, the perpetually moving goalposts have also dragged the word "vaccine" away from its classic definition and rebranded it as a form of prophylactic treatment. The profusion of "I just got Covid, so glad I'm triple-vaxxed" posts on Facebook and Twitter "would have made *no* sense to anybody merely 18 months ago," he remarked in early 2022. "That's how quickly the goalposts have shifted."[3]

Known as the "rapper with a difference," Zuby (full name Nzube Olisaebuka Udezue) was born in England and raised in Saudi Arabia, where he attended an international school. He turned to rapping while studying computer science at Oxford University. He has performed throughout Europe and the USA, released 5 albums with his own label, and reached #12 on the iTunes Hip Hop chart.[4] But his greatest fame comes from his pithy takes on culture and politics, which cheerfully deviate from the Black artist "script" and have earned him 1.5 million social media followers and over 20 million online video views. He refuses to use his race as a trump card, even after being harassed by police in a case of mistaken identity. "It would be easy for me [to] perceive myself as some kind of victim of injustice or something," he has said.[5] But "sometimes sucky things just happen. But you can control how you react and respond, right?"

Zuby is not the only Covid observer to note the shift in pandemic management goals—the boiling-frog progression from a two-week social compact to a protracted state of exception, with rewards proffered and pulled along the way. See that cookie? Jump through this hoop and you'll get it. Sorry, just one more hoop. Ok, here's your cookie. Keep jumping and you'll get the next one. Well, maybe not. Next hoop.

It's what psychologists call intermittent reinforcement: the delivery of a reward at irregular and unpredictable intervals.[6] This method has been shown to yield the greatest effort (in Covid terms, compliance) from the subject,[7] but it can also drive people crazy. (It drives rats crazy, too.) It's frustrating enough to watch Lucy yank the football away from Charlie Brown, but when you're the one standing behind the ball, you start to feel a lot like a rat.

The public health advisors and their acolytes insist they're not moving any goalposts, just responding to new information that calls for new containment measures. "The science has changed," they say. "It's still not safe enough." We've covered this ground before: the science doesn't "call for" anything. It's humans who make public policy decisions, based on the trade-offs they consider reasonable. And once you go down the "not safe enough" path, you can never return because it could always be a little safer.

In tandem with the shifting goalposts, Covid has pushed the concept of personal rights into uncharted territory—like the newly sprung notion that we have a right to perfect safety. Before Covid, we all understood that being alive carried the risk of infection, Zuby explains an interview for the UK talk show GBN Live.[5] "You now hear people say, 'someone doesn't have a right to make me sick.'" It's reasonable to expect that people won't intentionally infect you—"that would be crazy and perhaps even a form of assault"—but insisting on full protection from a virus doesn't jive with material reality. "There's no 'right not to get sick'," he says. "That's not even a right that is possible to have."

Also brand-new territory to Zuby: the religious fervor surrounding a virus. "It's extraordinarily cultish," he says, chatting with Megyn Kelly on her talk show.[8] Viruses, contagion, illness, death—all these things have existed since the beginning of time. "What is totally new is the paranoia and the hysteria, the way people are viewing each other and the hostility in some areas... It's just weird to me. That's not what should be running a society." To earn a membership in the cult, he tells podcaster Luke Storey, it helps to be afraid[9]: "To show you're a good person, you're supposed to be terrified of COVID. You're supposed to wear your mask forever, get your shots, scream at everyone else to get their shots, like the more fear you display now in this weird tribe or cult, as I call it, that's like virtue points to you."

Zuby's one-liners find a perfect home on Twitter, where he has steadfastly exposed the underbelly of the pandemic response. On July 5, 2021, he posted a series of tweets called "20 things I've learned (or had confirmed) about humanity during the pandemic,"[10] which garnered a million views within 4 hours. Three days later, 5 million views and an invitation from Joe Rogan to discuss the thread on his show. Six months later, 15 million views.

Several of Zuby's "20 things" converge on authoritarianism, offering an elegant distillation of the social forces behind Covid culture:

- At least 20% of the population has strong authoritarian tendencies.
- A significant % of people thoroughly enjoy being subjugated.
- When sufficiently frightened, most people will not only accept authoritarianism, but demand it.
- Humans can be trained and conditioned relatively quickly and easily to significantly alter their behaviors.
- Hedonic adaptation occurs in both directions, and once inertia sets in, it is difficult to get people back to "normal."

There we have it, folks: a BDSM analysis of the pandemic response. Jokes aside, Zuby's grasp of the dynamics of authoritarianism, the eternal *pas de deux* between the impulse to govern and to be governed, offers fresh insight into the Covid story.

* * *

Long before Zuby was born, Dave Mustaine was already making noise on his guitar. The veteran of many bands, including Metallica, Mustaine achieved his greatest fame as co-founder and primary songwriter for Megadeth, a thrash metal band that has sold over 50 million albums worldwide.[11] The group won a Grammy award in 2017 for the title track of their (presciently named, some would say) Dystopia album. Now over 60 years old, Mustaine has been ranked third in the top 25 rhythm guitarists of all time. He still has an enviable head of hair (or more likely a great hairpiece), but the deep creases in his face betray his four-plus decades as a hard-partying rocker.

Mustaine started out on Side A of the album, the stay-safe side. "I hope you guys are taking the time to stay indoors and quarantine yourselves and especially take time to wash your hands a lot," he said to his fans on YouTube on April 6, 2020, adding that he himself was staying indoors. "Stay safe and see you soon."[12]

By September 2021 he had flipped the album to Side B. "Look to your right, look to your left, and look how wonderful this is," he said, addressing his audience at a concert in Camden, New Jersey.[13] "We're all here together... We're not in fucking bags. We're not freaking out, and we're not yelling at people, 'Wear your fucking mask'."

Urging his fans to look up the word "tyranny" when they got home, he told them they had the power to make change, starting with "a sensation that we build right now. We feel together, we feel like strength in numbers. We feel like we are invincible. People will not be able to stop us."

Of course he got pushback: a complaint about medical tyranny in the middle of a pandemic was guaranteed to bring the shamers out in force. Even *Rolling Stone* called Mustaine's speech an "anti-mask tirade" and scolded him for disregarding his own high-risk status after his recent bout with throat cancer.[13] The reporter didn't get it: Mustaine's risk level and feelings about masks were beside the point. The message he aimed to communicate to his fans was that gathering to rock out and rage has social and even spiritual value. When the health bureaucrats fail to acknowledge this dimension of life, some people get pissed off.

It's reductive and insulting to presume that all "high-risk" people will want to live out the rest of their days in a protective shell. As David Zweig states in a *Boston Globe* op-ed,[14] "not everyone, including those more medically fragile and their caregivers, sees maximizing risk aversion as the primary goal." A heavy metal guy who has survived tragedy (which in Mustaine's case also includes a longstanding battle with substances) may conclude that tomorrow is never promised, so let's rock and roll today.

And also, let's get real: a masked heavy metal concert? Some things are...just no. I am reminded of the time, many moons ago, when my first husband and I went on a week-long trek in Northern British Columbia, hundreds of miles from civilization in any direction. When I suggested we wear bear bells while hiking, he told me that he wanted an immersive experience, not a jingling reminder to stay scared. I grumbled and pouted, but even at the time I understood that my need for safety didn't trump his need for a transcendent journey. I could always pull out of the trip (I didn't), much as music fans can skip a concert they don't feel safe attending.

Mustaine's age and status surely made it easier for him to stand up on that Camden stage and say his piece. He knew his career had the horsepower to weather a Twitter storm. But what about the younger folks, the artists just starting out? By and large, they have acquiesced to the rules without a peep—perhaps not a surprise, considering what's at stake for them. In an article called "Truth and Art in the Pandemic Era,"[15] Daniel Nuccio reports on a musician who admits that "If you're an artist and you're trying to grow your Instagram following and you start posting, you know, anything that calls into doubt like 'The Science,' you know you're going to be shadowbanned. You're not going to appear on that list. You're not going to be in front of those eyeballs."

For better or worse, gender roles also get mixed into all this. Western culture's slide toward values traditionally regarded as feminine, documented by Ann Douglas as early as 1998,[16] has turned such attributes as caution and congeniality into moral imperatives. (It goes without saying there are a ton of badass women out there, many of them my friends. I'm just reporting on a societal shift I don't quite vibe with. My ideal society would cast prudence and affability as supporting actors, rather than stars.)

My daughter tells me that the "be a good person" ethos has

infiltrated youth culture to the point that young artists suppress not just their words, but their essential selves. They *become* good—or at least, the far left's version of good, which means supporting all the "proper" causes and no others. To prove their goodness, some of them take it up a notch and censor other artists who fall out of line, evidently forgetting that their profession depends on free speech to survive.

In an essay called "The Obedient Generation,"[17] Clayton Fox blames his own generation for shepherding young people to this place. "The generation that 'turned on, tuned in, and dropped out' (and the slightly younger punks) raised you with none of their same rebelliousness," he writes. "So what did they give you instead? Obey, and you'll be rewarded... Shut up. Shut down. Lean in." He urges young people to stop putting their dreams on hold—dreams crushed by frightened old boomers like him—to go out and kiss someone, and to "ride your bike as high as you can."

I share Fox's wish for young people. I would like them to worry less about being good and more about challenging the definition of goodness they inherited. I would like to see them stand next to Mustaine on that Camden stage and rock out.

* * *

Just a couple of years shy of 80, Van Morrison continues to belt it out on stage. A legend who needs no introduction, Morrison found success early and his star never fell. His prolific performing and recording career has earned him six Grammys, two honorary doctorates, and a knighthood, among other honors.[18] Since his early days as a 13-year-old traveling musician, the magic of live performance has always infused his career.

With all the money and fame anyone could ever want, he certainly doesn't need to keep doing it. But live music matters to him, and a government interdiction doesn't make its importance suddenly go away.

In the fall of 2020, Morrison released three songs protesting the Covid lockdowns[19]: "No More Lockdown," "Born to Be Free" and "As I Walked Out." Northern Ireland health minister Robin Swann responded with a scathing op-ed in *Rolling Stone*, calling his songs "dangerous" and fodder for conspiracy theorists.[20] "He could have chosen to sing about how we all can help save lives" or about "poverty, starvation, injustice, racism, violence, austerity," Swann wrote, drawing straight from the list of SJW-approved topics. Swann might have paused for a minute to consider exactly what Morrison was protesting: not the legitimacy of the virus, but whether "stopping the spread" should eclipse all other dimensions of life and make performing arts expendable. The health bureaucrats' biomedical perspective left no room for a debate about that.

Tensions between Morrison and Swann escalated when Covid restrictions led to the last-minute cancellation of a show he was about to give in Belfast.[21] "Robin Swann has all the power," Morrison told his audience, leading the group in a "Robin Swann is very dangerous" chant and telling them "this stops when we say no." Upping the ante, Swann sued Morrison for defamation in November 2021.[22] Morrison sued right back in May 2022.[23]

Reading up on the feud, I had the impression of two people talking different languages, like a zoologist and a painter discussing the meaning of a flower. It's why Swann and Morrison will never bridge the gap between them, regardless of what happens in court.

In May 2022, Morrison released an album of protest songs called "What's It Gonna Take?"[24] The topics are not from Swann's approved list (and the album's title track, "Dangerous," appears to take a jab at the health minister), but people who speak Morrison's language may hear the strangled wail beneath the fighting words: that human connection and live performance matter, even when a virus is going around, and need to be part of the conversation.

- From "Dangerous": Somebody said I was dangerous, I said somethin' bad, it had to be good, well, I must be somebody lookin', seein' I'm close to it, maybe I'm getting' close to the truth.
- From "Nervous breakdown": Say depression is suppression, anger, man, it feels like it to me, when you're not allowed free expression, or to follow your obsession, showed you're not essential, it's a crime against humanity, is it any wonder at this time? Not much is working for me.
- From "Pretending": Pretending my life is not in ruins, pretending I'm not depressed, pretending I left it all behind, pretending most of the time, just pretending, just pretending.
- From "Damage and Recovery": How long can this go on this time? Guess they tried it on for size, took our rights before our eyes, fear-mongering media hypnotized, accountants, please tell my why, in our so-called free society, is freedom just a memory? I'm watching you, you're watching me.
- From "Absolutely positively the most": Pick your own salvation and your co-creation, we're all part of the same whole, got to come together, no separation, got to reach our goal.

TURN LEFT, TURN RIGHT: MATT TAIBBI, GLENN GREENWALD, AND TOBY YOUNG

f you object to lockdowns, mask mandates, or vaccine passports, you must be right-wing. Not just right-wing, but far-right. Or alt-right. Some kind of right, anyway. You're also white and you think racism is a leftist invention. I'm improvising a little, but you get the point.

Within days of the pandemic's inception, criticism of lockdowns and other restrictions became conflated with right-wing politics. This put lefties in a bind: if they didn't support the restrictions, they might be mistaken (the horror!) for a conservative—or worse, a soldier in Orange Man's army. They latched onto the mask, the left-wing answer to the MAGA hat, as a badge of their political allegiance. In the US, many people admitted as much[1]: *I wear a mask outside so people won't think I'm a Republican.* Lindsay Brown, a Canadian woman and prolific Covid tweeter, went a step further[2]: "If you think you're on the left and you're not wearing a mask in public indoor spaces, you're not."

Despite this enormous social pressure from their ranks, a small cadre of left-wingers stepped up to challenge the orthodoxy. In print, on air, and online, they argued that one-size-fits-all restrictions disproportionately impact working-class communities, who can't easily retreat to home offices tricked out with stained-glass lamps and WiFi and Alexa. They pointed out that school closures widen the educational gap between the privileged and the working class, who don't have the resources to hire tutors or speech therapists for their kids. They took issue with the censorship of dissenting views on pandemic policy, conveniently lumped together as "disinformation" by legacy media.

Suppression of dissent is the pandemic hill that Matt Taibbi has chosen to die on. To those who say that free speech does too much damage in a pandemic, he counters that a pandemic makes free speech more important than ever.

One of the most trenchant investigative journalists of his generation, Taibbi began reporting on politics for *Rolling Stone* in 2004 and received a National Magazine Award for his contributions to the publication.[3] He gained prominence (and displayed his leftist stripes) for his takedowns of Wall Street during the global financial crisis of 2008-2009. He has written several books, all colored with rage against the political machine. Politically, Taibbi has described himself as a "run-of-the-mill, old-school ACLU liberal" and unabashed Bernie bro.[4]

Mainstream media being an obviously unsuitable vehicle for exploring censorship by mainstream media, Taibbi took to Substack, an online newsletter platform that allows writers to send posts directly to paying subscribers. The lack of corporate oversight or advertisers limits opportunities to censor the content, making the platform a perfect match for the likes of Taibbi—articulate and well-respected malcontents who can finally say what they damn well please and get paid for it (in Taibbi's case, rather well).

An April 2020 article extolling the advantages of Chinese media control over American free speech in the Covid era had Taibbi all fired up. "The people who want to add a censorship regime to a health crisis are more dangerous and more stupid by leaps and bounds than a president who tells people to inject disinfectant," he wrote in his newsletter.[5] "It's astonishing that they don't see this."

A follow-up post two years later[6] finds him gnawing on the same bone, explaining that the censors utterly misunderstand the "calculus of free speech." They assume that scrubbing the Internet of "misinformation" will solve the pesky problem of non-compliance: the partiers will limit their social interactions, the anti-maskers will cover their faces, and the vaccine holdouts will roll up their sleeves. But "the opposite is true," he writes. "If you wipe out critics, people will immediately default to higher levels of suspicion. They will now be *sure* there's something wrong with the vaccine. If you want to convince audiences, you have to allow everyone to talk, even the ones you disagree with."

Taibbi also invites the official purveyors of pandemic information, such as Fauci and the CDC, to review their own track record: ventilator good, ventilator bad. Mask off, mask on. Use this mask. No, that one. Or maybe both. The vaccines stop transmission. The vaccines were never meant to stop transmission. Or this rather stunning *volte face* from White House Covid Response Coordinator Ashish Jha[7]: "We used to spend a lot of time talking about 6 feet of distance, 15 minutes of being together. We realize that's not actually the right way to think about this."

There's nothing wrong with changing a recommendation in the face of new data. What some of us can't forget, though, is the certainty (read: arrogance) with which the public health advisors made their pronouncements, insisting at every turn that "the science is settled." Nor do we take kindly to the "noble lies" they told us, as when Fauci nudged up the estimated herd immunity threshold in the hope of boosting vaccine uptake.[8] One can hardly fault Taibbi for stating that "the most dangerous misinformation is always, without exception, official."[6]

Taibbi has good reason to worry about censorship in the Covid era. In 2021, Human Rights Watch, a global organization that investigates and reports on human right abuses, determined that "at least 83 governments worldwide used the Covid-19 pandemic to justify violating the exercise of free speech and peaceful assembly."[9] They "attacked, detained, prosecuted, and in some cases killed critics" who failed to toe the line, as well as enacting laws criminalizing speech that didn't align with their public health objectives. The organization called on authorities to "immediately end excessive restrictions on free speech in the name of preventing the spread of Covid-19 and hold to account those responsible for serious human rights violations and abuses."

While Taibbi's 30,000 paying subscribers have made him a Substack superstar, not all his fans have followed him to his new sandbox. In a commentary called "What Happened to Matt Taibbi,"[4] journalist Doug Henwood, who once counted himself among Taibbi's admirers, lamented that "he's gone off the rails" and is now "obsessed with stupid shit." It's true that Taibbi's targets and topics have shifted: less raging about Wall Street, more criticism of woke campus life.

Instead of celebrating the diversity of thought within the Left, too many progressives view such criticisms as betrayals. To such purists, it's not good enough to like the tomatoes and cucumbers and green peppers in the left-wing salad—you also have to like the radishes, and if you don't, you're out. Some formerly staunch leftists are only too happy to oblige. Fed up with the policing and cancellations, they join communities such as #walkaway or #donewiththeleft. Their actual politics don't move, but the new Left no longer has a place for them. You may have seen the meme: a motionless stick-figure man, hovering over a horizontal line that keeps shifting leftward. The centrist of 2008 becomes the right-winger of 2022.

Taibbi is that stick-figure man: "It used to be that I was the one furthest to the left in any newsroom," he tweeted in early 2022.[10] "I am now easily the most conservative, frequently sparking tension by questioning identity politics. This happened in the span of about 18 months. My own politics did not change."

If questioning policies formerly considered illiberal, like government surveillance, medical coercion, and censoring of scientists, puts one's left-wing cred in jeopardy, it's a price Taibbi is willing to pay.

* * *

It's not a coincidence that Matt Taibbi and Glenn Greenwald are friends. They've both traversed the same ground, from representing the Left to railing against its excesses. Their free-ranging minds lead them to heterodox ideas that more timid souls won't touch. And the Right is now claiming both of them as its own.

In case anyone needs an introduction, Glenn Greenwald is an American writer and lawyer who has been called "the greatest journalist of all time."[11] A resident of Brazil since 2005, the vocal critic of the Iraq War and American foreign policy has contributed to such bastions of left-wing thought as *Salon* and *The Guardian*, where he published a series of reports about the global surveillance programs leaked by Edward Snowden.[12] In 2013 he co-founded a news outlet called *The Intercept*, for which he wrote and edited articles until resigning in 2020 on grounds of editorial censorship.[13]

Left-wing media groups often paint Greenwald and Taibbi as defectors who somehow got away with it, raking it in as independent journalists while refusing to admit they've joined the dark side. An article in *Current Affairs*[14] accuses the pair of spouting "dangerous conservative hyperbole about The Left." A *Washington Babylon* piece twists the knife still further, calling the defecting duo "rich pigs who seek to protect their class interests through their writing and social media presence."[15]

While rather tiresome, such reactions come as no surprise. Greenwald has committed the unforgivable leftie sin of appearing on Fox news—more than once, proving it wasn't just a whoopsie.[16] And his contention that the cultural Left "has become increasingly censorious, moralizing, controlling, repressive, petulant, joyless, self-victimizing, trivial and status-quo-perpetuating"[17] cannot have pleased all his old admirers.

Just as Taibbi sniffs out suppression of free speech, Greenwald tracks down (and takes down) hypocrisy. While he has apparently been enjoying this pursuit for some time, as evidenced by his 2008 book *Great American Hypocrites*,[18] the "rules for thee" politicians of the Covid era made his job easier than ever. Following Obama's maskless bash of 2021, he noted that liberals have "spent a full year relentlessly Covid-shaming anyone who went outside (unless for liberal protests) or questioning Fauci. But now that their icons threw themselves an opulent indoor maskless party, they announce that only pettiness or jealousy would make you notice."[19] Aside from rubbing Greenwald the wrong way, the hypocrisy undermined the rule makers' objectives, leading people to doubt or ignore their health decrees: "People aren't dumb. They see it."[20]

Does anyone remember how Covid temporarily "disappeared" during the BLM protests of May and June 2020? Greenwald remembers[21]: "After months of being told it's immoral to leave your house—the argument became: Don't worry! It's very hard to get COVID outside if masked." Before the protests, anyone who whispered costs and benefits was told to stop killing grandmas. Suddenly costs and benefits were all the rage. "We should always evaluate the risks and benefits of efforts to control the virus," Johns Hopkins epidemiologist Jennifer Nuzzo tweeted on June 2, 2020.[22] "In this moment the public health risks of not protesting to demand an end to systemic racism greatly exceed the harms of the virus." Skeptics called out the hypocrisy of supporting one flavor of protest (BLM) and opposing another (anti-lockdown), but not many people listened. In any case, after the riots ran their course, public health advisors lost interest in cost-benefit and the "crush the virus" soundtrack began playing again.

The double-standard of blaming conservative but not liberal politicians for Covid failures doesn't get past Greenwald, either[23]: "More Americans have died of Covid in 2021 than 2020, even though Biden had the benefit of universally available vaccines and improved treatments. Fortunately for Biden, all 2020 Covid deaths were blamed personally on the president but none in 2021 is."

Like Taibbi, Greenwald has found a congenial home on Substack, where he gets to say the quiet part out loud. "In virtually every realm of public policy, Americans embrace policies which they know will kill people," he writes in a post about the refusal to assign costs to the Covid policies.[24] "They do so not because they are psychopaths but because they are rational," reluctantly accepting a certain number of deaths in exchange for policies that make the world a better place. "This rational cost-benefit analysis, even when not expressed in such explicit or crude terms, is foundational to public policy debates—except when it comes to COVID, where it has been bizarrely declared off-limits."

It's what pundits dare not say in mainstream media outlets, where the "it if it saves one life" rhetoric has muzzled discourse since the start of the pandemic. But Greenwald understands that to do public health well, you need not only empathy but emotional distance. If a lone grandma pulls too hard on your heartstrings (or your political strings), you end up short-changing the circle of depressed young grandchildren around her. People who lack the fortitude to weigh benefits against costs should write books about puppies and rainbows, not set public policy.

Greenwald also recoils against the authoritarianism that comes with the territory of "crushing a virus" at all costs. "Australia has gone insane on COVID—so far to excessive authoritarian impulses—that it's hard to put into words at this point," he wrote in reaction to an Australian news clip showing police handcuffing young beachgoers. "But for some sectors of the liberal Left, this form of authoritarianism—the state controls your actions in the name of protecting you—is *appealing.*"[25]

Social psychologist Erich Fromm makes a distinction between rational authority, "based on competence and knowledge, which permits criticism," and irrational authority, "exercised by fear and pressure on the basis of emotional submission."[26] As Greenwald and others have noted, Covid pushed the needle over the dividing line.

In an attempt to explain "how the Left got duped" into an authoritarian position, Canadian writer Kim Goldberg points to the deliberate use of "pseudo-collectivist messaging designed to resonate with leftist sensibilities."[27] The feel-good slogans waved around by authorities, like "wearing is caring" or "my vaccine protects the community," backed leftists into a corner: conditioned to see themselves (and show themselves) as empathetic, they couldn't challenge these bromides without risking expulsion from their chosen tribe. In practice, Goldberg argues, such messages empower the exploitative systems traditionally opposed by leftists and grant governments and corporations "unfathomable authority over everyday life." Neither Goldberg nor Greenwald is down with that.

Mainstream progressives don't know what to make of people like Greenwald, who refuse to confine their opinions to a committee-approved list. Here's a thought for the tribalists: forget what side of the road he drives on. Trust that he has some interesting things to say about the pandemic. Have a read and have a listen, whether you end up agreeing or not.

* * *

Nobody has to wonder about Toby Young's political affiliations: he flies right and stays proudly on course. A UK writer and editor, Young has worked for *The Times*, *The Daily Telegraph*, and *Quillette*, the Internet's stomping ground for counter-narrative types.[28] His 2001 memoir, *How to Lose Friends & Alienate People*, reports on his employment at *Vanity Fair*. His passion for free speech led him to found the Free Speech Union in February 2020 (a rather well-timed launch, as things turned out).

Young has been called a conspiracy theorist, though an introductory note on his website clears up that misconception. Not one to imagine "sinister cabals at work, bent on some secret plot to subvert democratic institutions and usher in a New World Order," he ascribes the pandemic response to the "cock-up theory of history"— things go wrong because people do stupid shit.[29] "History can in rare circumstances be bent to the will of an extraordinary individual, but it is never planned."

Anti-vax? Wrong again. He's just "strongly inclined to postpone the decision about whether to get the vaccine until we have a clearer idea of the safety profile."[30] (If you're not sure the meat is fresh, you're not "anti-meat.") He also knows how to poke fun at himself, which is more than one can say for many of his left-wing counter-parts. In an article for *The Spectator*,[30] he imagines himself in the hospital with Covid, accepting a phone call from a left-leaning news outlet: "We're running a story about Covidiots who regret not being vaccinated and wondered if you'd like to comment?"

So he's not a conspiracy guy and he's not anti-vax. What he is, unabashedly, is anti-lockdown—for all the usual reasons[31]: shaky scientific rationale, infringement on civil liberties, impact on mental health, and disruption to the social fabric. Like many skeptics, he maintains that lockdowns have no place in a democracy because "they involve the arrogation of power by the executive branch of government at the expense of the legislative branch." They set a precedent that the state can always reactivate when the next crisis arrives, and to Young that's just not cricket.

Young's *Lockdown Sceptics* website (now rebranded as *The Daily Sceptic*[29]) performed an invaluable function in spring 2020: letting dissidents know they weren't alone and helping them find each other. People seeking more personal connections could hop over to the "Love in a Covid climate" section, the idea being that "if you're a Covid realist you don't want to go out with a hysteric who thinks the lockdown is being eased too quickly."[32] (As an aside, my own Q-LIT group spawned a romance that could easily take "cutest couple" honors in a school competition. I felt like a *yenta* who just scored a match.)

The *Daily Sceptic* offers a mix of articles written by Young and other iconoclasts from various disciplines. While perusing the archived posts, I stumbled on Newcastle University philosophy lecturer Sinead Murphy, who asks the same question that has been haunting me for three years: Why have democratic societies so quietly accepted the suspension of their freedoms? Drawing on her scholarly reading, she concludes that the new model citizen is basically a young girl, ruled by sentiment and "eminently prepared to relinquish heretofore absolute values."[33] This prototype has tilted the Covid discourse so far toward emotionalism that rational arguments are recast as "unsentimental, unemotional, and therefore inherently callous." Given women's tiresome reputation as the more emotional sex, it pleases me mightily that this diamond-cut observation came from a woman.

Young believes that health and the economy cannot be separated. In a thought piece on the health-economics of lockdowns,[34] he argues that "the choice politicians are making is not between saving lives and economic growth, but between sacrificing lives now and sacrificing them in the future." When economies contract, "life expectancy declines, due to, among other things, a rise in poverty, violent crime and suicide."

After taking us through some napkin math, he concludes that the £185 billion forked out to support lockdowns significantly outpaced the traditional upper limit for public expenditures on health: no more than £30,000 to add one year of perfect health to one person. What's more, the government could have spent the same money to save lives in less disruptive ways.

The outrage mob reacted with the usual epithets: cold, unfeeling, yada yada. *You wouldn't be talking this way if it were you on that ventilator.* As a matter of fact, he would: if keeping him alive came at too high a cost to the NHS, "my death would be acceptable collateral damage." Cold and unfeeling? I call it unselfish.

20

RIGHTS AND RESTRAINTS: JENIN YOUNES, STACEY RUDIN, AND DAVID BELL

Jenin Younes cares about things like civil liberties and human rights. A lot. She also has firm roots in social justice. A criminal and civil liberties lawyer, Younes spent many years working as a public defender in New York City, standing up for people who couldn't afford fancy lawyers. Righting social wrongs is what she does and who she is.

Bewildered at the the world's enthusiasm for lockdowns and eager to add her voice to the global conversation, Younes joined Twitter in September 2020. By mid-2022, her Twitter account, @ Leftylockdowns1, had attracted close to 100,000 followers. She began writing essays and appearing on talk shows to defend the role of foundational American principles in a pandemic.

Twitter also helped Younes find like-minded people, including several in New York. "We ended up meeting at an apartment," she told me when we spoke on the phone. "It was a lifeline at the time, and we kept meeting after that because the group meant so much to us." (I share the sentiment: my Q-LIT group kept me from tumbling down the abyss in the dark days of the pandemic.)

Not that it's been fun and games for Younes: "I lost a lot of friends. Some people distanced themselves from me, and in other cases I decided I no longer wanted to talk to people who paid lip service to caring about the underclass, but clearly didn't. Children living in poverty, children from abusive households, people starving to death because of lockdowns, they didn't want to hear any of it."

They especially didn't want to hear words like "freedom" or "civil liberties." Without asking a further question, "they would assume I had suddenly jumped over to the far right," Younes told me, chuckling through her words. "So I sometimes insert this disclaimer, 'I'm from the left,' when talking about Covid." I had to smile at this, recalling all the times I prefaced my concerns about a vaccine policy with a statement like "I myself am vaxxed" to reassure my interlocutor. Note to self: time to break this habit.

In February 2020, the Western world—including its progressive wing—still saw a place for civil liberties during a pandemic. On the second day of that month, the solidly left-leaning *The Guardian* ran an article about the human rights violations in China's response to the coronavirus.[1] Disturbed by the WHO's endorsement of the Chinese policies, the article warned that "the WHO is ignoring Chinese government suppression of human rights regarding the outbreak, including severe restrictions on freedom of expression." And a few paragraphs later: "That the Chinese government can lock millions of people into cities with almost no advance notice should not be considered anything other than terrifying."

When I review that article today, I'm not sure whether to laugh or tear my hair out. If nothing else, the piece serves as a breathtaking testament to the fickleness of people's commitment to human rights. In mid-March, the free world decided that human rights are disposable, as "non-essential" as the cleaning supplies and menstrual products at the dollar store. Not just that, but anyone who agreed with what *The Guardian* had written a month earlier was a selfish idiot.

The American Civil Liberties Union (ACLU) went along for the ride. Looking back, Younes views the group as "huge disappointment throughout this ordeal. They did nothing." Happily for Younes, a position at the Washington, DC-based New Civil Liberties Alliance (NCLA) opened up in 2021. She packed her bags and scooted down to the national capital, "basically starting my whole life again."

Back in 2008, long before Covid was a gleam in anybody's eye, the ACLU issued a white paper on pandemic preparedness[2] that stated: "There will always be a new disease, always the threat of a new pandemic. If that fear justifies the suspension of liberties and the institution of an emergency state, then freedom and the rule of law will be permanently suspended... The notion that we need to 'trade liberty for security' is misguided and dangerous. Public health concerns cannot be addressed with law enforcement or national security tools." UNESCO took a similar stance in its 2006 Universal Declaration on Bioethics and Human Rights[3]: "The interests and welfare of the individual should have priority over the sole interest of science or society."

In the early days of the pandemic, the ACLU had very little to say about civil liberties. If governments declared that people had to close their businesses and stay home, that was that. When the ACLU finally spoke out in 2021 to weigh in on vaccine mandates, they presented civil liberties as a reward to be earned, rather than a birthright in the free world. From the ACLU's official statement[4]: "By inoculating people from the disease's worst effects, the vaccines offer the promise of *restoring* [italics mine] to all of us our most basic liberties... Far from compromising civil liberties, vaccine mandates actually further them. They protect the most vulnerable among us, including people with disabilities and fragile immune systems, children too young to be vaccinated, and communities of color hit hard by the disease."

The statement has all the right pandemic talking points—"protecting the vulnerable" and "communities of color"—but falls remarkably short in upholding the ACLU's mission, which is to protect individual liberty, irrespective of medical, demographic, or cultural status. It also lacks subtlety, says Younes, who notes that "not all vaccine mandates are created the same." In an article for *Tablet*,[5] she explains: "Mandate proponents typically point to the list of immunization requirements for schoolchildren, along with a 1905 Supreme Court case, *Jacobson v. Massachusetts*, to support their belief that COVID vaccine mandates are legal." But "never in American history have schoolchildren been required to receive vaccines that had not already undergone years—usually at least a decade—of safety trials. Nor have we required children to receive vaccines for diseases that primarily pose a risk to adults or the elderly."

Such arguments evidently don't interest the ACLU. Their new interpretation of civil liberties requires people to cast their freedoms aside so they can enjoy them later—the opposite of the organization's stance in 2008. This about-face exemplifies the seismic moral shift accelerated by the pandemic. In a few short years, we've gone from "can't trade liberty for security" to "only security guarantees liberty."

Younes has found a much more congenial home at the NCLA, where she and her colleagues have been challenging Covid regulations imposed by executive decree and government-led censorship of debate around Covid policies. Remember the lawsuit (mentioned in Chapter 5) alleging the US government of colluding with social media outlets to suppress dissenting views? As it happens, the plaintiffs enlisted the NCLA to represent them. In October 2022, Younes and her team received some welcome news[6]: the judge overseeing the case granted their request to depose the defendants. The list includes White House senior Covid-19 advisor Andrew Slavitt, White House director of digital strategy Rob Flaherty, and former White House press secretary Jennifer Psaki. Oh, and Anthony Fauci. This could get interesting.

"It's strange to think that the pandemic policies have led me to my dream job," Younes reflects. "Not that it makes up for any of the damage they caused, but I'm glad I can help move the needle."

* * *

Whatever one may think of America, its Constitution has captured the global imagination as an enduring monument to freedom. Created as a restraining force to keep institutional encroachment on individual liberty in check, it belongs to the people, not to the government. "Our safety, our liberty, depends upon preserving the Constitution of the United States as our fathers made it inviolate," Abraham Lincoln has said.[7] "The people of the United States are the rightful masters of both Congress and the courts, not to overthrow the Constitution, but to overthrow the men who pervert the Constitution."

More than 150 years after Lincoln's assassination, Stacey Rudin still believes in the inviolability of the Constitution—free movement and free speech and all that jazz. A former litigator based in New Jersey, Rudin has found a new vocation in writing fiery essays about Covid. The tagline on her Medium webpage is "I say what I think."

In the early weeks of the pandemic, speaking out against the pandemic policies was like climbing a rockface without rappelling equipment: odds were you would fall, and fall hard. So people kept their doubts to themselves, leaving the impression that everyone was on board. "Many who were disquieted by the widespread elevation of fear into virtue never said a word due to concern over 'looking bad'," Rudin reflects in an essay for the American Institute for Economic Research (AIER).[8] They hoped "someone else would step up to fight against the absurd new moral construct calling good, hardworking people murderers if they won't sacrifice their entire lives and livelihoods for an indefinite period."

Rudin is that "someone else." She calls it as she sees it. Almost all of her essays touch on the same theme: the urgency of preserving constitutional rights and democratic principles. She understands that pandemics are complex and may test the Constitution's resilience—but if the document means anything at all, it must weather the storm. That's why she cheered when, in September 2020, the Pennsylvania Federal Court declared the indefinite emergency restrictions imposed by the executive branch—the limitations on gathering size, stay-at-home orders, and mandatory business closures—unconstitutional.[9] Reporting on the ruling in another AIER article,[10] she wrote: "While global pandemics pose challenges for governors—particularly when the population is panicked by a hysterical mass media—entire populations cannot be indefinitely subjected to tyranny and deprived of fundamental rights and liberties."

I remember that ruling. Judge Stickman's statement[10] brought tears to my eyes, and I'm not even American: "In times of crisis, even a vigilant public may let down its guard over its constitutional liberties only to find that liberties, once relinquished, are hard to recoup and that restrictions—while expedient in the face of an emergency situation—may persist long after the immediate danger has passed." But he's a *conservative* judge, some have said, as though this invalidated his reasoning. (That was the thrust of the *Washington Post*'s pushback piece.[11]) To my mind, the ruling has nothing to do with political affiliation and everything to do with democracy.

And here we arrive at a fork in the road that, in my experience, divides people pretty cleanly and intractably. The first camp thinks: Who the hell cares about individual rights and constitutional freedoms during a pandemic? The second camp thinks: hell yes, we care.

If you fall in Camp A, you may bristle (or rage) at the selfish idiots who carry on about rights and freedoms while a highly transmissible virus is making the rounds. I'll ask you to take it on faith that Camp B feels equally frustrated (and at times enraged). We don't understand why such freedoms matter so little to you. We view freedom as a condition of flourishing, its absence as an unhealthy way to live. It's like hanging out in a well-equipped jail cell, where we get nice meals served to us every day. We may even get free Internet and Thursday movie nights in the common room. All the bells and whistles, except the one thing that matters most. We may be willing to live this way for a short time, to keep the safetyists happy—but as a way of life, we say hell no.

Like Younes, Rudin feels moved to speak for people left behind by the safetyist policies—the small business owners who had to close shop, the babies growing up without seeing smiles, the elderly people instructed to remove themselves from the flow of life "for their protection." Lockdown skeptics "believe that all of these people, every single one, deserves a voice, a unique vote as to the philosophy of his or her life, and that no one else—even someone vastly more powerful—has the right to override it," she says.[12]

To Rudin, the political response to the pandemic also betrays a lack of courage—and humility. Rather than admit they can't control everything in nature, our leaders insisted the virus bend to their will, regardless of the suffering and indignities occasioned by their policies. (Plus: it didn't work.) In Rudin's view, centuries of first-world privilege have left developed nations with an illusion of control. "We are never forced to face our vulnerability because prosperity protects us," she says.[10] "But the pandemic has laid bare "our puny, pathetic fear... our fear of a *lack of control* over dying." As I said, she calls it as she sees it.

* * *

Control begets control, and sooner or later someone is bound to ask: Why leave pandemic control to individual countries' discretion? Why not manage pandemics under a single planetary roof? The WHO began exploring this idea in 2021: an international treaty to strengthen pandemic prevention, preparedness and response. At the end of the year, WHO members agreed to start drafting the document, and the European Council greenlit the proposal three months later.[13] In defense of the initiative, Olivier Véran, then-Minister for Solidarity and Health in France, stated that "COVID-19 has revealed the importance of international cooperation to fight global threats to people's health... The international community needs to come together to ensure equitable access to vaccines and therapeutics, guarantee timely sharing of data and information and address the links between human, animal and environmental health."[13]

Sounds reasonable, right? To David Bell, not so much. A physician with training in internal medicine and a PhD in population health, Bell has devoted most of his career to infectious diseases. Past appointments include program head for malaria and acute febrile disease at FIND, a global alliance for equitable diagnostics, and medical and scientific officer for the WHO.[14] He now contributes his expertise to PANDA [Pandemics Data & Analytics], a multidisciplinary group that champions open science and rational debate. In our Zoom chat, he spoke in thoughtful, measured tones, not to mention a lovely down-under accent.

Bell's experience with the WHO has given him front-row insight into the organization's approach to pandemics. "The WHO defines a pandemic quite loosely," he told me. "It doesn't have to kill people. It doesn't have to be severe. It just has to be widespread. And a respiratory virus will always become widespread." A treaty may enable the WHO to expand its surveillance role when a pathogen of concern trips their radar. And with a low bar for declaring a pandemic, "they're liable to find what they're looking for."

In theory, a WHO treaty wouldn't displace the laws of individual countries. But politics being politics, a treaty "can be used as an instrument to target countries," says Bell in an interview for the American Thought Leaders series.[15] A small, relatively powerless country may hesitate to push back on the WHO's guidance, fearing that more powerful countries will slap them with sanctions or withhold financial assistance. So even if a treaty "doesn't directly change sovereignty, in effect it does. It takes away the ability of the people of that country to make their own decisions."

Once the proposed WHO treaty was announced, anti-globalists sounded alarm bells on Facebook and Twitter: The WHO will have global control over human health! Unvaccinated people will be sent to prison! Legacy media hit back with "calm down" messages. Reuters contacted a WHO spokesperson who reportedly said that "any accord, if agreed by the WHO's Member States, would be expected to include the respect and promotion of human rights as a core component—including the right to health—and to facilitate personal freedoms."[16]

Sounds pretty in theory, but Bell doesn't buy it. It's not that he sees the WHO as evil. He doesn't believe they're out to "control human health," much less throw unvaccinated people in jail, and maintains that "in developing countries, the WHO has done good work that has saved lives." He just believes that giving so much control to a single organization can only lead to trouble, especially an organization that's already grown too big for its britches. "The WHO has ossified into a self-important bureaucracy," he told me. "It responds to the corporate donors who fund a lot of its programs." A treaty would only ratchet up this conflict of interest.

What's more, a unified pandemic strategy doesn't make practical sense in a world as diverse as ours. "The policymakers in their corner offices don't know how the mother in Burkina Faso is faring. They're so focused on getting a Covid vaccine into her child, but her child may already have caught the virus and may be at much greater risk of dying of malaria."

Treaty or no treaty, Bell holds that the WHO has lost sight of its own definition of health[17]: "A state of complete physical, mental and social well-being and not merely the absence of disease or infirmity." In responding to the pandemic, the WHO beamed all its attention on conquering a virus and threw mental and social health overboard. Not just the WHO, but the CDC, NHS, and a thousand smaller public health units. "Public health became Covid."

This disproportionate focus on the virus led other public health efforts to backslide. Even during the two-weeks-to-flatten-the-curve period, Bell knew that tuberculosis and malaria would start rising, "and the longer you keep the pressure on Covid, the more these other diseases go up." What's more, "we're spending about 3 or 4 times more on Covid vaccines in Africa than we spend every year on malaria—for a vaccine that doesn't stop transmission. This is not just insane, but is doing a lot of specific harm to people. It doesn't fit with what public health is supposed to be."

The people who create public health policies sometimes forget that "life is more than avoiding some particular illness or other threat. It's more than avoiding going rock fishing because you may run into large waves." Bell told me about a law, in the Australian state of Victoria, requiring people do complete a food preparation course before holding a community barbecue. What these lawmakers fail to grasp is that "community barbecues are important in bringing people together. Some of these people may be struggling mentally, and the barbecue may be the event that pulls them back from suicidal thoughts."

Public health institutions also have a strong "action bias," a.k.a. compulsion to Do Something. The Decision Lab defines action bias[18] as the tendency to "favor action over inaction"—to respond to a problem with "action as a default, automatic reaction, even without solid rationale to support it." We feel "compelled to act, even if there's no evidence that it will lead to a better outcome than doing nothing would."

This bias pervades pandemic surveillance and management. Public health organizations "will spend billions of dollars looking for new pathogens or variants," Bell told me. "If they find something, they'll recommend an action. It's how they justify their existence." Sometimes the best response may be no response at all, but when you've spent big bucks and a long career looking for monsters under rocks, "just leave that banshee where it is" doesn't give you the satisfying ending you seek.

To defend against the next pandemic, Bell favors a less-is-more approach. Less intervention and more institutional restraint. Less panic, less contact tracing, less money diverted to the problem, and more "community fitness and buildup of immunocompetence." This means no lockdowns, no gym closures, and no taped-up playground equipment. In essence, "the opposite of what we did in this pandemic."

SEEDS OF UNREST: RUPA
SUBRAMANYA AND RAQUEL DANCHO

On January 22, 2022, truck drivers from several points in Canada began driving east.[1] Along the way, more trucks joined the queue. Rag-tag crews lined the highways to cheer them on, their hands wrapped around steaming cups of coffee to keep the blood flowing.

A week later the first truckers arrived at their destination, Canada's capital city of Ottawa, joined by foot soldiers who had made the trek on their own. They all had the same message to the Canadian government: no more vaccine mandates. Not for the truckers, whose livelihoods rested on the ability to cross the border to the US, and not for anyone else.

For two weeks the truckers and their allies swarmed around Parliament Hill, where they gave impromptu speeches, set up bouncy castles for their children, huddled around campfires, and made lots of noise. Honk, honk!

It wasn't all squeaky-clean, of course. All protests attract extremists of one stripe or another, and this one was no exception. A confederate flag and a swastika flag turned up early on and some protesters allegedly harassed the staff at a soup kitchen[2]—an unfortunate sidebar that distracted from the main story and gave media

pundits a pretext to inject words like "racist" and "white supremacist" into their news dispatches.

Already polarized by pandemic politics, Canadians now had a new
issue to divide them: Were the truckers and their entourage heroes or
villains? Peaceful protesters or bigoted boors? Was the movement a
working-class uprising or a toddler tantrum on steroids?

To get my bearings I turned to Rupa Subramanya, already on
my Covid hero list for her *National Post* pieces on the pandemic.
A writer with graduate degrees in economics and international
affairs, Subramanya spent 10 years in India and now makes her
home in Ottawa, not far from Parliament Hill.[3] She has written about
economics and policy for major news outlets across the world and
co-authored a bestselling book called *Indianomix*.

Subramanya did what none of the journalists lambasting the
convoy thought to do: interview the protesters themselves. For
about 10 days, she bundled up every morning and walked over
to Parliament Hill, where she talked to the truckers and their
supporters. And above all, listened.

In a guest post for Bari Weiss's newsletter,[4] Subramanya
described some of the almost 100 people who shared their stories
with her. Some protesters, like Peter, refused the vaccine because
"the whole thing had become so politicized, and you couldn't be sure
who to trust." Others, like convoy spokesman B.J. Dicheter, were
vaccinated but showed up at the protest on principle. "I'm Jewish.
I have family in mass graves in Europe. And apparently I'm a white
supremacist." Ivan, 46, who emigrated from Ukraine with his wife to
start fresh in New Brunswick, told Subramanya that "we lived under
communism, and, in Canada, we're now fighting for our freedom."

To Subramanya, the ostensible motive for the protest—no vax
mandates—was almost beside the point: "What's happening in
Canada right now is bigger than the mandates." She saw the protest
as an outcry against authoritarianism by people who often lack a
voice. "The elites—the people who have Zoomed their way through
the pandemic—had better start paying attention to the fentanyl

overdoses, the suicides, the crime, the despair."

Don't just take Subramanya's word for it. Get it straight from Gord Magill, a trucker who spoke for the movement in a *Newsweek* opinion piece.[5] What united the protesters was "a general feeling of having had enough," he wrote. "Enough of lockdowns and coercion, enough of lives interrupted...of children's upbringings being marred by this psychological warfare."

Magill also cut through the outrage about the two offending flags. "The question you should be asking is not how two racists managed to find their way to a protest of 100,000 people," but rather why the media, "who until very recently were absolutely lavish in their praise of 'essential workers,' have turned on us." He warned the elites to tread carefully: "The working class of Canada have been inspired to action, and it is ever more obvious that we have no need for the assistance or approval of the classes who think they are so far above us."

On the same day that Subramanya's report from the trenches came out, she gave an update to *True North* podcaster Candice Malcolm, confirming that the offensive flags spotted in the first couple of never showed up again.[6] Or if they did, Subramanya didn't see them. What she saw was a spirit of conviviality and solidarity—the "all in it together" vibe that everyone had talked about, but never quite materialized, in the early days of the pandemic. "I can get a burger, I can grab a hotdog, it's all free," she said, adding that people in the downtown homeless shelters were spilling out into the street and joining in the festivities. "I've seen them dancing. I've seen them happy."

In Subramanya's view, Trudeau and his entourage misjudged the moment. "There's something bigger going on here," she told Malcolm. "Our political class is completely disconnected from what is happening here. And this is going to backfire."

My own support for the convoy made me an outlier in my largely progressive group of friends, who threw the usual left-wing talking points at me: "How could you, the child of a Holocaust survivor, support such a racist movement?" (My answer: What part of "no vaccine mandates" sounds racist to you?) "Are you OK with the disruption to local businesses caused by the protests?" (My rejoinder: So *now* you're worried about local businesses, after two years of hand-waving their pain?) "You're an intelligent person," one friend told me. "Do you know something that the rest of us don't?"

As a matter of fact, I did. Along with Subramanya's ground-level reports, I had intel from my own son, who drove from Montreal to Ottawa to attend the event. Twenty-four years old at the time, Jackson wanted to test the media reports against reality. He also wanted to register his displeasure with pandemic regulations that had stopped making sense to him many months earlier. (You know what they say about apples and trees.) He missed his Ottawa friends, too: no-nonsense types he had met during his three summers planting trees in Northern Ontario, with none of the packaged politics of his other friend groups. They would be joining him on Parliament Hill to watch, listen, and make noise of their own.

This is what he told me.

White faces? Yes, lots of them. Many of the protesters had come from small towns, which don't match the ethnic diversity seen in urban Canada, so it stood to reason that the crowd would skew white. White supremacy? "It was on my mind the whole time and I looked everywhere for it," Jackson said. "But I never found it. Zero, zip." As he and his friends swapped stories with other protesters, rubbing their gloves together to keep frostbite at bay, they learned that everyone had come for the same reason: frustration with restrictions that were ruining their lives. For some people, it was the vax mandates. For others, the curfew in the province of Quebec (one of Jackson's beefs). Still others just wanted their freedom back.

Having traveled long distances to attend the event, the protesters were fixing for a party. The icy weather cemented their bond, reminding them of their shared Canadian identity as they swapped stories, shared snacks, and broke into song, their breath condensing instantly as it escaped their lips. It was also, Jackson told me, a big Trudeau-bashing party, with "Fuck Trudeau" banners swaying alongside maple-leaf flags above the protesters' heads.

Like Subramanya, Jackson wanted more than the CBC News version of things. And what he saw reinforced what he already knew: Don't take people's word for it. Go see for yourself.

Why in Canada, people have asked. Aren't Canadians supposed to be polite? Well, polite people have a breaking point too, and it usually comes after a lot of pent-up frustration. I had an uncle like that: a big bear of a man, mild-mannered and affable, unflustered by the wild children scampering around him. But once every few years, when we pushed him too hard, his eruption shook the earth beneath our feet. Considering the Trudeau government's heavy-handed management of the pandemic, the only thing that surprises me is that the convoy didn't happen sooner.

* * *

I had no idea who Raquel Dancho was until she appeared on my computer screen on February 7, 2022, in the midst of the Ottawa trucker protest, and blew me away in ten short minutes.

It turns out she's from Manitoba, descended from four generations of farmers in a rural community. She attended McGill University in Montreal, exposing herself to people with a wide range of world views, and then went right back home. Anyone who makes that trek—from the prairies to Montreal and back—clearly has Canada's heartland in their blood.

Dancho now serves as a federal Member of Parliament, representing the conservative party and serving the Manitoba constituency of Kildonan-St. Paul.[7] Not many people know her outside her province, and certainly not outside Canada, but that 10-minute speech she gave in Canada's House of Commons[8] secured her spot on my hero list. This woman is going places.

Watch her stand up and look the Speaker of the House in the eye, clutching a sheaf of notes that she clearly doesn't need as she builds up her argument. "If there is any member in this house that does not believe Canadians have been through trauma these past two years, they clearly have not been doing their jobs and listening to their constituents," she says. "I have had widowed elderly women call and cry to me on the phone about how lonely they are and they don't want to go on. I've had grown men who've called me crying because their businesses are falling apart."

Despite effective tools to manage the pandemic, Trudeau has "repeatedly relied on harsh lockdown measures and divisive mandates to control this virus." Before his "600-million-dollar unnecessary election" of 2021, he positioned the vaccines as a choice. Within days of the election, he was "yelling into a microphone at a liberal rally that you have the right not to get vaccinated but you don't have the right to sit next to someone who is."

Dancho continues: "We are seeing other governments around the world step up [and tell their constituents], 'look, we hear you, you've been traumatized, we're moving forward... You can travel, you can live your life, you can hug each other again. Here's a date, this is a plan, here's a threshold.'" But there has been "none of that in Canada, absolutely none of that from the prime minister."

Indeed, Trudeau's fixation on vaccination made him an outlier even among liberal leaders. During the last half of 2021, he answered virtually all media questions with a plug for vaccination. You couldn't design a better pull-string doll if you tried.

– Do you think vaccine mandates are fair?
– The way we get through this pandemic is by getting all Canadians vaccinated.
– When do you think the country will move beyond mask mandates?
– Let's get all Canadians vaccinated.
– What are your thoughts about the rising cost of living in Canada?
– Let's get all Canadians vaccinated.

– How about those Ottawa Senators? Think they have a
chance at the playoffs this year?
– Let's get all Canadians vaccinated.

Using the vaccine as a bludgeon has ripped families and communities apart, Dancho tells the Speaker, with yesterday's healthcare
heroes recast as villains if they refused the vaccine. The people most
affected by Trudeau's policies have been "experiencing trauma for
two years, and no-one is listening to them." So what choice do they
have? "When you don't listen to these people, they mobilize."

It's as stirring a speech as I've ever heard: eloquent and proud,
not a hem or a haw breaking the stride, and above all, straight from
the heart. It's not often that a political speech can make me cry, but
this one gets to me every time I listen to it.

The only thing Dancho might have added, for Trudeau's benefit,
is a little excerpt from Canada's own 2015 Pandemic Influenza
Preparedness guide[9]: "When considering restrictive measures, it
is important to balance respect for autonomy against protection
of overall population health. In such situations, the principles of
proportionality, reciprocity and flexibility are involved, with a view
to safeguarding individual freedom to the extent possible while
[also] promoting protection."

To avoid facing the truckers' grievances, Trudeau created a
subplot of racism, white supremacy, and far-right ideology. During
a press conference, he described the truckers as a "fringe minority"
with "unacceptable views."[10] (In an earlier talk, he called unvaccinated Canadians a "sect" who were taking up space, did not believe
in science, and were "often misogynists, often racists."[11])

Instead, he could have talked to the people, as Subramanya
and Dancho did. He could have held a formal conference with the
protesters, sketched out a path toward normalcy, or simply acknowledged their pain. Something, anything.

In fairness, the truckers could also have done a few things differently. Their sweeping demands—no vaccine mandates, no more

Covid restrictions—were politically naive. They overstayed their welcome in Ottawa, and when their presence began choking up the city's business activity they lost a lot of social capital.

Could have, would have, should have. With Trudeau at the helm, it's unlikely that any of it would have made a difference. Dialogue wasn't on his agenda: he just wanted the truckers gone. On Feb. 14 he invoked the Emergencies Act, a move that also enabled him to cut off financial contributions to the convoy, and got the job done.[12]

On the face of it, the convoy failed in its mission: the truckers left and the mandates stayed. But it got the world's attention. The *New York Times*, *The Guardian*, and *Al Jazeera* reported on it, among countless other outlets. It inspired me-too protests across the world, from New Zealand to France,[13] and Trudeau's sledgehammer politics came under fire internationally. In its post-mortem of the event,[14] *The Spectator* described Trudeau's tactics as "totalitarian methods, not the methods of a justly governed, civilised nation," adding that "nobody in power appears genuinely concerned about anything other than maintaining control and saving face." Even such liberal stalwarts as *The Washington Post* deemed that Trudeau had gone too far[15]: "This is the stuff of authoritarian regimes. In a free society, the government doesn't get to decide whose views are 'unacceptable' or whether it will 'tolerate' them."

The convoy failed, but it also succeeded. It told the world that the Covid pendulum had swung too far and needed a course correction. Perhaps it didn't change the outcome of this pandemic, but significant political events take time to metabolize. When the next pandemic rolls around, political leaders may hesitate just a little longer before calling a lockdown or instating a vaccine mandate. Once a bird escapes its cage, you never know how far it will fly or where it will land.

* * *

This chapter has its own epilogue, set in the summer of 2022, after the flimsy basis for Canada's travel vaccine mandate came to light in court documents. Once again writing for Bari Weiss, Subramanya gives us the deets.[16]

As it turned out, nobody in the Transport Canada department in charge of the mandate "had any formal training in epidemiology, medicine or public health." With the clock ticking on implementation day, Aaron McCrorie, a Transport Canada official, requested stronger evidence to support the move: "To the extent that updated data exist or that there is clearer evidence of the safety benefit of vaccination on the users or other stakeholders of the transportation system, it would be helpful to assist Transport Canada supporting its measures," he wrote to the Public Health Agency of Canada. (Gotta love the bafflegab.) That "clearer evidence" never materialized, beyond a set of generic bullet points endorsing the vaccine. Even so, the mandate kicked in on October 30, leaving 5 million Canadians unable to travel until its expiry eight and a half months later.

Also in summer 2022, Salman Rushdie got stabbed 10 times at an event in New York state, 33 years after Iran issued a fatwa against him.[17] Recognizing the opportunity to display his progressive stripes, Trudeau promptly tweeted his support for the writer[18]: "The cowardly attack on Salman Rushdie is a strike on the freedom of expression that our world relies on. No one should be threatened or harmed on the basis of what they have written."

OK, then. Let's hear what Rushdie himself has to say about freedom of expression—like the fact that "without the freedom to offend, it ceases to exist."[19] Or that, if you're going to defend the principle, "you have to defend the Ku Klux Klan as well as Martin Luther King." Or that you only discover how you feel about free speech "when people really upset you."[20]

The "unacceptable views" guy may want to brush up on his Rushdie. Just saying.

22

THE LIMITS OF CONTROL: CARL HENEGHAN AND ROBERT DINGWALL

Ever since lions roamed the savannah and windstorms tore down grass huts, humans have sought to control their environment. The Covid narrative—by acting together we can beat this thing—offered the two-for-one deal of controlling nature and controlling other people, the latter a means to achieve the former. The story appealed to the innate human drive to control.

And then the virus began to tell its own story, a story of guile and grit. It stickhandled around every obstacle we threw at it. It took the measure of our human hubris and had a good belly laugh.

Eventually, people could no longer ignore the laughter. Covid abolitionists, whose narrative rose to prominence in 2021, began to defect the cause. Even countries like Australia and New Zealand, which initially threw all their institutional muscle at the elimination strategy, eventually called it a day. Sooner or later people get tired of running on a treadmill with no off-button.

It's called acceptance. Some people have to go through the stages of grief before getting there: shock, anger, bargaining, and all the rest. Others reach the acceptance stage more quickly and easily. One of them is Carl Heneghan, who attributes his sanguine perspective to his complementary professional roles: head of the Centre for

Evidence Based Medicine at Oxford University during the week, urgent care doctor on weekends. This dual persona allows him test predictive models against the patients at his door, the academic cloister against the dirt road.

From the earliest days of the pandemic, Heneghan maintained that lockdowns would achieve nothing, because the battle was already lost by the time the WHO made the call. "There can be little doubt that covid-19 may be far more widely distributed than some may believe," he and a colleague wrote in April 2020.[1] "Lockdown is going to bankrupt all of us and our descendants and is unlikely at this point to slow or halt viral circulation as the genie is out of the bottle."

He called the revolving door of restrictions "utter chaos"— especially the practice of sending an entire class of schoolchildren home when one student tested positive—and urged his government to "slow down its thinking," rather than panicking at every uptick in cases.[2] If he were in charge, school policy would look something like this[3]: "If you're symptomatic, you stay out of school. Once you're back to normal, you go back to school." Looking ahead, he urged governments to accept the virus's presence in society, manage its risks, and balance them against the physical, mental, and spiritual drag of living in a recurring loop of restrictions and fear.[2]

The following year, the UK government branded July 19 as Freedom Day, the day that restrictions would cede to normality.[4] But two months later, as children were gearing up for a new school year, Groundhog Day was still playing in people's homes. "People are still very fearful about going about their daily lives," Heneghan said to *The Telegraph* columnist Allison Pearson in a *Planet Normal* podcast.[3] UK schoolchildren and their parents still faced the apparatus of lateral flow testing, masking, distancing, and isolating erected the previous year.

At the same time, Heneghan sensed some public movement toward "accepting that the virus is endemic." He called this process phase one of the endemic cycle. Phase two would hash out the fine points—how to engage with Covid as a normal respiratory virus, rather than a special case. To Heneghan, this phase couldn't come soon enough. "When do we start to have a grownup debate about how we go into phase two [and] learn to live with this virus?"

Part of being a grownup (one might say the whole point of it) is having free agency. You don't tell your partner it's past their bedtime. If your friend wants to eat her dessert before (or instead of) her broccoli, you don't threaten to confiscate her iPad. That's why Heneghan doesn't like mandates: they treat adults like children. "I never tell people what to do," he says. "You have to inform people... If you do that well, people come to the right conclusions."

At the end of 2021, amid rumblings of new restrictions, Heneghan pointed out that adults of sound mind "are able to respond to information or adapt their behaviour accordingly."[5] If a tiger is roaming the streets, they will stay inside without being told. Once again he asked: "When are we going to treat people like adults? [It's] the only sustainable policy."

Apparently not to his detractors. Throughout the pandemic, the people who wanted more control, more restrictions, pelted him with the epithets familiar to any Covid policy dissenter: irresponsible, dangerous, disgraceful. The professor of evidence-based medicine and author of over 400 peer-reviewed publications had joined the band of "willful heretics" (to use Pearson's term) and deserved to be punished for it.

He was named in an article that linked anti-lockdown views to right-wing lobbying to "revive herd immunity," without providing any evidence for the claim.[6] He had to defend himself against the accusation that he had claimed Covid was over.[7] Facebook labeled his report on the zero-benefit DANMASK-19 study "false information,"[8] and Twitter temporarily suspended his account after he shared a study that downgraded Britain's estimated death toll from Covid.[9]

(The pattern was set by then: any public figure who "downplayed" Covid or opposed a restriction faced the prospect of suspension, while the purveyors of doom got away scot-free, allegedly because the former group was "putting people at risk." I found it curious that the risks of alarmism never got a mention.)

"Isn't the professor of evidence-based medicine quite angry?" Pearson asked him during their chat, referring to the smear campaigns against opponents of the lockdown orthodoxy.[3] "Has it been painful or shocking for you, Carl, to be painted as someone who is at odds with the scientific evidence, when evidence is the air you breathe?"

While conceding that "the level of vitriol is quite something," Heneghan told Pearson that keeping a steady eye on "what's best for the next generation" has helped him stay calm and carry on. By continuing to speak out, he also hopes to encourage other academics who hesitate to come forward because of "what might happen to them in the public arena."

And this, folks, is why professors have job security. The mob may have pelted Heneghan with their rotten tomatoes, but he's still standing, still employed, still free to poke holes at the orthodoxy. Tenure rocks.

People resist the idea of "living with the virus" not just because of its public health implications, but because it represents an admission of defeat. From the get-go, governments across the world positioned the virus as an enemy in an planetary battle.[10] In the UK, Boris Johnson created a "war cabinet" to fight the virus, while the late Queen Elizabeth drew on the Vera Lynn wartime song "We Will Meet Again In France." Emmanuel Macron declared France at war with an "invisible enemy." Helicopters sliced through the air, showering rose petals on frontline workers, in displays of institutional might that medical anthropologist Carlo Caduff has described as "militarized state spectacles."[11]

To Caduff, such pomp represents an "overidentification in a hegemonic discourse of power." (As an aside, Caduff's "What Went Wrong" paper,[11] published in *Medical Anthropology Quarterly* in July 2020, is essential reading for pandemic scholars interested in a sociocultural analysis of the Covid policies.) The pandemic response itself "lacks imagination" in its reliance on "the crudest intervention of all: the full stop."

In a paper called "Homo Pandemicus,"[12] Fabio Vighi, a critical theory professor at Cardiff University, puts it still less politely: The only goal is "to win the war, regardless of how much it costs, who pays for it, who benefits from it, and what happens next." And a war that "exists primarily as a media representation, just as hell existed in the altarpieces of medieval churches, requires first of all obedience [and] *denkverboten*, a prohibition against articulating critical thinking that deviates an inch from the official line."

This militaristic stance originated in China, where Xi Jinping declared a "people's war" on the coronavirus.[10] To US lawyer and writer Michael Senger, the Chinese lockdowns embody the concept of *fang kong,* an ideologically loaded philosophy that incorporates both prevention and control. "Xi's lockdown of Wuhan had been inspired by [this] pet hybrid of public health and security policy," he writes in his book *Snake Oil: How Xi Jinping Shut Down the World.*[13] It's "the same policy that inspired the re-education and 'quarantine' of over one million Uyghur Muslims and other minorities 'infected with extremism' throughout Xinjiang and Tibet."

Such concepts lead us to the subterranean layers of human psychology, where the desire to control a virus melds with the naked impulse to control other people. To borrow from H.L. Mencken, "the urge to save humanity is always a false front for the urge to rule it."[14]

During the height of the vax pass period, Quebec's Ministry of Health decreed that unvaccinated shoppers in large retail stores such as Walmart or IKEA, or any retail businesses with a sales area of 1,500 square meters or more, could only buy pharmacy products and *had to be accompanied at all times by an employee* [italics mine].[15] It is difficult to interpret this level of interference as anything but a compulsion to control (and in this particular scenario, to humiliate).

This compulsion comes naturally to many of us. It must be "a yearning deep in human heart to stop other people from doing as they please," says novelist Robert Heinlein, by way of one of his characters.[16] "Rules, laws—always for [the] other fellow." That said, the impulse to control doesn't animate all humans with the same force. Some people have a special talent for it, while others prefer to chill and strum their guitars. Again from Heinlein[17]: "The human race divides politically into those who want people to be controlled and those who have no such desire."

Both the do-as-I-say and the do-as-you-wish factions believe the other side has it all wrong. In a pandemic, the first group grabs the moral high ground, insisting that everyone act in a certain way (their way) to subdue the offending pathogen. This approach has some basis, but only to a point and for a time. Once the pathogen settles in for the long haul, the chill-and-play-guitar crowd reminds us that life is to be lived, not trapped in glass like a museum artefact.

Anthony Furey, a *Toronto Sun* columnist whose observations about Covid psychology have consistently hit the mark, contends that the pandemic helped natural control freaks "come into their true selves...delighting in badgering people about what they can do."[18] Even when the epidemiologic situation no longer requires it, these "Covid busybodies" (as Furey calls them) "get a kick out of the idea of punishing and excluding people who aren't behaving exactly like them."

Starting in early 2022, the busybodies began invoking people with compromised immune systems as a justification to keep bossing the world around a little longer, or forever. This argument rests on at least two wobbly legs. For one thing, studies do not bear out the notion that a weakened immune system spells mortal danger from Covid. In late 2021, a study of 200,000 adults hospitalized with Covid found that "overall, patients taking immunosuppressive drugs do not face increased risk of being put on a ventilator or death."[19] Another study, which considered the effect of four types of serious immunosuppression on Covid outcomes, concluded that "in these four populations, iatrogenic or disease-related immunosuppression is not clearly associated with poor prognosis."[20] (This is not to say that immunocompromised people face no excess risk, just that the excess has been overplayed.)

Second, immunocompromised people have ways to protect themselves that don't depend on what others do, like wearing respirators or taking antivirals if they catch the virus. Their needs matter, but so too do the needs of the millions of people without immune dysfunction. I'm all for making life easier for people with health challenges and acutely aware I could join their ranks at any moment, having lost both my parents to cancer decades ahead of their time. But mandates in perpetuity aren't the way to do it.

The other grab-and-go justification for continued restrictions, long Covid, has the same built-in problem: no end-game in sight. Covid isn't leaving us anytime soon, so long Covid will remain a risk for the foreseeable future. However we choose to manage this risk today, we must be prepared to do it forever. We have two basic options here: controlling other people's behavior or focusing on our own.

At some point, the Covid control freaks become a fair target for their own "don't be selfish" slogan. As Oscar Wilde famously stated, "selfishness is not living as one wishes to live, it is asking others to live as one wishes to live. And unselfishness is letting other people's lives alone."[21] Aaron Schorr, a Yale University student on immune-suppressing medication, understood this when he wrote that he "didn't expect the government to structure its entire [Covid-19] response around my personal well-being" in the *Yale Daily News*.[22] "Feeling unsafe? By all means take extra precautions, but 4,664 undergraduates should not be forced to adhere to the same standard." Schorr is not betraying the disability community by acknowledging that the only rational way to run a campus, or a society, is to balance the needs of the few with the needs of the many. If anyone merits the "unselfish" prize, it's him—not the campus activists calling for mandates until the end of time.

Relinquishing the urge to control comes more easily to some

than to others. (It certainly doesn't come easily to me. I have an abiding impulse to meddle in my grown children's lives, although I know full well that I can control them as readily as I control the wind.) Seen through the lens of control, learning to live with the virus exemplifies the spiritual practice of letting go.

* * *

Robert Dingwall, a UK medical sociologist and professor at Nottingham Trent University, has a lot to say about control and surrender. Involved in the UK's pandemic strategy since 2005, when the government invited him to join a committee devoted to the ethical aspects of pandemic planning, Dingwall has also served at NERVTAG, an advisory group devoted to assessing the threat posed by new respiratory viruses.

Writing for *Social Science Space*,[23] Dingwall reflects on the cultural damage that flows from presuming that "the aim of medicine should be to control every virus or bacteria" rather than doing damage control on the worst ones. "Is every death a defeat for medicine or a natural part of the human condition? Do aggressive medical interventions at the end of life get in the way of care and compassion?" Like many others, Dingwall reminds us that the drive to impose medical control on nature "comes with huge social and economic costs."

Death as a part of the human condition? One cannot say such things anymore without evoking the Wrath of Twitter, but Dingwall takes on the challenge. In an interview with Alastair Benn of *Reaction* magazine, he discusses the damage of refusing to accept disease and death as part of life.[24] "Death is a moment in living," he observes. "It is our ultimate experience." But we no longer look upon death in this way. Emboldened by medicine's quantum leaps over the past few years, "we have developed this conceit that we could live forever if only the technology were right or if only we might micro-manage our health correctly. In the process, we have lost sight of the fact that pretty much anything we do merely prolongs life, and that it often does so at the expense of the quality of life we live towards the end."

Nobody exemplifies this shift in attitude more than Ezekiel Emanuel, the oncologist and bioethicist who wrote an essay called "Why I Hope to Die at 75" for *The Atlantic* in 2014.[25] I read the piece shortly after it came out and applauded Emanuel for resisting the "manic desperation to endlessly extend life" at all costs. "By the time I reach 75, I will have lived a complete life," he wrote. "I will have loved and been loved [and] pursued my life's projects." While death is a loss, "living too long is also a loss... It robs us of our creativity and ability to contribute to work, society, the world. It transforms how people experience us, relate to us, and, most important, remember us." Fast-forward to 2022, which finds Emanuel, now 65 years old, lecturing at the University of Pennsylvania with "four HEPA filters going in my classroom for 140 students. We bought N-95 face masks. You have to wear it in class twice a week... I haven't gotten COVID-19. I've gotten over 80 tests. And I am determined not to get COVID-19."[26] Like, dude, what happened to that dauntless spirit of 2014?

As Dingwall notes, we cannot save life, only prolong it. With Covid settling into endemicity, "we may have to accept that most of us will get this once or twice, or three or four times in our lives. It may be the thing that accelerates our death at the point that we are already frail from other causes."

It's what we used to call the cycle of life, as encapsulated in the fable of a rich man who asks a Zen monk to write him a blessing. The monk writes, "father dies, son dies, grandson dies." The rich man responds with the Old Japanese equivalent of "WTF?" The monk tells him, "Well, how would you like it if it happened in a different order?"

We would do well to take our biomedical hats off for a moment and allow insights from other fields, like anthropology and sociology, to modulate our thinking. We can stop to ask the questions, rarely considered by the techno-scientific approach but vital to the likes of

Dingwall: "What is the point? What are we trying to achieve here? What is achievable?"

In its presumption of moral rectitude, the biomedical view of life fails to honor alternative perspectives on death. Dingwall told me how this cultural blind spot came to the fore during the Ebola virus epidemic in West Africa, when Western doctors drove up to remote villages and carted off the dead in body bags—and then wondered why villagers threw stones at them and tried to hide the corpses. It took some input from anthropologists for these first-world saviors to understand "the significance of the dead body in the traditions of the people in those villages." Once the doctors tuned into this reality, they were able to bring the outbreak significantly under control.

Before Covid, the UK government had a much broader view of pandemic management, Dingwall told me in a personal interview. "Our whole-government approach, which saw pandemics as a societal threat rather than a public health threat, was much admired in Europe, where most countries thought it was just a medical problem."

In the immediate response to Covid, the work Dingwall and his colleagues had carried out for almost 20 years "was completely ignored." Instead of providing leadership from the Cabinet Office, the government shunted the portfolio to the health department. As a result, "the whole thing fell into the hands of people with a bioscience background rather than an emergency response background." This meant the biomedical perspective ruled the day, abetting rather than allaying the social panic building up around the virus.

Dingwall likens the Covid panic to the alarm surrounding HIV and AIDS in the 1980s. In time, people came to realize they could "manage the disease through simple precautionary measures that are not disruptive to ordinary life."[24] Forty years on, "we still don't have a vaccine but we have an effective preventive therapy. We learned to live with it. The question with Covid-19 is how long it takes to accept that this is not something we can eradicate."

I asked Dingwall one of my standard questions: What does living with the virus mean to you? "It means accepting it as a second influenza," he said. "It means accepting that outbreaks will happen from time to time. It means not panicking and not structuring our lives around it." Above all, "it means relinquishing the fantasy of control, which people have struggled with ever since Darwin revealed the essential randomness of the universe."

During our interview, Dingwall ranged affably and effortlessly across medicine, sociology, anthropology, and history. He told stories from earlier pandemics, quoted arcane studies on "the mingling of human breath," and rolled words like "proxemics" (the study of spacing between people) off his tongue. A horizontal man in a vertical age, he offered the holistic perspective that many biomedical types seem to lack (or keep hidden from view). If I had my way, I would put him in charge of managing the remainder of the pandemic—and the next one.

An admirer of the Austrian-born philosopher Ivan Illich, Dingwall suggested I check out Illich's book *Medical Nemesis*[27] as an articulation of a holistic world view. The book did not disappoint. While written in 1975, it speaks clearly to our times. If health is taken to include an environment that favors "self-reliance, autonomy, and dignity," Illich asserts that modern medicine represents makes people sicker, not healthier, because it destroys their ability "to deal with human weakness, vulnerability, and uniqueness in a personal and autonomous way." That includes death. Today's version of end-of-life care, with tubes and machines beeping around a slack-jawed patient in a hospital bed, represents "the culmination of a public worship organized around a medical priesthood struggling against death" that deprives people of a culturally meaningful death experience. He has a name for this state of affairs: social and cultural iatrogenesis. If any healing needs to take place in modern society, he argues, it's in the realm of culture, not medicine.

In the same way, Dingwall views the recovery from the Covid-19 pandemic as more of a social than an epidemiological challenge— and doesn't expect the scars to heal quickly. "The traditional partnership between public health medicine and the people it served was sacrificed to the quick fix of intimidation," he says.[23] From the detritus of fear, exhaustion and mistrust washed up by this tactic, "it will be hard to rebuild the goodwill on which public health practice has rested for a hundred years."

In the meantime, we need to get on with Heneghan's phase two: how to live with the virus as we do with other respiratory pathogens. A metaphor for uncertainty, the proposition continues to make people anxious. The virus gets the match point, steps up to the podium, and accepts the gold. We can't let that happen, can we?

Well, why not? If a sports team loses a game, the teammates form a queue and shake hands with the victors. And if they look back on their strategy, they can always learn something that will help them play the next round with more grace.

ANONYMOUS

One day in April 2020, I entered "against Covid lockdowns" in my Google search box and discovered a Reddit group called Lockdown Skepticism. Formed a month earlier, the group had about 2,000 members when I chanced upon it. I became an active participant and, months later, joined a team of moderators curating the community. (I sometimes joke that I must be the oldest moderator on Reddit, which overwhelmingly attracts people under 50.) Membership eventually grew to over 56,000 people and the pandemic story sprouted several new branches, leading the group to broaden its focus to include mask and vaccine mandates.

For the uninitiated, Reddit is a network of global communities (called subreddits or just "subs"), each devoted to a region, topic or well-known person. There are subs devoted to Kim Kardashian photos and to pansexuality, to the Los Angeles Rams and the philosophy of science. Members share content by posting news articles, opinions, images, or videos. Posts can be upvoted or downvoted, with the most popular posts rising to the top of the feed. Rather than using their own names, Redditors create a handle, often something random and off-the-wall like Ornithator211 or BowelsOfTheBeast. The comments section is where a lot of the action takes place. The anonymity encourages free expression, though people who repeatedly break sub rules can be banned.

Our moderation team ran a fairly tight ship, rejecting posts from unreliable sources and deleting uncivil comments, which may have helped the community emerge unscathed from the great Reddit purge of 2021. Over the months and years I formed close bonds with my co-moderators and with a few other participants, who include health professionals and academics and fall everywhere along the political spectrum.

This chapter shines a spotlight on the individuals who contributed to the community: their hopes, fears, and moments of despair. Below, you'll find a compilation of comments posted by sub members at various stages of the pandemic. I've made light edits for spelling, grammar and brevity, but otherwise kept the content intact. It's raw, it's rough, and it's part of the story.

ON WHAT MAKES LIFE WORTH LIVING

They all think we should live in a sterilized, dead, grey world without human interaction, joy, art, culture, living. Life is no longer worth living, frankly, and I do not see that changing much as the goalposts continue to move.

ON EXISTING VS. LIVING

If "living" just means "not dying" now, I don't see why I'm supposed to try so hard anymore anyway—especially as a young person who is not allowed to do any of the things that people do to get their lives started. Like, what am I allowed to do in the name of "living" anymore? What should I expect to have as my options in the future? What can I actually count on that isn't subject to being taken away from me now at the whim of some shitty mayor or governor?

Go out, meet people, date, meet my soulmate, decide to settle down, and marry them at a wedding? No. Decide to start a family, get pregnant, and be able to have my husband with me during the agonizing labor and delivery so we can welcome our child into this world together? No. Have and raise a child, giving them basic opportunities in life like a decent education and socialization? No.

Attend graduation for my current educational program? No. Get professional experience during summer internships (which are essentially mandatory in my profession) so I can launch my career? No. Pursue the career that I've spent too many years and too much money investing in, a profession which exists only in the realm of in-person gatherings of human beings in rooms together? No. Go to a gym so I can better my health/appearance/happiness? Make memories at a concert or on a vacation to take a break from the drudgery of school/work? No.

Tell me why I should fight so hard to preserve "life" when all "living" means anymore is breathing and having a beating heart.

ON THE EXCESSES OF PUBLIC HEALTH

In much the same way that an overactive immune system can destroy a human body, an overactive public health system can destroy a society.

ON COVID POLICIES AND LIFE PLANS

You know what I feel anxious about? Not being able to pay my bills if this goes on for much longer. Losing my business and my home, and the ten years we spent saving to get it. I'm worried about starting over again with nothing in my late 30s. Not being able to have the happy family I've longed for my whole life with the man I love, because I'm running out of time and the goddamn specialists won't return my calls because "Covid!" takes priority in an ob-gyn office and my diagnostic tests for infertility have been postponed, indefinitely.

ON SOCIAL ISOLATION

The isolation I experienced during Covid had me constantly wanting to jump from the nearest window to escape the suffering I was dealing with and am still dealing with. The fact that it took more than two years for these stupid people to realize that humans are social beings, and to shut them away can cause mental health problems, is astounding. There needs to be a reckoning. They can't get away with what they've done.

ON COVID POLICIES AND MENTAL HEALTH

So my 'work routine' on the surface has hardly changed. However, the lockdown and my existential struggles with the depressing big picture and long-term ramifications of it has my mental health in the shitter. I've been sleeping 9 to 11 hours a night staying in bed till noon and haven't been able to correct my schedule. I wish I was one of those people who can "focus on work" when they get depressed. I'm the opposite. When I'm feeling down I can't fucking focus at all or get motivated to work. Everything's so grim right now and at this point I wonder how high of a death rate I'd be willing to accept just to take my chances at living a normal fucking life. 20%? Probably.

I'm in my mid-30s, single, and at this rate what the fuck am I even striving for or looking forward to? I have no wife or kids to live and die for, and it seems I'll never own a fucking house. All of the things I did in the past to keep my mental health good have been taken away.

ON THE LOSS OF WILL TO LIVE DURING LOCKDOWN

So the other night I got kind of high, as one does to deal with this world we live in. But I was lying in bed and wondering WHY was I so upset when the world shut down in March 2020. Why didn't I just take it as an opportunity to spend time with my family and get paid for it? For 3 months I was suicidal. I had no will to live, I didn't care if I got the "scary virus" because I wanted to die anyway.

I'm not really proud of who I was as a parent, but my son finished ridiculous virtual school and his needs were met. Somehow losing my shitty waitressing job made it worse even though I was planning on getting a new job anyway. I didn't want to make sourdough bread or read books or make the best of it. I wanted to die, and I drank a lot to numb the pain. From the very beginning,

I felt something was *wrong*.

Was my soul grieving because it knew the extent of the destruction this would cause?

ON FEELING NUMB

If I die, good, at least that would be more interesting than sitting here thinking about a very boring virus and not living anything remotely resembling a life.

I am out of all patience. I am out of any concern after this slow-moving ache of impending, terrible news that never comes to fruition. They just say "you're going to die, so you need to stay home" or "your grandmother will die." (Pro-tip: she's going to die anyways—she's 95 years old, and I would have enjoyed going to her funeral, which because of Covid I won't be able to do, as she now lives shuttered away and unable to live out her final days in peace.)

There's no place for me in this world anymore. I am the devil incarnate because I value freedom very highly and think that people dying from viruses is just life. Society is trying to play God and I don't think it's going very well. I don't want to live in a world that says I'm bad.

People's delusions of immortality consign others to living as if dead. San Francisco county just said we should act "as if" we had Covid already. We don't, but they told us to envision ourselves as a biohazardous viral vector rather than a living human being, and that is dehumanizing and sick, sociopathic even. Numbness is the only appropriate response.

ON FEELING HOPELESS

All this messaging—"the next pandemic" or "the next variant that will evade the vaccines"—has been more than enough to absolutely fucking break me. It lets me know that not only do I not own my own life today, but I do not own my own future either, and that I better never make a single plan or invest anything or any time in some plan because anything can and will be taken from me whenever the media, bureaucrats, spineless institutions, and corporations decide that it's time for the "next" time.

ON LIVING THROUGH LOCKDOWN WITH DISABILITIES

I became a heavy alcoholic and tried to kill myself by trying to drink myself to death. I'm shocked I don't have organ or brain damage. I cried almost every day. I'm autistic and going deaf in one ear so seeing facial expressions is crucial. Masks went against everything social for me. I had panic attacks and dizzy spells being forced to wear them. I felt like everything I had to learn socially was ripped away and it was like a big F-you slap in the face.

I'm absolutely terrified it will all come back. It's like my brain got stuck. I have nightmares and lingering physical illness from all the stress, anger and depression I suffered during all of it. I had no support from family or doctors. Here, just take this med. My doctor sympathized but said there was nothing he could do.

ON THE COVID VIRTUE SIGNALERS

I refuse to believe you give a fuck about my grandma's well being, or anyone else's for that matter. You are fucking lying. Virtue signaling does not mean you care; it is a cheap imitation of empathy. You are the real sociopaths.

You're the type of person to tell someone expressing suicidal thoughts after losing their job and sanity over this bullshit to just "shut up and wear a mask." Your narcissistic need to appear as if you care has destroyed our economy and left society deformed and twisted. I cannot fathom the mental gymnastics you must go through to convince yourself this has all been worth it, that the government's insistence of "just two more weeks" isn't actually just the cry of a petulant, spoiled child screaming for "FIVE MINUTES MORE" on their favorite video game before bedtime.

Just continue to blame us when the government decides to once again to move the goalposts, despite the vast majority of us begrudgingly adhering to your draconian, ever-changing rules out of fear of being beaten to death by a mob of masked moral crusaders hypocritically breaking social distancing protocol or being carted off by the police for thought-crimes to an undisclosed facility for "re-education." It won't change the fact that you don't care: never have, never will.

ON HUMAN INTERACTION DURING A PANDEMIC

I am vaccinated but have lost friends because we simply don't have the same world view. I am not endlessly selfless and I don't believe zero tolerance for human interaction is realistic, sustainable, or the basis for sound public policy. Considering that thousands of people die every single day even during non-pandemic times, I don't think that "how can you go to a restaurant when people are dying?" makes any sense. I'm not in favor of interrogating people about their vaccine status before deigning to be in their presence. I'm also not in favor of medical coercion, vaccine mandates, or vaccine passports. But apparently these viewpoints make me heartless and cruel. Go figure.

ON BETRAYING CORE VALUES

I often see people here saying that the only way out of this is non-compliance with mandates, and I agree. The issue, obviously, is that it's becoming less and less possible to openly resist without suffering severe and life-altering consequences. Refusal to comply on my part would only lead to initial negative interactions and then probably my being permanently banned from all of the grocery stores near me, not to mention the public transportation I rely on. Since I don't have the option of outright noncompliance, I feel mentally broken down to some extent, and at a genuine loss for what to do going forward.

In addition to the mental health effects of being coerced to go against my core values on the daily, I feel morally culpable (and horribly guilty) for not doing my part to fight the measures and be a visible example of resistance to others. Rationally, I know that I have little ability to prevent what's happening. I'm a recently recovered drug addict and alcoholic with bad mental issues, no job and no local community. I don't have any true social or financial power to help or change anything. But I still feel like I should be doing something to resist all of this.

ON COSTS AND BENEFITS

In the US, cost-benefit analysis has become anathema and people seem to regard it as a prelude to death camps. In reality, it's just a matter of practicality. Our medical system and insurance companies will not authorize a million-dollar surgery if it's expected to extend someone's life by ten minutes. Even the most every-life-matters person has to admit that would be a poor use of resources. So right there we've agreed that we are not willing to pay any price to save a life (which actually means delaying that person's death—in the long run, there's no such thing as saving a life because that person will eventually die).

Like in the old joke, we've already agreed what's going to happen, and now we're just haggling about the price. From there, we can get into arguments about what expenditures are desirable for what gain. But this punishingly idealistic insistence that any price is worth paying to save a life is simply not true. If our public health officials said, "the virus is so bad that it's necessary to have strict lockdowns for the rest of your life in order to save the vulnerable," everyone would snap out of it eventually and realize that the benefits aren't worth the costs.

ON CARING ABOUT DIFFERENT THINGS

My sympathy is with the old people who can't see their relatives, those who've lost their businesses, victims of domestic violence stuck inside with their abusers 24/7, young people who missed out on the heady freedom of university and traveling, people who have had their cancer treatment postponed or have committed suicide, all the misery people have had to endure. I feel sad for silly things like the zoo animals who missed having visitors, for the pets who will be abandoned after this ends, for the environment which is now littered with masks. Those things make me sad. I do feel sorry for people who've died of Covid, but only as much as anyone who has died. Its sad, but life must go on.

ON THE ROLE OF MEDICINE IN LIFE
Medicine is *supposed* to occupy a limited, background role with the aim of promoting normal life. It is *not* and was *never* supposed to take over running the entire world and every daily interaction as though it were a hospital or doctor's office. Healthcare exists—at least used to—in order to help people get back to real living ASAP. But over the decades it has undergone massive mission creep. And yes, the implications of that are profoundly disturbing.

ON SPEAKING FOR THE ELDERLY
My parents are both 81. They don't care. Their friends of a similar age do not care. They don't speak for everyone at that age, but they absolutely want everyone to stop speaking for them. They aren't helpless or ill informed. They like agency in their life just like the people in this sub.

ON THE LIFE CYCLE
They had their lives. They had their decades of peace and prosperity. They had their lavish pensions, home ownership, and nice cars. Part of being old is stepping aside to make room for the young, not feeding off them like vampires to extend your life for another precious few weeks of watching daytime TV. Eventually it will be my turn to step aside. That's called life.

ON DISMISSING THE HARDSHIPS OF LOCKDOWN
It's a crime against humanity to have our suffering dismissed and trivialized and to be told that it's all in our heads and we're terrible people. Ever notice how the people who got through it and write

sappy crap about how the lockdowns were OK are always the ones who were privileged to begin with? They're not people struggling with autism or hearing loss or people like me, building an alternate support structure to cope with family dysfunction and neglect.

ON DISMISSING THE PLIGHT OF THE YOUNG
My brother is dead, and it's like feeling him dying again each time I see people dismissing the blighting of young lives in favor of extending those of the old.

ON LOSING YEARS OF HARD WORK
I still clearly remember the 24-hour window when everything shut down and basically every gig I had was canceled (and then being unable to book anything for another whole-ass year or longer). Have you ever literally lost tens of thousands of dollars in a single day? I have. It's not fun. People like me had damn near everything taken from us. We were told to sit down, shut up, and stop killing grannies for two years. This has set us back *years* in terms of professional and socioeconomic development, and now we're being told, "What's the big deal? Everything is open. Stop complaining about mandates that don't exist."

ON COVID ALARMISM
We know: The virus has a fatality rate of 2% at least. Millions will die. Herd immunity is not possible. The virus is killing tons of young, healthy people. We must be in lockdown till a vaccine. Society will never recover. We will have to social distance for the rest of our lives. Sports and concerts are forever gone. Sex will have to be outlawed. No more restaurants. Walking on the beach is basically murder. Does that cover it?

ON INDEFINITE MASKING
They want a forever-masked society. That's not a society or world I want any part of. The fact that these experts talk about it like it's

no big deal chills me to the bone. We're talking children growing up and never seeing each other's faces again. This is a cold, inexpressive, dystopian society and I am in awe that healthy, feeling human beings would be OK with it.

ON STAYING ALIVE VS. LIVING

Physicians are myopic, and that is both a curse and a blessing. To them, all that matters is that your heart is beating and there is enough activity in your brain that you can breathe. That's it. Their focus is *life*, not *living*. As a psychologist I'm interested in living, and let me tell you: lockdowns completely thwart the three basic human needs of relatedness, autonomy, and competence.

These people have engaged in psychological warfare, whether they know it or not. Health is not just physical: mental well-being is an integral part of it. We knew for decades that loneliness kills. We knew the strong effects of mere touch. That's not new. Yet we threw it down the shitter and psychologists were happy to lead the way in shaming.

To add: in my opinion, anyone who automatically assumes that you are heartless for opposing a previously untested and dubious mass intervention gives absolutely no shits about mental health. That's another way of saying that society, including everyone's favorite leaders including lord Fauci, give no shits about your well-being.

ON BLAMING PEOPLE FOR TRANSMITTING A VIRUS

My mom literally died of a cold that went into pneumonia. It never crossed my mind to blame whoever she got the cold from for "killing her." That is just ridiculous logic and completely unprecedented in society.

ON MEDIA FEARMONGERING AND LOSS OF PUBLIC TRUST

The media has been on a bender of Covid fear porn, delivered via kegstand and with about as much subtlety as a brick to the face. They're not even bothering to try to hide it anymore. They have openly embraced the "restrictions: eternal" message for Covid, which is not what anyone agreed to at the beginning of this cluster-fuck. People just aren't listening anymore, and the savvier politicians have read the room.

What we're witnessing (in agonizingly slow motion) is the death of trust in media, and the death of trust in *experts* who refuse to move on and have elected to chain themselves to the prow of this (sinking) ship so they can shriek louder before it goes under. Their message of doom has never changed even for a minute, *and that's precisely why they've lost.*

ON THE BOILING FROG PHENOMENON

Covid is just a whole sequence of gaslighting and apologism until one day we all wake up and few of us can quite remember what it "used to be like" and the talking heads say, "it isn't so bad" and we all live nice long half-lives in a tech-obsessed, atomized consumer society.

But the scariest part is that when you get to the bridge of the ship and expect to confront the Illuminati, or the Lizard People, or the Fat Cat of the Elite, instead you find no-one. There was no-one captaining the ship. Instead, the ship turned all by itself, through the invisible and far more sinister mechanism of bureaucratic inertia, anti-intellectualism and self-censorship.

ON COVID AND THE SENSE OF TIME

During the COVID idiocy, we were all ordered to live in a time which is not ours. Someone else's time: the virus's time, Fauci's time, Neil Ferguson's or Boris Johnson's time. Time was truly 'out of joint," as Hamlet says. As a philosopher, I'm interested in the questions: Who owns our common time? Who is going to submit and live in the other person's time?

ON A FATE WORSE THAN DEATH

When I think of the list of things that horrify me the absolute most, loss of identity and loss of freedom rank FAR higher than loss of life. I don't want to live long enough to get dementia and not even recognize myself or the people I love anymore. I don't want to "fight" a terminal illness if the word "fight" just means submitting to such torturous medical interventions that I'm incapacitated and miserable. I don't want to "live" through a pandemic if survival means hiding forever, or being left in a dystopian hellscape war zone with nothing that makes life *worth* living.

Basically, yeah. Dying is one of the lowest fears on my list, and just "being alive" has no inherent value to me as an end in itself. I fear loss of self, loss of freedom, loss of quality, and loss of community FAR, FAR more. I don't care about "life" in the sense of a pulse; I care about life in the sense of a purpose, and the ability to carry it out. And would ya look at that? Our idiotic Covid response tried to take all of those away.

ON SAFETYISM

People in rural America are used to a fairly rough, hardscrabble existence; they work in forestry, construction, railways, and face actual dangers in life and on the job. I'm beginning to think that the more coddled a person is, the more they're prone to safetyism and to acting like Covid is an extinction-level event. The people who know actual risk, fear, and need are able to quickly assess Covid because they have context and experience.

ON THE PUSH FOR PERMANENT RESTRICTIONS

Honestly? You want to create a permanently masked society, to serve yourself, and allow no one but you to have a choice in any of it? You didn't care about anyone else's feelings this entire time, and you didn't care about the damage you inflicted by removing the human FACE from society? FOR TWO YEARS? You see nothing wrong with forcing the whole world to accommodate YOU, permanently?

ON SELFISHNESS

Being forced to wear a mask as a healthy person, to appease someone else's hypochondria, is in my opinion the definition of selfishness.

And being accused of possibly harboring a sickness that I could somehow spread to said hypochondriac, even though I'm perfectly healthy and work out, is also in my opinion the definition of selfishness. If you're so scared of dying, stay the fuck home. I have a family to support and the stress and risk of financial loss as a result of these bullshit lockdowns and restrictions has wrecked my mental health.

ON COVID DYSTOPIA

At this point I'm comfortable saying this: there are indeed worse things than death. Living a perpetual dystopian pandemic life with no days brighter than the ones before—the life it sounds like you're willing to live—would be one of them. At some point, you'd have thought that those who were afraid before would have grown sick and tired of being afraid. Look up Churchill Picnics on the Rhine.

It's why many of us are refusing the vax. Not because of an epidemiological cost-benefit to our own health, but because we're trying to do our part to prevent society from going in this terrifying direction. So no amount of statistics on how the vaccine helps in the short term will convince us because we're much more afraid of totalitarian dystopia than we are of going to a hospital.

ON HOW IT ALL HAPPENED

No-one pushed the strings, there was no mastermind, it actually was just millions of people reading Twitter, doing what the person who shouted the loudest did, and amplifying that signal by tweeting that they also did it. Someone did something in panic, and everyone else followed along, because the first person looked like they knew what they were doing, and most importantly, they were *Doing Something* when people were screaming at politicians to *Do Something*. Lockdown was Something. So we did it.

WE'RE OVER IT: BILL MAHER AND BARI WEISS

"I 'm done with Covid." On January 21, 2022, journalist Bari Weiss spoke those words on the *Real Time with Bill Maher* TV show,[1] echoing what Maher himself had told *Deadline* magazine in an earlier interview[2]: "I'm over Covid."

When Weiss spoke, the audience broke into applause. The boos came later: in news reports, in talk shows, on Twitter. "She needs to grow up, because she's acting like a child," said CNN medical analyst Jonathan Reiner.[3] "Done pretending to care about anyone but themselves! You go girl!" comedian Sara Schaefer tweeted.[4] And here's Whoopi Goldberg, addressing Maher[5]: "How dare you be so flippant, man?" Some people chided the pair for disrespecting the Covid dead. Others hit back with the "you may be done with Covid, but Covid isn't done with you" trope, which they evidently saw as a gotcha.

It isn't. When people say they're done with Covid, they're not denying that the virus still exists or that it carries a risk. They're not disrespecting the dead. Nor are they suggesting they'll never follow a precaution again, much less go out and cough on people. They're simply stating that they're done living in crisis mode. In essence, they're saying: "It's not healthy for Covid to keep ruling our lives. Even if the virus still lurks among us, we need to put it on the back burner, where we place the other risks in our midst."

Maher, the world-famous comedian known for poking fun at both liberals and conservatives, has been broadcasting his common-sense thoughts about Covid since the earliest days of the pandemic: eat well, live well, keep calm and carry on. *Common Sense* is also the title of Weiss's Substack newsletter, which she launched after concerns about editorial censorship led her to resign from the *New York Times*. She has invited several of the intellectuals featured in this book, from Jay Bhattacharya and Vinay Prasad to Rupa Subramanya and Jennifer Sey, to write guest columns about the pandemic.

Maher and Weiss perform a vital function in the Covid ecosystem: recalibration. They speak for the millions of people who have sensed, but don't have the platform to say out loud, that not all chapters in the Covid story were necessary or good or right. They shine a light on a needle that got stuck and show us how to get it unstuck.

> *I went so hard on Covid. I sprayed the Pringles cans that I bought at the grocery store, stripped my clothes off because I thought Covid would be on my clothes. Like, I did it all. And then we were told, you get the vaccine. You get the vaccine and you get back to normal. And we haven't gotten back to normal. And it's getting ridiculous at this point.*[1]

That's Weiss talking, and her sentiments reveal her not as a petulant toddler, but as a healthy human experiencing pandemic fatigue. In an analysis for *The Conversation*,[6] a pair of academics from Griffiths university describe pandemic fatigue as a "gradual exhaustion and inability to engage with government public health messaging," noting that it is "not unusual and is part of a complex interplay of factors, including those relating to risk and control." Far from a sign of weakness or childish impatience, pandemic fatigue is a rational response, an intuitive recalibration of risk tolerance in response to a persistent threat. There's only so much crisis the human brain can take.

Policymakers don't always understand this. They view pandemic fatigue as no more than a loose brick in the edifice of pandemic management, a hole to patch up. If not for that tricky little brick, we could all keep following the science and all would be well.

But here's the thing: pandemic fatigue is *part* of the science. It's a feature of pandemic management, not a bug—a predictable human response that decision makers must factor into their policies if they want the public to buy in. Researchers have even developed instruments to measure it, such as the aptly named Pandemic Fatigue Scale[7] and the Covid Burnout Scale.[8]

> *I don't want to live in your paranoid world anymore—your masked, paranoid world. You go out, it's silly now! You have to have a mask, you have to have a card, you have to have a booster. They scan your head, like you're a cashier and I'm a bunch of bananas. I'm not bananas. You are.*[1]

People cheered, people booed. Most disappointing of all, some people interpreted Maher's comments in the most literal, prosaic sense. They decried Maher for "arguing against masking" and "making fun of Covid protocols," evidently forgetting the dude earns his keep as a comedian.

What comedians do is poke fun at excesses. They shine a light on absurdities. Wearing a mask to a walk-in clinic, where many sick people congregate, is nothing remarkable. Asking all the passengers in a Boeing 747 to get off a plane because a toddler in row 15 isn't wearing a mask properly? For a comedian, that's money in the bank. (Or for Seinfeld fans: "That's gold, Jerry. Gold.") Comedians take kernels of truth and turn them into giant vats of popcorn, which is precisely why they make us laugh. When Maher made those statements, he was doing no more and no less than plying his trade.

*I got the vaccine. I walked out of the CVS. I hadn't been that
thrilled coming out of the drugstore since I got the birth
control pill in 1981. I've had cancer. I'm triple vaxxed. If it
gets me, fair play to it because it will put up a fight against
me but I'm not staying in my house again.*[9]

That's what Caitlin Flanagan, a staff writer for *The Atlantic*,
told Maher. She also compared Covid to an abusive boyfriend from
whom she had finally broken loose. She had reached that crucial
point in the stay-or-go conundrum: ready to take her chances with
the uncertain world out there, rather than living another minute
under her abuser's iron thumb.

Life is all about calculated decisions, and the calculus naturally
shifts over time. Given the choice between indefinite restrictions
and an extra increment of risk, a rational person may conclude:
"On balance, plan B gives me a better shot at a good life. It gives
my loved ones a better life, too. What time does that jazz festival
begin already?"

If we kept responding to a recurring stimulus at peak intensity,
we could never get on with the business of living. That's why people's
willingness to follow public health mandates erodes over time: they
reach a point where avoiding disease becomes less important than
making a new friend or putting on a theater production, and there's
nothing unscientific about that.

*Everyone knows Corona is no walk in the park. But at
some point the daily drumbeat of depression and terror
veers into panic porn. Enough with the 'life will never be
the same' headlines. You don't have to put hot sauce on
a jalapeño.*[10]

Maher said this on April 17, 2020, already fatigued by the
alarmism and fear. He wasn't the only one. In the fall of 2020,

having noted the creep of pandemic fatigue into its member states, the WHO's European Office published a paper called "Pandemic Fatigue: Reinvigorating the Public to Prevent COVID-19."[11] The architects of the document, to their credit, showed a welcome grasp of human psychology. They recommended acknowledging people's hardships, striving for the highest level of fairness in restrictions, transparently sharing the rationale for restrictions, understanding which restrictions may be "unbearable" (their word) in the long term, and conceding the limits of science and government.

Too bad nobody got the memo. Policymakers continued to view pandemic fatigue as a problem to stickhandle around, rather than a human propensity to respect. To offset pandemic fatigue, a August 2021 *Nature Human Behaviour* article[12] encouraged policymakers to figure out "how to motivate steady physical distance adherence, with additional focus on groups [that have] shown the largest drop-off." A few months later, an Italian paper[13] proposed combatting pandemic fatigue through "fear of the disease's consequences modeled with the death rate in mind"—a polite way of saying, "let's strike some terror in people's hearts." Speaking directly to the Covid-fatigued public, the American Medical Association offered a string of bromides[14]: seek mental health care, focus on what you can control, practice positive affirmation. The underlying theme was always the same: change the people, not the policies.

Public health pundits chided the public for losing its focus—for "capitulating to Covid," to borrow cardiologist Eric Topol's ill-tempered locution.[15] Or they insisted we all double down. "Very simply, we need judiciously targeted mask and vaccine mandates and widespread testing to, once again, flatten the curve of infections," public policy researcher Henry Miller wrote in a June 2022 opinion piece.[16] The flatten-the-curve meme got the public's attention in March 2020. Coming in mid-2022, it was just noise.

One health professional who appears to understand pandemic fatigue is Leana Wen, an American physician and prominent public health communicator during Covid. Practically overnight, her messaging shifted from "be scared, stop killing people, take every precaution you can" to "life isn't just about reducing risk. Your mileage may vary, but go forth and live."

Before 2020, this advice would have landed right in the common-sense bucket. But it didn't sit well with the Covid vigilantes, who argued that removing restrictions hurts vulnerable populations the most and is thus unfair. When Wen was invited to speak at the 2022 American Public Health Association meeting, a group of health professionals petitioned to have her removed from the lineup and replaced with "someone whose work is consistent with anti-racist, anti-eugenicist public health practices and community health."[17]

First of all, this twisted interpretation of "eugenics" has got to go. Seriously. "It's a disingenuous conflation of living life normally, including caring for your loved ones, with deliberate, active policies designed to eliminate a sub-section of the population," says Seb Thirlway, my philosopher friend from the UK. "It absolutely boils my brain."

Second, the "Covid equity" game has no endpoint: if restrictions must continue until everyone is equally and perfectly safe, they must continue forever. Thankfully, the number of people who think this way is shrinking. For most of us, the healthy impulse to reengage with the world overtakes the fear of catching a disease. The distorted sense of responsibility brought forth by Covid, which blames individuals for inadvertently transmitting a virus that cannot be stopped, collides with biological reality. Nobody can live life with that kind of weight on their shoulders—and before Covid, nobody did.

Pandemic fatigue is the life force waking up again. It's the caged bird that hears the leaves rustling outside and one day decides to bust through the bars. It's the warmth that greeted me when I returned to Brazil in February 2022, fixing to reconnect with all the friends I was unable to see two years earlier. The skin-on-skin smorgasbord began as soon as I arrived: hugs, kisses, more hugs, group photos with everyone's faces touching. The annual Carnival was officially canceled, but people found ways to celebrate. (The inclination to bend the rules, using little tricks that Brazilians call *jeitinho,* is part of what I love about the culture.) A friend took me to a Samba party, where I danced under an open sky and she kissed a stranger. The world's warmest and most gregarious culture will only put up with "distancing" for so long.

We saw the life force assert itself in April 2022, when a Florida judge struck down the transportation mask mandate in the US. As soon as flight attendants made the mid-air announcement, passengers erupted into cheers.[18] Just for a moment, people saw that everyone else wanted this, too. Since that time, the dwindling mask use throughout the world makes it clear that most people see a fundamental difference between masks and underpants, masks and seatbelts. The remaining #mandatesforever warriors haven't disappeared, but their ranks are shrinking and their death rattles no longer have the sting to infect public opinion.

Even Covid-cautious Twitter heaped derision on a *New York Times* article[19] listing the measures needed to stay safe at Christmas gatherings—in 2022. In youth parlance, total ratio. My personal favorites (with due NSFW warning): "An election season, where no fear can go unturned." "Would eating indoors topless count as ventilating your space?" "Step 1: DGAF." When news outlets misread the public mood so egregiously, they have only themselves to blame for this type of response.

Pandemics have both a medical and a social end, and the social end often comes first. Shifts in behavior set the course of a pandemic as much as any transmission curves or reproduction numbers. "People, Not Science, Decide When a Pandemic Is Over"—that's the title of a March 2022 *Scientific American* article[20] on how pandemics wind down. "I believe that pandemics end partially because humans declare them at an end," says Marion Dorsey, a pandemic historian interviewed for the piece. The medical transition to endemicity doesn't have a clear demarcation line, and nobody rings a bell to declare the end of a pandemic. "Every time people walk into stores without masks or even just walk into stores for pleasure, [they are] indicating they think the pandemic is winding down, if not over."

We can't expect politicians or public health officials to return normality to us. Knowing they will face blame for the slightest hiccup, they will choose excess caution over common sense every time. As Alan Richarz says in an op-ed for CBC News,[21] which garnered over 7,000 responses before the news outlet closed the comments section, the target needed for a return to normal "will always be n+1. Meet one metric, and be met with two more."

It's not up to the scientists, either. "An epidemiologist with a model is very good within a narrow professional remit," says Mike Hulme, a Professor of Human Geography at the University of Cambridge, in an interview with Alastair Benn of *Reaction News*.[22] "But that certainly doesn't give [epidemiologists] automatic authority over how and when policy measures should or should not be relaxed. That should be in the public realm."

It's the same point we've been hearing from the people featured in this book. Epidemiologists can do epidemiology. Public health experts can do public health. But none of these experts can do society or human nature any better than the rest of us. They have neither the legal nor the moral authority to tell us how to lead our lives. When enough of us choose normal, we get it.

Normality *has* largely returned, over the protestations of the pandemic shamers and moralizers. People are doing all the things they assured us would never come back, from dripping sweat at the gym to attending shoulder-to-shoulder street festivals and live music events. A significant increase in airline prices didn't stop millions of tourists from making so-called "revenge travel" plans in 2022.[23] I joined the fray in September, when I went to Barcelona and Milan to report on a couple of dermatology conferences. I saw almost no masks, even in small-group meeting rooms. Evidently, thousands of doctors from all over the world understood the social value of seeing faces. Several of them shook my hand, a custom the doomsayers had pronounced dead in the water. (It's not that I love shaking hands so much. What I love is the trust that it symbolizes, the willingness to touch and make oneself vulnerable to another human.)

I'll admit it: there's something satisfying about seeing how much the prognosticators got wrong. They had hoped Covid would fundamentally change human behavior. That it would make us keep our distance from each other, retreat into ourselves, dedicate more of our lives to gardening (assuming we had a garden) and sourdough breadmaking (assuming we had a functioning kitchen). They wanted this. They really wanted this. But it turns out that human nature, with its glorious and messy contradictions, overrides their smug and sterile vision.

So what's the problem, then?

In a gorgeously written essay, author Naomi Wolf describes the sense of grief that follows her as she drives through her Hudson Valley neighborhood.[24] At first she can't put her finger on it: her loved ones are safe and well, the daffodils and forsythias in bloom. Many of the businesses that shut down have reopened.

And then it comes to her: in their eagerness to move on, people are pretending that none of it ever happened. The "cruel moral judgments, the two-tier society, the mandates, the coercions, the nasty looks, the desperate masked children with their laboring breath, the loneliness, the desolate centrally-planned economies"— all evaporated and memory-holed.

"I started to realize what my sense of sorrow really was," she writes. Not grief, but rage. And what she wanted was closure. "I wanted people to face what they had been, what they had done... To be healing, there has to be justice."

Some of the architects of the Covid policies have started to talk more openly about their misgivings and their mistakes—perhaps too little and too late for Wolf, but better than nothing. In a August 2022 interview with *The Spectator*,[25] UK politician Rishi Sunak reflected on his culpability as a bystander when UK went into lockdown. "We shouldn't have empowered the scientists in the way we did," he said.

"You have to acknowledge trade-offs from the beginning. If we'd done all of that, we could be in a very different place." Responding to Sunak's disclosure, the *Wall Street Journal* agreed there has to be a "political reckoning over lockdowns, and not only in the United Kingdom."[26]

I sometimes imagine a lineup of politicians and public health officials in a courtroom, fielding questions from a roomful of plaintiffs traumatized by their policies. Questions like these:

- Why did you jettison all the wisdom from pre-Covid pandemic guidance documents?
- Why did you put a patch over one eye and ignore the costs of your policies?
- Less destructive ways of saving lives were proposed to you. Why did you refuse to listen?
- Why did you use fear and shame as bludgeons?
- Why did you show so little understanding of human nature?
- Why did you rob children of their childhoods?
- Why did you let people die alone?

When the defendants admit they have no suitable answers, the presiding judge calls an end to the proceedings. The spectators in the courtroom stand up and everyone hugs each other. And then it's over. Really, really over.

NOT THE END

We need to keep talking about it.

Three years ago, two years ago, even one year ago, we couldn't talk about it. We could not point out the bad songs on Side A, or suggest listening to some of the better ones on Side B, without being told we "want people to die."

That's what's so wholesome about time: it takes some of the knee-jerk emotionality out of our reactions, allowing us to reflect more maturely on a situation. Anyone who has been dumped by a lover knows this all too well: in the fullness of time, "how could he *do* this to me, I'll never be happy again" alchemizes to "it was all for the best, we were clearly mismatched."

Three years in, time has done its work and we can begin talking about pandemic policy with a modicum of sanity. And it's important that we do. You know what they say about history, right? If we don't understand what fed the narrative of panic and the destructive policies it set in motion, we're sitting ducks for a repeat performance. (And it will be easier the next time, because we've already done it once.)

Some people don't want to talk about it—they want to pretend it didn't happen or was never that bad. Michael Senger lays out this revisionist narrative in a must-read essay called "The Great

Gaslighting"[1]: "Lockdowns never really happened, because governments never actually locked people in their homes...and even when things were shut down, the rules weren't very strict; [and] when the rules were strict, we didn't really support them." We need to keep talking about it so this fairy tale doesn't paper over reality.

You know what else they say about history: it doesn't repeat itself, but rhymes. The next global crisis may not be a virus, perhaps not even a pandemic, but will undoubtedly set off the same impulse to panic. If we keep the memory of the Covid madness alive, we may pause just a little longer before yelling "fire" and hosing down the world.

We need to talk about why things got so crazy in 2020. About why democracies so readily adopted a policy developed by and for a very different sociopolitical regime, a turn of events that leaves even historian and *Bloomberg* columnist Niall Ferguson scratching his head[2]: "It continues to puzzle me that so many smart people were convinced that the People's Republic of China should be the role model for a free society faced with a pandemic."

We need to talk about why countries across the world fell like Humpty Dumpties, locking down in lockstep, without concern for any outcomes beyond suppressing a virus. About why governments didn't trust us to behave like adults and chose instead to quarterback our every step, reaching into the most intimate aspects of our lives. (I don't know about you, but I'll never forget the glory holes.) We need to figure out why we decided, as a society, that freedom and personal agency have no place in a pandemic.

We need to talk about why decision makers refused to consider alternative approaches to managing the virus—not just refused, but heaped scorn on the idea. About why they withdrew from adult conversations about costs, benefits and managing risk.

We need to talk about the lack of a braking mechanism to interrogate the imposition of restrictions and mandates never before enacted in peacetime. I was encouraged to see lawyer Adam Wagner explore this topic in late 2022 in *The Guardian*[3] (a sign that even mainstream liberal publications may be ready for some self-reflection). Of the 109 lockdown laws imposed in the UK, "only eight were considered by parliament before coming into force, usually only a day before," Wagner reports. "The rest became law (literally) as soon as [the health secretary] put his signature at the bottom of the page." While conceding that emergency law-making has to move swiftly, Wagner argues that "it did not have to be like *this*... The ease with which ancient freedoms [were removed] should be a wake-up call. It is only a matter of time before a new crisis will arise."

We need to talk about why so few intellectuals spoke out against the damaging and dehumanizing measures. In an essay exploring the topic,[4] Jeffrey Tucker offers a clue: academics typically have "nonfungible" skills, meaning skills they can't easily transfer to another setting, unlike a hairdresser who can simply take her craft to the next salon. "It is extremely hard to move from one academic position to another," Tucker writes. Knowing that getting fired could end their careers, academics "hold onto their jobs for dear life," which means toeing the party line. Ditto for journalists: "Everyone in this industry knows that rocking the boat is the worst possible way to advance in your career." This sets up a troubling reality: "We want these people to be brave and independent—we need them to be—but in practice they are the complete opposite."

We need to understand what Side A and Side B were *really* arguing about (it wasn't just science; it was never just science) and why they could never truly hear each other, no matter how loudly they yelled. We need to understand all this so we can do better the next time around.

Many people died. This doesn't mean we *had* to keep playing Side A, over and over and over again. With the growing body of research concluding that lockdowns didn't make an appreciable difference in Covid outcomes, the claim that "it would have been 10 times worse without lockdowns" has lost its luster. Even Michael Osterholm, the epidemiologist and public health professor who served on Biden's Covid-19 advisory board, has admitted that "we've ascribed far too much human authority over the virus" and that its ebbs and flows "have little to do with what humans do."[5]

Even if the Covid policies did help slow the spread, they violated at least two of the four core principles of medical ethics, known as beneficence, nonmaleficence, autonomy, and justice.[6] The first two principles hark back to the Hippocratic Oath, which enjoins physicians to help and do no harm.[7] The Covid policies most assuredly caused harm. The nonmaleficence principle requires the treating physician to "weigh the benefits against burdens of all interventions and treatments, to eschew those that are inappropriately burdensome, and to choose the best course of action for the patient"[6]—exactly the cost-benefit perspective that went AWOL during the pandemic.

The concept of personal autonomy during a pandemic grew out of the civil rights movement in the middle of the last century.[8] The Hastings Center, a nonpartisan think tank that helped establish the field of bioethics starting in 1969, asserts that mitigation measures "work with the most benefit and least friction when they are voluntary, respect and rely on individual autonomy, and avoid the use of police powers."[8] With Covid, we threw the ethical principle of autonomy under a bus.

Pandemics are more about people than about viruses, and managing a pandemic is a social endeavor as much as a scientific one. We somehow lost sight of that. As Lord Jonathan Sumption, the UK's Covid critic par excellence, points out in *The Sunday Times*,[9] "the scientists said it was not their job to think about the social or economic implications of their advice. They were right about that. The problem was that it turned out to be no one else's job."

Precisely, m'Lord. Governments gave epidemiologists and public health experts carte blanche to dictate policy, leaving no room for experts from other disciplines to enter the chat. They replaced the time-honored "keep calm and carry on" with "stay scared and do as you're told." Had they boned up on Donald Henderson, to whom we owe the eradication of smallpox, they might have learned that "communities faced with epidemics or other adverse events respond best and with the least anxiety when the normal social functioning of the community is least disrupted."[10]

That's pretty much what Side B has been saying. As the people quoted in this book have argued, again and again, Side B is about striking a balance: between personal agency and collective action, between biological subsistence and quality of life, between scrambling to safety and working to create a healthier tomorrow. It's a world view that eschews biomedical supremacy, looks morally fraught trade-offs in the eye, and accepts the limits of human agency over natural forces.

I'm not suggesting Side B has always been polite and reasonable. We've been mad, hopping mad, in great part because of a media (and social media) apparatus that declared our objections null and void. The thought leaders gathered in this book help us understand why Side A grabbed the megaphone and Side B never got a fair hearing.

In the summer of 2020, when it became clear the Covid policies would be hanging around for some time, groups of experts in several countries wrote impassioned letters to their governments arguing for more balanced policies. (The letters fell on deaf ears, but they live on as a testament to the pockets of sanity that existed at the worst of times.) One of these groups, the UK's Recovery, penned a document called "Five Reasonable Demands" to help society recover from Covid.[11] Reproduced below (with UK-specific terms removed), these demands can serve us just as well in the next crisis.

1. Behave with humanity

Curbing the liberty and essential freedoms of large swaths of the population, many of whom will suffer long term consequences, is inhumane. Fear and isolation are killers in themselves. No-one should be barred from a dying parent's bedside. We ask the Government to pledge that it will always act with humanity.

2. Give equal regard to all lives

Scaremongering and the prioritisation of treatment for Covid-19 are costing lives. Thousands will die because screening and treatment for terminal diseases is being postponed or canceled. We face an addiction timebomb and a mental health crisis. We ask the Government to pledge that its policy on Covid-19 will give equal regard to all lives, allowing for the normal consideration of life-years in its assessments, and remove any restriction immediately if it cannot be proved that it is saving more lives than it costs.

3. Hold a comprehensive public inquiry and a balanced public debate

We need to examine every aspect of the response to Covid-19. That includes the huge impact on other aspects of health care, such as cancer; the economic impact and consequent mortality; mental health; and the role of Government and media in stoking fear. We need to hold those responsible for mistakes to account and ensure that they do not happen again, as this will not be the last time we face a threat from an infectious disease. Right now, experts need the freedom to challenge bad policies. We ask the Government to pledge to hold a comprehensive public inquiry and to remove rules which prevent balanced reporting.

4. Safeguard all that makes life worth living

We are all used to balancing decisions about quality of life against quantity of life in what we do every day—we do it even when we decide to cross the road. The emergency policies take that out of our hands, saying that quantity of life is the absolute goal and quality of life must be destroyed to achieve it. The reaction to Covid-19 has seen livelihoods ruined, performing arts banned, grandparents told they can't hug their grandchildren, young people forced to live for months in isolation. We ask the Government to pledge that it will balance the risk from Covid-19 with safeguarding all that makes life worth living.

5. Get the economy moving for the sake of our children

There is much talk of choosing between saving lives and a healthy economy, but the truth is that lives depend on a healthy economy. Our children will have to live for decades with the consequences of current policies: How many will be condemned to live in poverty as a result? We've mortgaged their future. We can't afford to do more damage. We ask the Government to pledge that it will not recklessly put the mental health, jobs and futures of the young people of this country at risk.

I'm one of those people who can never follow a recipe as written—watch me sneak in some cilantro leaves or replace the ricotta with goat cheese, usually while Drew isn't looking—so I'll take the liberty of amplifying on these demands, drawing inspiration from the pandemic thought leaders who have filled the pages of this book.

To the first demand, "act with humanity," I would add that pandemic planning guidelines should prioritize mental health and human rights alongside viral mitigation. At the government level, executive powers should include checks and balances to ensure that no measure can be enacted or perpetuated without due process.

To the demand to consider not just lives, but life years, I would add that our analyses must also consider well-being—because ultimately it's not how many breaths we take that matters, but how much living we do. And to safeguard what makes life worth living, we must have permission to talk about it. Mocking people for caring about things like performing arts or weddings or spiritual communion doesn't move the conversation forward.

The much-needed public debate about pandemic policy needs to include transparent communication about risks, benefits, and areas of uncertainty. Norway appears to have gotten this part right. From the start of the pandemic, decision makers resolved to "communicate openly with the public about uncertainties and disagreements and the difficulties and dilemmas involved with managing a crisis," says Camilla Stoltenberg, director of the Norwegian Institute of

Public Health.[12] The leaders of our "great nations" showed none of this consideration.

Even worse, they refused to acknowledge their mistakes. To all the politicians and advisors bemoaning the loss of public trust in your words, there's your answer: if you don't come clean when you were wrong (say, about sterilizing immunity from the vaccines), people won't trust you. In case anyone needs a script, here's a suggestion: "We initially believed the vaccines would block transmission, but this hasn't proven to be the case." See? It's not that hard. (The hard part is overriding the human instinct to save face. Perhaps we need public apology workshops for that.)

Communication also means listening. As stated in the Ethical Principles of Public Health developed in 2022 by the Academy for Science and Freedom,[13] "it is critical for public health scientists and practitioners always to listen to the public, who are living the public health consequences of public health decisions, and to adapt appropriately." To facilitate this dialogue, pandemic advisory teams should include not just scientists and public health specialists, but (at the very least) mental health experts, ethicists, and economists.

If our young people deserve a moving economy, they also deserve a more general sense of normality. We all do. Governments could have created a lot more good will, even among skeptics, by signaling their intent to end the state of emergency and showing us an exit ramp beyond "when it's safe." When you're sitting for hours in an airplane awaiting departure, the least the crew can do is to explain how they're working to end the delay and when you can reasonably expect to leave the ground.

Instead, we got what Ari Schulman calls the "lockdown logic" of rolling restrictions. The initial weeks of lockdown, while troublesome on many levels, were arguably forgivable as "a desperate, temporary, last-ditch Band-Aid," he writes in a pandemic post-mortem for the *National Review*.[14] But "this same logic still prevailed years into the pandemic, because leaders showed so little urgency in actually using the time purchased at such terrible cost to create other options." The early claim that we had no choice "held less and less water because it became clear that we were choosing not to have a choice." The skeptics, the Side B people, maintained that we always had choices.

Side B resists the temptation to control other people and to blame governments for failing to win an unwinnable war. The question Daniel Hannan asks in *The Telegraph*[15] should concern us all: "Will coronavirus deaths be treated like stroke or cancer deaths — an ugly reality in an imperfect world? Or will they become the medical equivalent of terrorist fatalities, blamed on state policy?"

From the start of the pandemic, Side B has clamored for an honest discussion of trade-offs—a discussion that never happened. A *New England Journal of Medicine* article[16] attributes this conspicuous absence to "the ascendance of social media as a dominant platform for public conversation" and (in the US) the 2020 presidential election. Does this let our world leaders and communicators off the hook? Three years of social upheaval say no.

Side B has its own excesses, its own scratchy songs. But it served and continues to serve an essential purpose. We needed it during the worst of the pandemic, as a counterweight to the runaway fear and the groupthink, and we need it now, as Covid steps off the world stage and the next major pandemic casts as-yet unseen shadows on our planet.

"You Can't Always Get What You Want," that immortal Rolling Stones song, originally appeared on Side B of the *Honky Tonk Women* album. It's a simple tune, with a limited vocal range, but the refrain strikes at the heart of the human condition. In a pandemic, we can't get what we want, and we must choose our poisons to get what we need. Side B reminds us of that. Ω

ACKNOWLEDGEMENTS

I t all starts with my publisher, the Brownstone Institute. Jeffrey Tucker, who founded the Institute, has given a voice to intellectuals across the world who had something important to say about the Covid-19 policies and needed the right place to say it. Throughout the manuscript development process, Jeffrey showed a remarkable—and much appreciated—level of trust in me. I view Jeffrey and the Brownstone crew as my traveling companions and friends.

Heidi Buxton, who reviewed the manuscript, zeroed in on problems large and small, from typos and tonal wrong notes to arguments that needed strengthening. I could not ask for a more astute reviewer. While too numerous to list, my co-pilots in the Reddit community we curate deserve a big shoutout for their encouragement and support as I worked on the book. My grown children (Tara and Jackson), brother (Robert), and therapist (Dr. Zoom) merit special thanks for putting up with my "pandemic obsession" for three years.

When I informed my husband (Drew) that I would be writing this book, he told me I had better get used to his beef stew and shepherd's pie, because he would be doing all the cooking for the next six months. His unfailing support, which I seek to return but never manage quite as gracefully, is one of the many reasons he's a keeper.

To all of you who spoke out against the Covid monoculture: whether you're in this book or not, whether I know about you or not, you have a special place in my heart.

ABOUT THE AUTHOR

Gabrielle Bauer has been earning her living as a health and medical writer since 1995, producing materials for both health professionals and the general public. She has written for most major magazines in Canada and has won six national awards for her health journalism. Her first memoir, *Tokyo, My Everest,* was co-winner of the Canada Japan Book Prize. A later memoir, *Waltzing The Tango,* was a finalist for the Edna Staebler Award for Creative Non-fiction. Bauer's essays about the Covid-19 pandemic have appeared in several Canadian, US and UK publications. She lives in Toronto.

ABOUT THE PUBLISHER

The Brownstone Institute is a nonprofit 501(c)(3) organization founded May 2021. Its vision is of a society that places the highest value on the voluntary interaction of individuals and groups while minimizing the use of violence and force including that which is exercised by public or private authorities. This vision is that of the Enlightenment which elevated learning, science, progress, and universal rights to the forefront of public life. It is constantly threatened by ideologies and systems that would take the world back to before the triumph of the ideal of freedom.

The motive force of Brownstone Institute was the global crisis created by policy responses to the Covid-19 pandemic of 2020. That trauma revealed a fundamental misunderstanding alive in all countries around the world today, a willingness on the part of the public and officials to relinquish freedom and fundamental human rights in the name of managing a public health crisis, which was not managed well in most countries. The consequences were devastating and will live in infamy.

APPENDIX 1: THEMATIC SNAPSHOT

CHAPTER	FEATURING	KEY THEMES
1	[Introduction]	• The two divergent stories behind the pandemic
2	Laura Dodsworth	• How governments stoked fear in the interest of achieving compliance with restrictions • Ethics of "nudging" techniques to influence behavior
3	Mattias Desmet	• Conditions needed to create mass formation (an intense form of crowd psychology) • Link between mass formation and authoritarianism
4	Zubin Damania	• How moral intuitions (or "flavors") shape people's response to the pandemic policies • Benefits of celebrating people with different views
5	Jay Bhattacharya Sunetra Gupta Martin Kulldorff	• Alternative pandemic management strategy based on protecting the vulnerable • Toxicity of Covid shaming culture
6	Vinay Prasad	• Role of science and values in shaping public policy • Lack of high-quality data to support policies

CHAPTER	FEATURING	KEY THEMES
7	Zeb Jamrozik Mark Changizi	• Dangers and social costs of the precautionary principle • Advantages of the proportionality principle • Rational risk assessment and risk tolerance
8	Lucy McBride Jennifer Sey	• Importance of keeping children in school • Dubious ethics of sacrificing young people's current and future well-being for a virus that doesn't threaten them
9	Matthew Crawford Lionel Shriver	• Importance of personal agency in a public health crisis • What freedom does and does not mean
10	Paul Kingsnorth Daniel Hadas Ann Bauer	• Narrative underlying the vaccine campaign • Dystopian dimension of the "new normal" • Mutability of expert opinion
11	Giorgio Agamben Angie Hobbs	• Lopsided emphasis on "bare life" (metabolic survival) at the expense of integrated living • Importance of human flourishing in society
12	Aaron Kheriaty Julie Ponesse	• Bodily autonomy and other principles of medical ethics • Problematic ethics of mandating the Covid vaccines

CHAPTER	FEATURING	KEY THEMES
13	Robert Freudenthal Father Raymond de Souza	• Why a legislative and criminal response to a pandemic constitutes overreach • Importance of placing limits on government power
14	Charles Walker Udi Qimron	• Importance of considering mental health and livelihoods in shaping pandemic policies • Toxicity and futility of organizing society around Covid
15	Anders Tegnell Mark Woolhouse	• Principles of harm reduction • Futility and social costs of elimination policies
16	François Balloux Stefan Baral David Leonhardt	• Role of centrists in the Covid discourse • Adapting pandemic strategy to different populations • Psychology of doom
17	Sanjeev Sabhlok Paul Frijters	• How economists see the world • Crucial role of cost-benefit analyses (CBAs) • Importance of including well-being in CBAs
18	Matt Taibbi Glenn Greenwald Toby Young	• Toxic politicization of the pandemic • Changing meaning of liberalism • Rationality and emotionalism in the Covid discourse
19	Zuby David Mustaine Van Morrison	• Moving goalposts and mission creep • Importance of preserving arts and culture during a pandemic

CHAPTER	FEATURING	KEY THEMES
20	Jenin Younes Stacey Rudin David Bell	• Human rights and civil liberties in a pandemic • Danger of centralizing pandemic response strategies without regard for local conditions
21	Rupa Subramanya Raquel Dancho	• Deeper meaning of Covid protests • Government responsibilities toward protesters
22	Carl Heneghan Robert Dingwall	• Limits of human control over nature • Importance of balancing harms
23	Anonymous	• People's unfiltered thoughts about the Covid policies
24	Bari Weiss Bill Maher	• The logic of pandemic fatigue • Medical vs. social end of a pandemic
25	[Conclusion]	• How to do better the next time

APPENDIX 2: RESOURCES

Here's a short list of organizations with an interest in balancing priorities during a pandemic, documenting the harms of monolithic policies, broadening the concept of public health, upholding democratic ideals, and promoting freedom in scientific and public discourse.

Academy for Science and Freedom: Housed in Hillsdale College in Washington, DC, this group seeks to combat violations of individual and academic freedom perpetuated in the name of science and to communicate the importance of free, reasoned and civil discourse in science and in public health. https://dc.hillsdale.edu/Academy-for-Science-and-Freedom/Overview/

Brownstone Institute: Founded in response to the Covid-19 policies, this organization seeks to come to terms with what happened, understand why, and advocate for reforms to prevent a recurrence. The Institute hopes to assist in the recovery from the collateral damage, while offering "a different way to think about freedom, security, and public life." https://brownstone.org/

Collateral Global: This research and analysis group seeks to understand and communicate the effectiveness and collateral harms of the non-pharmaceutical interventions mandated in response to the COVID-19 pandemic—in a nutshell, to "figure out what we got right and what we got wrong." https://collateralglobal.org/

Freedom House: Through a combination of analysis, advocacy, and action, this organization works to defend human rights throughout the world, with a focus on democratic rights and civil liberties. The group includes "democracy during a pandemic" in a list of core issues it seeks to address. https://freedomhouse.org/

Pandemic Data & Analytics (PANDA): Formed in April 2020, this organization aims to use international data to increase knowledge about pandemics and inform policy. The group stands for open science and debate, and opposes the call for a socially damaging "new normal." https://www.pandata.org

Rational Ground: This group seeks to develop and curate a set of high-quality data sources to gauge the impact of Covid-19, promote reasoned and fact-based analysis of the pandemic, and provide evidence to drive balanced and rational public policies in the US and elsewhere. https://rationalground.com/

Urgency of Normal: This group of physicians, infectious disease specialists, and mental health experts seeks to counteract the damage to children caused by the Covid-19 policies, provide data to help people frame and balance risks, and broaden the definition of public health as it applies to children. https://www.urgencyof-normal.com/

REFERENCES

CHAPTER 1

1. Hartford T (2020, October 9). Lockdown sceptics v. zero Covid: who got it right? *Financial Times.*
2. Allen DW (2022). Covid-19 Lockdown Cost/Benefits: A Critical Assessment of the Literature. *International Journal of the Economics of Business*, 29, 1.
3. Herby J et al (2022, May 20). A literature review and meta-analysis on the effects of lockdowns on Covid-19 mortality—II. Johns Hopkins Institute for Applied Economics. *Studies in Applied Economics*, 200.
4. Sabhlok S, Gavrilis J (2022, August 24). Lockdowns increase even Covid deaths. India Policy Institute.
5. Pandemic lockdowns had severe consequences for women in the developing world (2022, April 1). *Science Daily.*
6. Reading and mathematics scores decline during COVID-19 pandemic (2022). The Nation's Report Card.
7. Park WJ, Walsh KA (2022). Covid-19 and the unseen pandemic of child abuse. *BMJ Paediatrics Open*, 6, e001553.
8. Onyeaka H et al (2021). COVID-19 pandemic: A review of the global lockdown and its far-reaching effects. *Science Progress*, 104.

CHAPTER 2

1. Mangan L (2019, February 19). 100 vaginas review—an extraordinary and empowering spread of the legs. *The Guardian.*
2. Dodsworth L (2021). *A State of Fear.* Pinter & Martin.
3. Victoria State Government (2020, July 7). Statement from the Premier. https://www.dhhs.vic.gov.au/updates/coronavirus-covid-19/statement-premier
4. Christensen J (2020, June 10). Covid-19 is Dr. Anthony Fauci's 'worst nightmare'. CNN.
5. Beck J (2017, June 23). Anthony Fauci on Americans' overblown fear of pandemics. *The Atlantic.*
6. Braddick I (2021, November 22). Merkel warns Germany's Covid nightmare is 'worse than anything we've seen' as THREE countries are plunged into lockdown. *The Sun.*
7. Coronavirus: 'virus does not discriminate'—Gove (2020, March 27). *Sky News.*

8. Booth A et al (2021). Population risk factors for severe disease and mortality in Covid-19: a global systematic review and meta-analysis. *PLoS One*, 16, e0247461.
9. Carbert M (2020, April 2022). MP who contracted Covid-19 recovers, warns virus doesn't discriminate. *The Globe and Mail*.
10. Covid hypocrisy: policymakers breaking their own rules (2022, February 24). Heritage.org.
11. Cecco L (2020, December 30). Canadian politician faked Twitter posts to conceal Caribbean holiday. *The Guardian*.
12. Partygate. Wikipedia. https://en.wikipedia.org/wiki/Partygate
13. Criminal investigation opened against Swiss 'National Covid-19 Science Task Force' for committing Covid fraud (2021, May 25). *The Exposé*.
14. Aaronovitch D (2021, June 11). A State of Fear by Laura Dodsworth review—a covidiot's guide to the pandemic. *The Times*.
15. QCovid® risk calculator. University of Oxford. https://qcovid.org/
16. Ioannidis JPA et al (2020). Population-level COVID-19 mortality risk for non-elderly individuals overall and for non-elderly individuals without underlying diseases in pandemic epicenters. *Environmental Research*, 188, 109890.
17. Dodsworth L (2022, March 4). The collective and the self. *Laura Dodsworth Substack*.
18. Rhoads S et al (2021). Global variation in subjective well-being predicts seven forms of altruism. *Psychological Science*, 32, 1247.
19. Milton Friedman quotes. BrainyQuote. https://www.brainyquote.com/quotes/milton_friedman_382646

CHAPTER 3

1. Martensen C (2021, December 3). The monster that devours its own children. Peak Prosperity podcast. https://peakprosperity.com/mattias-desmet-on-mass-formation/
2. Academy of Ideas (2021, February 26). Is mass psychosis the greatest threat to humanity?
3. Astin-Gregory D (2021, September 21). Why do so many still buy into the narrative? Pandemic Podcast. YouTube. https://www.youtube.com/watch?v=uLDpZ8daIVM
4. Astin-Gregory D (2022, June 16). Mattias Desmet: why were so many people willing to sacrifice their freedoms? Pandemic Podcast. YouTube. https://www.youtube.com/watch?v=ANHaHNr4qxU
5. Moffic SH (2022, January 31). Mass formation psychosis and the need for a DSM of social psychopathologies. *Psychiatric Times*.
6. Dewals P (2021, March 4). The emerging totalitarian dystopia: an interview with Professor Mattias Desmet. *Daily Sceptic*.

7. Bernstein W (2021). *The Delusions of Crowds.* Grove Atlantic. https://groveatlantic.com/book/the-delusions-of-crowds/
8. WHO chief calls Covid-19 'enemy against humanity (2020, March 18). *Medical Xpress.*
9. Saverio-Eastman L (2022, October 25). Parochial and pathological altruism. Brownstone Institute.
10. Nardi C (2020, April 15). Covid-19 pandemic is turning Canada into a nation of snitches. *National Post.*
11. Desmet M (2022). *The Psychology of Totalitarianism.* Chelsea Green Publishing.
12. Olsen J (2021, November 22). Associated Press. Report: democracy backsliding across the world amid pandemic.
13. Basen R (2022, January 22). Just what is mass formation psychosis? *Medpage Today.*
14. Joe Rogan Experience #1757 (2022, January 3). Congressman Troy Nehls website. 2022. https://nehls.house.gov/posts/joe-rogan-experience-1757-dr-robert-malone-md-full-transcript
15. No evidence of pandemic 'mass formation psychosis' (2022, January 7). Reuters Fact Check.
16. Baba S, Hafsi T (2022, April 20). Did governments around the world initially overreact to the Covid-19 pandemic? *The Conversation.*
17. Helmore E (2022, January 8). Houston woman charged after allegedly isolating Covid-positive son in car trunk. *The Guardian.*
18. Wood T (2022, January 13). Episode 92: Mattias Desmet on mass formation (psychosis) and Covid-19. *Trish Wood Is Critical* podcast. https://www.trishwoodpodcast.com/podcast/episode-92-mattias-desmet-mass-formation
19. Ryan H (2021, June 17). Halifax family questions delay in treatment after son, 19, dies of meningitis. CBC News.
20. Bagus P et al (2021). Covid-19 and the political economy of mass hysteria. *International Journal of Environmental Research and Public Health*, 18, 1376.
21. Cravis T, Sexton B (2022, March 15). Dr. Mark McDonald on America's mass delusional psychosis. NewsRadio 840 WHAS.

CHAPTER 4

1. Zubin Damania website. https://zdoggmd.com/about-z/
2. Damania Z (2020, May 3). Masks and the Moral Matrix. YouTube. https://www.youtube.com/watch?v=Eiy71RpATBQ
3. Schuman J (2018, July 15). The righteous mind: moral foundation theory. Divided We Fall.
4. Moral Foundations.org. https://moralfoundations.org/

5. Damania Z (2021, October 20). Covidians vs. Covidiots: an Alt Middle
    View. YouTube. https://www.youtube.com/watch?v=jZIJoekD_HE
6. Damania Z (2021, November 9). Covid Chill Chat. YouTube. https://
    www.youtube.com/watch?v=-cExZi6bxvU

CHAPTER 5

1. Great Barrington Declaration. https://gbdeclaration.org/
2. Mallapaty S (2020, August 28). The coronavirus is most deadly if you
    are older and male—new data reveal the risks. *Nature.*
3. Covid-19 deaths and hospitalizations by age (2020, August 10).
    CS319360-A (infographic). CDC. https://stacks.cdc.gov/view/
    cdc/91856
4. Nonpharmaceutical public health measures for mitigating the risk
    and impact of epidemic and pandemic influenza (2019). WHO
    Global Influenza Programme. https://apps.who.int/iris/bitstream/
    handle/10665/329438/9789241516839-eng.pdf
5. Community Mitigation Guidelines to Prevent Pandemic Influenza (2017).
    CDC. https://www.cdc.gov/mmwr/volumes/66/rr/rr6601a1.htm
6. Open letter (2020, July 6). Balanced Response (archived document).
    http://web.archive.org/web/20200927152940mp_/http://
    balancedresponse.ca/open-letter/#content-content-inner
7. A balanced response to Covid-19. Covid Plan B. https://www.
    covidplanb.co.nz/
8. Magness P, Harrigan JR (2021, December 19). Fauci, emails, and
    some alleged science. American Institute for Economic Research.
9. Gonsalves G (2020, October 8). Focused protection, herd immunity,
    and other deadly delusions. *The Nation.*
10. John Snow Memorandum. https://www.johnsnowmemo.com/john-
    snow-memo.html
11. Higgins-Dunn N (2020, October 15). CNBC. Dr. Fauci says letting
    the coronavirus spread to achieve herd immunity is 'nonsense' and
    'dangerous.'
12. Gillespie N (2022, April 22). Facing Fauci's fury: Q&A with Jay
    Bhattacharya. *Reason.*
13. Bhattacharya J (2020, October 17). Ask Me Anything. Reddit.
    https://old.reddit.com/r/LockdownSkepticism/comments/jcxsb1/
    ask_me_anything_dr_jay_bhattacharya/g9479wy/
14. Kulldorff M, Bhattacharya J (2021, May 27). It's mad that 'herd
    immunity' was ever a taboo phrase. *The Telegraph.*
15. Tucker J (2022, April 5). Lockdowns shredded the social contract:
    interview with Sunetra Gupta. Brownstone Institute.

16. Gupta S (2020, October 30). A contagion of hatred and hysteria: Oxford epidemiologist Professor Sunetra Gupta tells how she has been intimidated and shamed for backing shielding instead of lockdown. *The Daily Mail.*

17. Sunetra Gupta. Wikipedia. https://en.wikipedia.org/wiki/ Sunetra_Gupta

18. Tucker J (2022, February 26). The feudal symbolism of restaurant closures. Brownstone Institute.

19. Gupta S (2022, April 29). Our failure to protect care homes was the original sin of lockdown. *The Telegraph.*

20. Bauer G (2022, March 14). Those who chose shaming over science. Brownstone Institute.

21. Kulldorff M (2022, March 16). Twitter. https://twitter.com/ MartinKulldorff/status/1504149146176999427

22. Martin M (2020, December 19). Epidemiologist on why 'pandemic shaming' isn't working. National Public Radio.

23. Editorial Board (2021, December 21). How Fauci and Collins shut down Covid debate. *The Wall Street Journal.*

24. Harry Truman quotes. Goodreads. https://www.goodreads.com/ quotes/17832-once-a-government-is-committed-to-the-principle-of-silencing

25. Murtha R (2017, November 5). The highest form of patriotism. *Talkin' Bout Praxis.*

26. Louis Brandeis quote. Libquotes. https://libquotes.com/ louis-brandeis/quote/lbl2h1o

27. Case 3:22-cv-01213-TAD-KDM (2022, August 2). Western District of Louisiana. https://nclalegal.org/wp-content/uploads/2022/08/ Doc.-45-First-Amended-Complaint.pdf

28. Impelli M (2021, March 8). Jay Bhattacharya, Stanford doctor, calls lockdowns 'the biggest public health mistake we've ever made.' *Newsweek.*

29. Rau N et al (2022, September 14). Opinion: draconian Covid measures were a mistake, let's not repeat them. *National Post.*

30. McKie R (2022, January 2022). Britain got it wrong on Covid: long lockdown did more harm than good, says scientist. *The Guardian.*

31. Lewis D (2022, September 7). What scientists have learnt from Covid lockdowns. *Nature.*

32. Wright K (2022, October 19). 'Brutal" Australian Covid lockdowns hurt vulnerable, review says. BNN Bloomberg.

33. Kulldorff M (2022, September 12). Twitter. https://twitter.com/ martinkulldorff/status/1569312119002112001

34. Raghunathan N (2022, September 18). 2022 Doshi bridgebuilder award given to Stanford professor Jay Bhattacharya. *IndiaWest Journal.*

35. Aschwanden C (2021, March 18). Five reasons why Covid herd immunity is probably impossible. *Nature.*

36. Robertson D (2022, March 25). How we got herd immunity wrong. *Stat.*

37. Stokel-Walker C (2022). What do we know about covid vaccines and preventing transmission? *British Medical Journal*, 376, 0298.

CHAPTER 6

1. Prasad V (2013, February). Twitter. https://twitter.com/VPrasadMDMPH

2. Vinay Prasad, oncology and Twitter star, locked in debate over precision medicine (2018, June 22). *The Cancer Letter.*

3. Keshavan M (2017, September 15). Did he really just tweet that? Vinay Prasad takes on big pharma, big medicine, and his own colleagues—with glee. *Stat.*

4. Prasad V (2022, July 24). Twitter. https://twitter.com/vprasadmdmph/status/1551365457495539712

5. Prasad V (2022, July 17). Twitter. https://twitter.com/VPrasadMDMPH/status/1548847594293452800

6. Prasad V (2022, July 22). Twitter. https://twitter.com/VPrasadMDMPH/status/1550553502639804417

7. Prasad V (2020, November 23). Op-ed: what does 'follow the science' mean, anyway? *Medpage Today.*

8. Sapiens: notes and critical review (2017, April 28). *Vialogue.*

9. Harari Y (2021, February 26). Yuval Noah Harari: Lessons from a year of Covid. *Financial Times.*

10. Hume on *Is* and *Ought*. Philosophy Now.

11. Prasad V (2021, September 23). Follow the Science is a broken, empty slogan. YouTube. https://www.youtube.com/watch?v=xSqQuY-s3yE

12. Prasad V (2021, August 17). Seven cognitive distortions poisoning COVID debates. *Medpage Today.*

13. Prasad V (2022, May 30). Memorial day travel: experts vs. Americans. *Observations and Thoughts.*

14. Prasad V (2021, March 3). Op-ed: the hidden costs of avoiding death. *Medpage Today.*

15. John S (2021, December 2). Harm versus benefits in medicine: not just a decision for experts. *The Conversation.*

16. Winston Churchill quote. Quotes.pub. https://quotes.pub/q/nothing-would-be-more-fatal-than-for-the-government-of-state-342523

17. An address to the nation by Federal Chancellor Merkel (2020, March 18). The Federal Government (Germany). https://www.bundesregierung.de/breg-de/themen/coronavirus/statement-chancellor-1732296

18. Prasad V, Damania Z (2022, July 22). Ep. 23: Trust Issues, Sensible Medicine, Ideologic Possession. The VPZD Show. https://podcasts.apple.com/us/podcast/ep-23-trust-issues-sensible-medicine-ideologic-possession/id1596335407?i=1000570830641

19. Prasad V (2021, September 2). The downsides of masking young students are real. *The Atlantic*.

20. Smelkinson M et al (2022, January 26). The case against masks at school. *The Atlantic*.

21. *Unmasked* book review (2022, Spring). *The Independent Review*.

22. Cassata C (2022, June 22). In the era of Omicron, masks aren't working. Vaccines are. *Healthline*.

23. Prasad V (2022, February 26). Twitter. https://twitter.com/VPrasadMDMPH/status/1497666734613950465

24. Kim D, Lyons J (2022, February 11). Commentary: masks in schools do more harm than good. *Seacoastonline*.

25. Wood G (2022, March 9). What are the long-term consequences of masking kids? *Vancouver is Awesome*.

26. Prasad V (2022, May 29). If a few more people choose to wear masks, we will increase protection to the immunocompromised person wearing an n95 in our ranks. *Observations and Thoughts*.

27. Prasad V (2022, September 29). Biden says the pandemic is over. YouTube. https://www.youtube.com/watch?v=2_cNez3_1kQ

28. Prasad V (2022, October 1). I am going to mask because I want to get fewer colds & other flawed ideas. *Observations and Thoughts*.

29. Li JTC (2021, April 21). Hygiene hypothesis: does early germ exposure prevent asthma? Mayo Clinic.

30. Stadtmauer G (2016, September 16). Farm living study confirms the hygiene hypothesis. *Medscape*.

CHAPTER 7

1. Aguilar B (2020, October 4). Toronto school to close for a week 'out of an abundance of caution' after confirmed COVID-19 case. CTV News.

2. USDA statement on the confirmation of COVID-19 in a tiger in New York (2020, April 5). US Department of Agriculture.

3. Actions taken out of abundance of caution (2021, June 3). Singapore Ministry of Health. https://www.moh.gov.sg/news-highlights/details/actions-taken-out-of-abundance-of-caution

4. Doucleff M (2021, November 27). What we know about Omicron, the new variant. National Public Radio.

5. Goldstein BD (2001). The precautionary principle also applies to public health actions. *American Journal of Public Health* 91:1358.

6. Precautionary principle. *ScienceDirect*. [from Information Resources in Toxicology, 4th Ed, 2009].

7. Report of the United Nations conference on environment and development (1992, August 12). United Nations. https://www.un.org/en/development/desa/population/migration/generalassembly/docs/globalcompact/A_CONF.151_26_Vol.I_Declaration.pdf
8. Bonneux L, Van Damme W (2011). Health is more than influenza. *Bulletin of the WHO*, 89, 539.
9. Kauffman J (2022, February 5). Ask Me Anything. Reddit. https://www.reddit.com/r/LockdownSkepticism/comments/slmyo4/hi_im_jesse_im_a_historian_of_modern_europe_ask/
10. COVIDSurg Collaborative (2021). Effect of COVID-19 pandemic lockdowns on planned cancer surgery for 15 tumour types in 61 countries: an international, prospective, cohort study. *The Lancet Oncology* 22:1507.
11. Emergency department visits for suspected suicide attempts among persons aged 12-25 years old before and during the COVID-19 pandemic (2021, June 18). Morbidity and Mortality Weekly Report. CDC.
12. Dunlop T (2021, November 1). How Britain betrayed the elderly. *UnHerd*.
13. Neidell J et al (2019, October). Be cautious with the precautionary principle: evidence from the Fukushima Daiichi nuclear accident. National Bureau of Economic Research.
14. Ioannidis JPA (2020, March 17). A fiasco in the making? As the coronavirus pandemic takes hold, we are making decisions without reliable data. *Stat*.
15. Prasad V (2021, November 9). COVID-19 failures—scientific and ethical—with ID ethicist Zeb Jamrozik. YouTube. https://www.youtube.com/watch?v=1MmlHVgwscM&t=7s
16. Cohen R et al (2021). Pediatric Infectious Disease Group (GPIP) position paper on the immune debt of the COVID-19 pandemic in childhood, how can we fill the immunity gap? *Infectious Diseases Now*, 51, 418.
17. Kraaijeveld SR, Jamrozik E (2022). Moralization and mismoralization in public health. *Medicine, Health Care and Philosophy*, 1.
18. Jackson-Meyer K (2020, April 1). The principle of proportionality: an ethical approach to resource allocation during the COVID-19 pandemic. *Bioethics Today*.
19. Mark Changizi. Wikipedia. https://en.wikipedia.org/wiki/Mark_Changizi
20. Changizi M (2021, July 12). https://twitter.com/MarkChangizi/status/1414609765762797572
21. Changizi M (2020, May 6). Twitter. https://mobile.twitter.com/MarkChangizi/status/1258212493396238336
22. COVID-19 opinion tracker (2020, July 15). KEKST CNC. https://www.kekstcnc.com/media/2793/kekstcnc_research_covid-19_opinion_tracker_wave-4.pdf

23. Rothwell J, Desai S (2020, December 22). How misinformation is distorting COVID policies and behaviors. Brookings Institute.

24. De Bruin WB et al (2020). Political polarization in US residents' risk perceptions, policy preferences, and protective behaviors. *Journal of Risk and Uncertainty*, 61, 177.

25. Harkness T (2020, May 7). It's worth taking a risk over Covid-19. *UnHerd*.

26. Dougherty MB (2022, January 7). No to vaccine passports. *National Review*.

27. Soave S (2021, December 20). Against Faucism. *Reason*.

28. Macheras A (2021, December 19). Twitter. https://mobile.twitter.com/AlexInAir/status/1472646855234400256

29. Changizi M (2022, October 7). The trouble with face coverings is that they cover our f***ing faces. *Mark Changizi Newsletter*.

30. Changizi M, Barber B (2022). *Expressly Human*. BenBella Books.

31. Civil Action No.: 2:22-cv-1776. Changizi, Senger & Kotzin vs. Ohio Department of Health & Human Services (2022, April 22). New Civil Liberties Alliance. https://nclalegal.org/wp-content/uploads/2022/04/Declaration-D.-Kotzin-Filed.Stamped.pdf

CHAPTER 8

1. Study finds schools are not at higher risk for COVID-19 (2021, June 22). UBC Faculty of Medicine.

2. Onishi N et al (2020, November 30). Positive test rate of 11 percent? France's schools remain open. *The New York Times*.

3. O'Brien A (2021, October 23). Toronto students told not to speak during lunch to reduce the spread of COVID-19. CTV News.

4. Frizzell S (2021, October 5). Ottawa music teachers want wind instruments back in classrooms. CBC News.

5. Covid-19 information: Guidance for schools (K-12) and school buses (2022, January). Government of Alberta. https://open.alberta.ca/dataset/eca63dc4-1fd4-4eb4-9e3d-572d6004c0f8/resource/c031cf85-acab-43fa-8077-e9fee09e780c/download/health-covid-19-information-guidance-schools-k12-school-buses-2022-01.pdf

6. Downing S (2021, January 19). Class warfare: students in Anchorage will be forced to kneel for hours, no recess. *Must Read Alaska*.

7. Lucy McBride website. https://www.lucymcbride.com/

8. McBride L (2022, March 2). Testimony to Subcommittee on Oversight and Investigations on Energy and Commerce. House Committee on Energy and Commerce. https://energycommerce.house.gov/sites/democrats.energycommerce.house.gov/files/documents/Witness%20Testimony_McBride_OI_2022.03.02.pdf

9. Elgot J, Grover N (2021, June 29). Ministers set to end automatic isolation for pupils in England. *The Guardian*.

10. Wolfe-Robinson M, Adams R (2022, June 22). A quarter of a million children in England missed school last week due to Covid. *The Guardian.*

11. Furey A. (2021, February 27). Experts call Peel guidelines to place children in solitary quarantine 'cruel punishment.' *Toronto Sun.*

12. Rawlinson O (2021, November 29). Child with 'Covid symptoms' develops hypothermia after being isolated in outdoor classroom. *News & Star.*

13. The Urgency of Normal. https://www.urgencyofnormal.com/about

14. Henderson J (2022, January 28). Doc group calling for kids' prompt return to normal met with swift criticism. *Medpage Today.*

15. Prasad V (2022, January 7). We forgot about mental health and focused only on COVID-19. YouTube. https://www.youtube.com/watch?v=ylnOIVavnBw

16. McBride L (2021, August 13). Fear of COVID-19 in kids is getting ahead of the data. *The Atlantic.*

17. Cortina L (2022, March 19). Twitter. https://twitter.com/liliacortina/status/1505246939356573697

18. Caminiti S (2022, February 17). Former Levi Strauss executive Jennifer Sey on decision to leave company over Covid 'free speech' controversy. CNBC.

19. Elite gymnastics not all it's 'chalked up' to be (2008, May 1). National Public Radio.

20. Sey J (2022, February 14). Yesterday I was Levi's brand president. I quit so I could be free. *Common Sense.*

21. Genoa L (2022, January 5). Chicago public schools shut down amid teachers union protest of Covid protocols. *Politico.*

22. McKean C (2022, January 27). First, you decide that kids belong in school. *The Atlantic.*

23. Jacques I (2022, August 28). Teachers unions want parents to forget what happened during Covid. Don't let them. Yahoo!News.

24. Daugherty EH (2021, May 4). Q&A: Lucy McBride '95 on Covid-19, risk, and mental health. *Princeton Alumni Weekly.*

25. Reading and mathematics scores decline during COVID-19 pandemic (2022). The Nation's Report Card.

26. Basen N (2020, May 29). Covid-19: former Ontario medical officer of health responds to criticisms. TVO Today.

27. Park WJ, Walsh KA (2022). Covid-19 and the unseen pandemic of child abuse. *BMJ Paediatrics Open*, 6, e001553.

28. Breathnach A (2020). Covid-19 elimination: should we force our young to sacrifice their freedoms so the older generation can live a bit longer? *British Medical Journal*, 371, m3880.

29. Williams J (2021, September 5). The push to vaccinate kids shows our moral compass is askew. *The Telegraph.*

30. Gutentag A (2021, November 21). What they did to the kids. *Tablet.*

31. Collins S. (2021, June 25). Older generation needs to return favour after sacrifices of young people. *The Irish Times.*

32. Butler K, Bannock C (2021, June 2). A 'sacrificed generation': psychological scars of Covid on young may have lasting impact. *The Guardian.*
33. Prasad V (2022, June 9). Interview with Lilia Cortina, Ph.D. *Observations and Thoughts.*
34. Hoeg TB. (2022, August 12). Sacrificing children's health in the name of Health. *Sensible Medicine.*
35. Lance S (2022, January 20). I'm a schoolteacher. The kids aren't alright. *Common Sense.*

CHAPTER 9

1. Crawford M (2020). *Why We Drive.* HarperCollins.
2. *Shop Class as Soul Craft* quotes. Goodreads. https://www.goodreads. com/work/quotes/6444549-shop-class-as-soulcraft-an-inquiry-into-the-value-of-work
3. Crawford M (2020, May 15). The danger of safetyism. *UnHerd.*
4. Repucci S, Slipowitz A (2021). Democracy under siege. Freedom House.
5. Crawford M (2022, May 15). Covid was liberalism's endgame. *UnHerd.*
6. Tucker J (2020). *Liberty or Lockdown.* American Institute for Economic Research.
7. Hart J (2022). *Gone Viral.* Regnery.
8. Lionel Shriver. Wikipedia. https://en.wikipedia.org/wiki/ Lionel_Shriver
9. Domenech B (2021, April 5). Lionel Shriver & the importance of difficult people. Ben Domenech podcast. Fox News Radio. https://radio.foxnews. com/2021/04/05/lionel-shriver-the-importance-of-difficult-people/
10. Women more likely to embrace behaviors aimed at preventing the spread of COVID-19 (2020, October 5). *Science Daily.*
11. Galasso V et al (2020, October 15). Gender differences in COVID-19 attitudes and behavior: Panel evidence from eight countries. *Proceedings of the National Academy of Sciences*, 117, 27285.
12. Levy A (2020, May 25). Lionel Shriver is looking for trouble. *The New Yorker.*
13. Shriver L (2020, October 17). Covid has killed off our civil liberties. *The Spectator.*
14. Shriver L (2005, September 17). No kids please, we're selfish. *The Guardian.*
15. The right to self-determination: freedom from involuntary sterilization. Disability Justice.
16. O'Neill B (2020, May 5). The cruelty of social distancing, with Lionel Shriver. Spiked Online podcast.

17. Kroning A (2021, December 30). De facto ist eine gesamte Gesellschaft entmündigt worden. *Welt.* English translation: https://www.reddit.com/r/LockdownSkepticism/comments/rs4qyo/many_people_have_long_since_come_to_terms_with/

CHAPTER 10

1. Kingsnorth P (2021, November 24). The vaccine moment, part one. *The Abbey of Misrule.*
2. Paul Kingsnorth. Wikipedia. https://en.wikipedia.org/wiki/Paul_Kingsnorth
3. Paul Kingsnorth website. https://www.paulkingsnorth.net/cross
4. Kingsnorth P (2008, July 6). Here's the thing. *The Guardian.*
5. French D (2021, July 22). America's disinformation dilemma is more difficult than it seems. *The Dispatch.*
6. Campion-Smith B (2021, August 28). Toronto Star front-page design exacerbated divisions between readers. Greater care should have been taken. *The Toronto Star.*
7. Kingsnorth P (2021, December 9). The Vaccine Moment, part two. *The Abbey of Misrule.*
8. Dougherty MB (2021, August 6). Ignoring them is the only way out. *National Review.*
9. Kingsnorth P (2021, December 20). The Vaccine Moment, part three. *The Abbey of Misrule.*
10. Hadas D (2021, December 10). The agony of the anti-lockdown centrists. *UnHerd.*
11. Hadas D (2022, October 15). Nitter. shorturl.at/cux06
12. Hadas D (2022, August 5). After Covid. *City Journal.*
13. Ann Bauer website. https://www.annbauer.com/about.html
14. Bauer A (2021, October 27). I have been through this before. *Tablet.* Oct. 27, 2021.
15. Addendum guidelines for the prevention of peanut allergy in the United States (2017). NIAID.
16. Ioannidis JPA (2005). Why most published research findings are false. *PLoS Medicine*, 2, e124.
17. Howick J et al (2022, August). Most healthcare interventions tested in Cochrane Reviews are not effective according to high quality evidence: a systematic review and meta-analysis. *Journal of Clinical Epidemiology*, 148, 160.

CHAPTER 11

1. Giorgio Agamben. Wikipedia. https://en.wikipedia.org/wiki/Giorgio_Agamben
2. Agamben G (2021). *Where are we now? The epidemic as politics.* Rowman & Littlefield. [Includes Swedish interview.]
3. Kotsko A (2020, March 17). Giorgio Agamben: clarifications. *An und Für Sich.*
4. Aleksandr Solzhenitsyn quotes. Goodreads. https://www.goodreads.com/quotes/8560898-but-i-had-begun-to-sense-a-truth-inside-myself
5. Mounk Y (2022, February 9). Open everything. *The Atlantic.*
6. Kauffman J (2022, January 15). Is this our World War I? Brownstone Institute.
7. Daley J (2020, December 19). Our drastic Covid response reflects the state's new moral duty to end death. *The Telegraph.*
8. Oshinskie M (2022, June 18). Covid exposed the medical-medical-pharmaceutical-government complex. Brownstone Institute.
9. Dennis M (2022, June 5). ASCO22: Enhertu halves risk of disease progression in HER2-low breast cancer study. *FirstWord Pharma.*
10. Kolata G (2022, June 7). Breast cancer drug trial results in 'unheard-of' survival. *The New York Times.*
11. Kotsko A (2020, May 2). Giorgio Agamben: medicine as religion. *An und Für Sich.*
12. Godwin S (2021, June 3). Twitter. https://twitter.com/samanthaagodwin/status/1400305718843133954
13. The Biopolitics of immunity in times of COVID-19: An interview with Roberto Esposito (2020, June 16). *Antipode Online.*
14. Pedgen W (2020, December 12). Twitter. https://twitter.com/WesPegden/status/1337965623301836801
15. Dolan P (2020, December 14). For the middle aged, by the middle aged: how the responses to COVID have ignored the preferences of those most affected. LSE School of Public Policy.
16. Reuters staff (2020, October 22). "I'm 83, I don't give a sod"; UK pensioner sums up frustration with new COVID curbs. Reuters.
17. Peif S (2020, October 8). Greely nursing home residents protest pandemic lockdown: "I'd rather die of COVID than loneliness." *Complete Colorado.*
18. Favaro A et al (2020, November 19). Facing another retirement home lockdown, 90-year-old chooses medically assisted death. CTV.
19. Gavroche J (2021, May 4). Giorgio Agamben: on the government of the faceless and deathless. *Autonomies.*
20. Chambers J (2021). Interview with Angie Hobbs—the double-wicked challenge: Covid and Brexit. *Jericho Conversations.*

21. Hobbs A (2020, October 15). The ethics of the pandemic: life or quality of life? *Prospect.*

CHAPTER 12

1.   COVID-19 vaccine incentives (2021, October 19). National Governors Association. https://www.nga.org/center/publications/covid-19-vaccine-incentives/
2.   Allen A (2021, October 16). Covid immunity through infection or vaccination: are they equal? *ASBMBToday.*
3.   Ponesse J (2022). *My Choice.* The Democracy Fund.
4.   Roos D (2021, December 9). When the Supreme Court ruled a vaccine could be mandatory. History.
5.   Ponesse J (2021, November 22). Why are so many choosing life in a cage? Brownstone Institute.
6.   Kheriaty A (2015, November 9). Letter to the American Medical Association. https://s27589.pcdn.co/wp-content/uploads/2017/02/Kheriaty-AMA-letter-1.pdf
7.   Kheriaty M. Desmond JF (2022, January 18). Interview: Dr. Kheriaty discusses COVID-19, vaccine mandates and his dismissal from UC-Irvine. Ethics & Public Policy Center.
8.   Kheriaty A (2021, September 17). Ask Me Anything. Reddit. https://www.reddit.com/r/LockdownSkepticism/comments/pq5d16/i_am_aaron_kheriaty_md_as_me_anything/
9.   Kheriaty A, Bradley GV (2021, June 14). University vaccine mandates violate medical ethics. *The Wall Street Journal.*
10. Aaron Kheriaty biography. Zephyr Institute. https://www.zephyr.org/People/AARON-KHERIATY
11. Kheriaty N (2022). *The New Abnormal.* Regnery.
12. Huston WT (2022, August 1). First-of-its-kind victory in covid shot mandate suit: workers awarded millions after having religious exemptions denied. *Western Journal.*
13. Vitagliano B (2022, October 25). New York State judge reinstates fired sanitation workers who did not comply with New York City's vaccination mandate. CNN.
14. Dolmetsch C (2022, October 25). NYC ordered to reinstate workers fired for Covid vaccine refusal. *Bloomberg.*

CHAPTER 13

1.   Ahearne G, Freudenthal R (2021). The health/power/criminality-nexus in the state of exception. *Journal of Contemporary Crime, Harm, Ethics,* 1, 108.

2. Prasad V (2021, April 1). The role of government in public health and in COVID-19 policy with Robert Freudenthal. Plenary Session podcast. YouTube. https://www.youtube.com/watch?v=Un3fUgv5RLg

3. Jackman R (2021, March 19). How Britain lost the lockdown battle. *Reason*.

4. Freudenthal R (2022, October 2). Covid-19: are we handing over too much unchecked power? *Labour Hub*.

5. Freudenthal R et al (2020). Lack of safeguards in response to restrictive public health measures. *The Lancet* 2020, 396, e70.

6. Freudenthal R (2021, September 28). Psychiatry will not save us from lockdown harm. Brownstone Institute.

7. Freudenthal R (2022). Was lockdown necessary? *British Medical Journal*, 376, 0776.

8. Lukianoff G, Haidt J (2018). The truth of fragility: what doesn't kill you makes you weaker. From *The Coddling of the American Mind*. Penguin Books. https://www.thecoddling.com/chapter-1-antifragility

9. Freudenthal R (2021, December 3). Three tragic assumptions behind lockdown strategy. Brownstone Institute.

10. Freudenthal R (2021, August 10). Brownstone Institute.

11. Raymond J. de Souza. Wikipedia. https://en.wikipedia.org/wiki/Raymond_J._de_Souza

12. de Souza R (2021, October 23). Raymond J. de Souza: Government overreach on vaccines has been about power, not the pandemic. *National Post*.

13. de Souza R (2021, December 17). Raymond J. de Souza: O come all ye faithful—faithfully vaccinated, that is. *National Post*.

14. Blackwell T (2022, June 13). Ohio bill calls for Canada to be put on religious freedom watchlist over Covid restrictions. *National Post*.

CHAPTER 14

1. Charles Walker. Wikipedia. https://en.wikipedia.org/wiki/Charles_Walker_(British_politician)

2. Carpani J (2020, November 24). Sir Charles Walker demands PM responds after 'elderly lady peacefully protesting' is arrested. *The Telegraph*.

3. Coronavirus lockdown restrictions (2020, May 4). Sir Charles Walker MP. https://www.charleswalker.org.uk/news/coronavirus-lockdown-restrictions

4. Covid-19: road map (2021, February 2021). Sir Charles Walker MP. https://www.charleswalker.org.uk/news/covid-19-road-map

5. Covid-19: Government 'bordering on the dangerous' (2021, February 21). Sky News. YouTube. https://www.youtube.com/watch?v=qje2mpTwiBc

6.   Patrick DM et al (2006). An outbreak of human coronavirus oc43 infection and serological cross-reactivity with SARS coronavirus. *Canadian Journal of Infectious Diseases and Medical Microbiology*, 17, 330.

7.   Mulholland H (2012, December 26). Charles Walker MP: 'I've made peace with it. I've got it off my chest.' The Guardian.

8.   Mulholland H (2013, September 4). Charles Walker MP: 'mental illness is not a weakness.' *The Guardian*.

9.   Freedom of expression (2016, December 6). Sir Charles Walker MP. https://www.charleswalker.org.uk/news/freedom-expression

10. Freedom of protest (2021, March 15). Sir Charles Walker MP. https://www.charleswalker.org.uk/news/freedom-protest

11. Freedom of protest (2021, March 25). Sir Charles Walker MP. https://www.charleswalker.org.uk/news/freedom-protest-0

12. Grace J (2021, March 25). Tory milkman delivers speech surreal even by Commons' standards. *The Guardian*.

13. Harel A (2020, September 6). Israeli physicians, scientists warn against lockdown, call to adopt Swedish model. *Haaretz*.

14. Eldar A (2020, October 29). The pandemic is revealing Israel's festering sore. *Al Jazeera*.

15. Ben Zion I (2021, February 20). Israel's ultra-Orthodox reject criticism, defy virus rules. Associated Press.

16. Aschkenazy B (2020, September 23). Lawsuit by Israel doctors urges high court to revoke national lockdown. *Haaretz*.

17. Qimron E (2022, January 10). Ministry of health, it's time to admit failure (translated from Hebrew). Swiss Policy Research. https://swprs.org/professor-ehud-qimron-ministry-of-health-its-time-to-admit-failure/

CHAPTER 15

1.   Paterlini M. (2020, April 21). 'Closing borders is ridiculous': the epidemiologist behind Sweden's controversial coronavirus strategy. *Nature*.

2.   Country comparison. Hofstede Insights. https://www.hofstede-insights.com/country-comparison/spain/

3.   Anders Tegnell. Wikipedia. https://en.wikipedia.org/wiki/Anders_Tegnell

4.   Anderberg J (2022). *The Herd*. Scribe UK.

5.   Milford C (2021, May 18). 10 things the Covid-19 crisis has taught us about Sweden. *The Local*.

6.   Letter to the European Centre for Disease Control (2020, April 5). Public Health Agency of Sweden. https://drive.google.com/file/d/1FqUIDPZWA5AkBY57YNbB9EIHeJCDSFHv/view

7. Nonpharmaceutical public health measures for mitigating the risk and impact of epidemic and pandemic influenza (2019). WHO Global Influenza Programme. https://apps.who.int/iris/bitstream/handle/10665/329438/9789241516839-eng.pdf

8. UK Influenza Pandemic Preparedness Strategy (2011). UK, Welsh & Scottish Governments. https://assets.publishing.service.gov.uk/government/uploads/system/uploads/attachment_data/file/213717/dh_131040.pdf

9. CDC community mitigation guidelines to prevent pandemic influenza (2017). *Recommendations and Reports*, 66, 1. https://www.cdc.gov/mmwr/volumes/66/rr/rr6601a1.htm

10. Siglaugsson T (2022, July 8). Excess mortality same in Denmark and Sweden. *From Symptoms to Causes*.

11. Hallin AE et al (2022). No learning loss in Sweden during the pandemic: evidence from school reading assessments. *International Journal of Education Research*, 114.

12. Silver L, Connaughton A (2022, August 11). Partisanship colors views of covid-19 handling across advanced economies. Pew Research.

13. Rolfe B (2020, June 3). 'Was it necessary'?: The PM who regrets taking tough coronavirus lockdown measures. Yahoo!News.

14. Mark Woolhouse. Wikipedia. https://en.wikipedia.org/wiki/Mark_Woolhouse

15. Woolhouse M (2022). *The Year The World Went Mad*. Sandstone Press.

16. 1968 flu pandemic. Britannica. https://www.britannica.com/event/1968-flu-pandemic

17. Spitznagel E (2020, May 16). Why American life went on as normal during the killer pandemic of 1969. *New York Post*.

18. Principles of harm reduction. National Harm Reduction Coalition.

19. Ferguson N et al (2020, March 16). Report 9: impact of nonpharmaceutical interventions (NPIs) to reduce COVID-19 mortality and healthcare demand. Imperial College COVID-19 Response Team. https://www.imperial.ac.uk/media/imperial-college/medicine/sph/ide/gida-fellowships/Imperial-College-COVID19-NPI-modelling-16-03-2020.pdf

20. Hayes A (2022, March 9). Covid-19 expert claims he was told to 'correct his views' after criticizing 'implausible graph' shown during official briefing. Sky News.

CHAPTER 16

1. François Balloux. Wikipedia. https://en.wikipedia.org/wiki/
   Francois_Balloux
2. Prof François Balloux. Twitter. https://mobile.twitter.com/
   ballouxfrancois/with_replies
3. Pelling R, Phelps P (2022, February 4). The interview: François
   Balloux. *Perspective.*
4. Balloux F (2021, May 20). Twitter. https://twitter.com/
   ballouxfrancois/status/1395566547964506112
5. Plüddemann A et al (2017). Positive results bias. Catalogue of Biases.
6. Tucker I (2021, August 7). Prof François Balloux: 'The pandemic has
   created a market for doom and gloom.' *The Guardian.*
7. Epstein D (2019, June). The peculiar blindness of experts. *The
   Atlantic.*
8. Balloux F (2022, July 17). The best of times, the worst of times...
   That's science in the age of Covid. *The Guardian.*
9. Heffernan V (2019, March 25). The beautiful benefits of contemplating
   doom. *Wired.*
10. Shen H (2018, June 28). The despondent mind: are our brains wired
    for doom and gloom? *Scientific American.*
11. Babylon A (2008, August 1). The psychology of doom. Alan Weiss
    website.
12. Madrigal AC (2020, January 28). How to misinform yourself about
    the coronavirus. *The Atlantic.*
13. Binks-Collier M (2021, November 25). 'We're deviating from what
    makes us Canadian': An interview with Steven Baral. *Healthy Debate.*
14. The Canadian Press (2015, September 10). Union says Ontario nurses
    can't be forced to wear masks in flu season. CBC News.
15. Baral S (2022, September 25). Twitter. https://twitter.com/sdbaral/
    status/1574114449409146881
16. Baral S (2021, April 8). Twitter. https://twitter.com/sdbaral/
    status/1380229071548862469
17. Baral S (2021, March 8). Twitter. https://threadreaderapp.com/
    thread/1368943302423293952.html
18. Baral S (2021, August 8). Twitter. https://twitter.com/sdbaral/
    status/1424446346329690113
19. Chait J (2021, March 3). Zero Covid risk is the wrong standard.
    Intelligencer.
20. Baral S (2021, February 22). Twitter. https://twitter.com/sdbaral/
    status/1363894813041524743
21. David Leonhardt. Wikipedia. https://en.wikipedia.org/wiki/
    David_Leonhardt#cite_note-7
22. Kenen J (2022, January 27). The NYT's polarizing pandemic pundit.
    Politico.

23. Leonhardt D (2021, December 10). Covid malaise. *The Morning* newsletter. *The New York Times.*
24. Tomori C (2022, January 26). Twitter. https://twitter.com/DrTomori/status/1486501069996064768
25. Adler-Bell S (2022, February 24). David Leonhard, the pandemic interpreter. *Intelligencer.*
26. Barbaro M (2022, January 26). We need to talk about Covid, Part 1. The Daily podcast (transcript). https://www.nytimes.com/2022/01/26/podcasts/the-daily/omicron-coronavirus-behaviors.html?showTranscript=1

CHAPTER 17

1. What it takes to think like an economist. American University Washington DC.
2. Sabhlok S (2022, May 17). Lockdowns did more harm than good. *Spectator Australia.*
3. Hochman N (2022, April 21). The tyranny of public health. *National Review.*
4. Sabhlok S (2021). *The great hysteria and the broken state.* Connor Court Publishing.
5. Sabhlok S (2020, March 6). Age-based risk management of coronavirus. *The Times of India.*
6. Sabhlok S (2020, March 24). Lockdowns won't defeat the virus but will definitely destroy us all. *The Times of India.*
7. Sabhlok S (2020, April 3). Risk-based analysis, not models, will defeat coronavirus. *The Times of India.*
8. Who am I? Sanjeev Sabhlok blog. https://www.sabhlokcity.com/who-am-i/
9. Executive order 12291 (Feb. 17, 1981). National Archives. https://www.archives.gov/federal-register/codification/executive-order/12291.html
10. Lemoine P (2021, March 11). The lockdowns weren't worth it. *The Wall Street Journal.*
11. Soetenhorst B (2021, June 22). Ministerie van economische zaken verzette sich tegen 'intelligente' lockdown. *Het Parool.*
12. Greve JE and agencies (2020, March 21). US state governors impose tighter restrictions to slow coronavirus spread. *The Guardian.*
13. Davies A, Harrigan JR (2020, April 29). The "if it saves just one life" fallacy. Intercollegiate Studies Institute.
14. Carter S (2022, September 6). Covid school shutdowns were disastrous and we should have known. *Bloomberg.*
15. Frakt A (2020, May 11). Putting a dollar value on life? Governments already do. *The New York Times.*

16. Hannan D (2021, January 17). Freedom won't survive a world where every lethal virus triggers another lockdown. *The Telegraph*.
17. Pokhrel S (2021, June 9). Why standard ways of valuing health were set aside during the pandemic. *The Conversation*.
18. Allen DW (2022). Covid-19 Lockdown Cost/Benefits: A Critical Assessment of the Literature. *International Journal of the Economics of Business*, 29, 1.
19. Herby J et al (2022, May 20). A literature review and meta-analysis on the effects of lockdowns on Covid-19 mortality—II. Johns Hopkins Institute for Applied Economics. *Studies in Applied Economics*, 200.
20. Sabhlok S, Gavrilis J (2022, August 24). Lockdowns increase even Covid deaths. India Policy Institute.
21. Foster G, Frijters P, Baker M (2021). *The Great Covid Panic*. Brownstone Institute.
22. Frijters P (2022, July 4). Well-being cost-effectiveness applied to Covid policies (presentation). PANDA. https://www.pandata.org/prof-paul-frijters-wellbeing-cost-effectiveness-analysis-applied-to-covid-policies/
23. Daley J (2020, December 19). Drastic Covid response reflects state's new moral duty to end death. *The Telegraph*.
24. Frijters P (2020, March 21). The corona dilemma. Club Troppo.

CHAPTER 18

1. Zuby (2021, September 13). Nitter. https://nitter.net/i/status/1437493315151220738
2. Zuby (2021, November 12). Twitter. https://twitter.com/ZubyMusic/status/1459142519841828868
3. Zuby (2022, February 1). Nitter. https://nitter.net/i/status/1488398712959381509
4. About Zuby. Zuby Music. https://www.zubymusic.com/about
5. Zuby gives his view on Covid finger-pointers and health entitlement (2021, December 7). GBN Live. YouTube. https://www.youtube.com/watch?v=OXn1nNzFah4
6. Wig more I. Intermittent reinforcement. WhatIs.com.
7. Arabi S (2022, February 1). Intermittent reinforcement: the powerful manipulation method that keeps you trauma bonded to your abuser. *Thought Catalog*.
8. Kelly M (2022, January 4). Zuby on COVID doom addiction, the harms of closing schools, and how to fight back. Megyn Kelly Show. YouTube. https://www.youtube.com/watch?v=W-c_e7NUUvg
9. Storey L (2021, November 9). Zuby: the antidote to wokeness, cultural Marxism, and social division (podcast transcript). https://www.lukestorey.com/transcripts/zuby-the-antidote-to-wokeness-cultural-marxism-tyranny-social-division-377

10. Zuby (2021, July 5). Twitter. https://twitter.com/ZubyMusic/status/1412012537986568193
11. Dave Mustaine. Wikipedia. https://en.wikipedia.org/wiki/Dave_Mustaine
12. Ken C (2020, April 6). Dave Mustaine of Megadeth urges fans to stay in to prevent spread of Covid-19. Audio Ink Radio.
13. Kreps D (2021, September 16). Dave Mustaine rails against mask mandates: 'This is called tyranny'. *Rolling Stone*.
14. Zweig D (2022, August 18). An absurd and disturbing cancel campaign in public health. *Boston Globe*.
15. Nuccio D (2022, August 16). Truth and art in the pandemic era. Brownstone Institute.
16. Douglas A (1998). *The Feminization of American Culture*. Farrar Strauss Giroux.
17. Fox C (2022, January 20). The obedient generation. Brownstone Institute.
18. Biography. Van Morrison website. https://www.vanmorrison.com/about/biography
19. Van Morrison announces three protest songs against lockdown (2020, September 18). Van Morrison website.
20. Newman J (2020, September 21). Northern Ireland's health minister would like a word with Van Morrison. *Rolling Stone*.
21. Cambridge J, Black R (2021, June 11). Ian Paisley insists he does not believe health minister Robin Swann is dangerous. breakingnews.ie.
22. Paul L (2021, November 8). Van Morrison sued by Northern Ireland health minister over Covid-19 criticism. *Rolling Stone*.
23. Snapes L (2022, May 30). Van Morrison takes legal action against Northern Ireland health department and minister over Covid article. *The Guardian*.
24. Morrison V (2022). What's It Gonna Take lyrics. Genius. https://genius.com/albums/Van-morrison/Whats-it-gonna-take

CHAPTER 19

1. Fatima S (2021, April 30). Why some won't ditch their masks outdoors: 'I'm not about to look like a republican'. *Boston Globe*.
2. Brown L (2022, September 10). Twitter. https://twitter.com/Lidsville/status/1568504280424005632
3. Matt Taibbi. Wikipedia. https://en.wikipedia.org/wiki/Matt_Taibbi
4. Barka R (2021, October 21). What happened to Matt Taibbi? *Intelligencer*.
5. Taibbi M (2020, April 30). The inevitable coronavirus censorship is here. *TK News by Matt Taibbi*.
6. Taibbi M (2022, January 27). The folly of pandemic censorship. *TK News by Matt Taibbi*.

7. Breaking911 (2022, August 16). Twitter. https://twitter.com/ Breaking911/status/1559615892614533122
8. Prasad V (2020, December 29). Op-ed: Why did Fauci move the herd immunity goalposts? *Medpage Today*.
9. Covid-19 triggers a wave of free speech abuse (2021, February 11). Human Rights Watch.
10. Taibbi M (2022, January 4). Twitter. https://twitter.com/mtaibbi/ status/1478361757823369219
11. Burns N (2021, August 12). Glenn Greenwald: the greatest journalist of all time? *New Statesman*.
12. Glenn Greenwald. Wikipedia. https://en.wikipedia.org/wiki/ Glenn_Greenwald
13. Flynn K (2020, October 29). Glenn Greenwald is quitting The Intercept, claiming editors 'censored' his article about Joe Biden. CNN Business.
14. Robinson N (2021, June 17). How to end up serving the right. *Current Affairs*.
15. Silverstein K (2021, May 20). Glenn Greenwald Hates the Tech Oligarchy! OK, but How Did the World's Biggest Hypocrite Get Rich From Tech Oligarch Money? *Washington Babylon*.
16. Grove L (2021, June 2). Is Glenn Greenwald the new master of right-wing media? *Daily Beast*.
17. Greenwald G (2021, May 24). Twitter. https://twitter.com/ ggreenwald/status/1396973746410475522?s=20
18. Greenwald G (2008). *Great American Hypocrites*. Crown.
19. Greenwald G (2021, August 19). Twitter. https://twitter.com/ ggreenwald/status/1424730022087204871
20. Greenwald G (2021, January 4). Twitter. https://twitter.com/ ggreenwald/status/1346191535700848640
21. Glenn Greenwald (2021, August 1). Twitter. https://twitter.com/ ggreenwald/status/1427684833849921545
22. Nuzzo J (2020, June 2). Twitter. https://twitter.com/JenniferNuzzo/ status/1267885076697812993?ref_src=twsrc%5Etfw
23. Greenwald G (2021, December 20). Twitter. https://twitter.com/ ggreenwald/status/1472920991076651009
24. Greenwald G (2021, August 21). The bizarre refusal to apply cost. *Glenn Greenwald Substack*.
25. Glenn Greenwald (2021, August 23). Twitter. https://twitter.com/ ggreenwald/status/1429786126815010820
26. Authority (2014, December 11). Erich Fromm Online.
27. Goldberg K (2021, December 28). Mass formation: how the left got duped. *Kim Goldberg Substack*.
28. Toby Young. Wikipedia. https://en.wikipedia.org/wiki/Toby_Young
29. About the Daily Sceptic. https://dailysceptic.org/about/
30. Young T (2022, January 22). I got Covid (again)—is it time I got jabbed? *The Spectator*.

31. Young T (2020, November 20). 10 reasons why a second lockdown is a terrible idea. *The Critic.*

32. Young T (2020, August 15). I've started a dating site for lockdown sceptics. *The Spectator.*

33. Murphy S (2021, January 27). Preliminary materials for a theory of Devi Sridhar. *The Daily Sceptic.*

34. Young T (2020, March 21). Has the government overreacted to the coronavirus crisis? *The Critic.*

CHAPTER 20

1. Eve F (2020, February 2). China's reaction to the coronavirus outbreak violates human rights. *The Guardian.*

2. Pandemic Preparedness: the need for a public health approach (2008). American Civil Liberties Union. https://www.aclu.org/sites/default/files/pdfs/privacy/pemic_report.pdf

3. Universal Declaration on Bioethics and Human Rights (2006). UNESCO. https://unesdoc.unesco.org/ark:/48223/pf0000146180

4. Cole D, Mach D (2021, September 2). Civil liberties and vaccine mandates: here's our take. American Civil Liberties Union. https://www.aclu.org/news/civil-liberties/civil-liberties-and-vaccine-mandates-heres-our-take

5. Younes J (2022, January 4). Are COVID vaccine mandates for kids legal? *Tablet.*

6. Case 3:22-cv-01213-TAD-KDM (2022, August 2). Western District of Louisiana. https://nclalegal.org/wp-content/uploads/2022/10/order-granting-request-for-depositions.pdf

7. Abraham Lincoln quotes. Goodreads. https://www.goodreads.com/quotes/100343-our-safety-our-liberty-depends-upon-preserving-the-constitution-of

8. Rudin S (2020, September 1). Will you choose freedom? American Institute for Economic Research.

9. Judge rules Pennsylvania governor's COVID-19 restrictions unconstitutional (2020, September 14). Reuters.

10. Rudin S (2020, September 2020). Federal court holds "stay-at-home" orders and mandatory business closures unconstitutional. American Institute for Economic Research.

11. Littman L (2020, September 17). A conservative judge just made it even harder to stop Covid. *The Washington Post.*

12. Rudin S (2020, October 26). Who deserves your trust in the Covid debate? American Institute for Economic Research.

13. Council gives green light to start negotiations on pandemic treaty (2022, March 3). European Council.

14. PANDA Exco members. https://www.pandata.org/team/

15. Behind the pandemic treaty (2022, May 21). American Thought Leaders. YouTube. https://www.youtube.com/watch?v=e8G7jgEQR3Q

16. The WHO is not planning to implement a 'pandemic treaty' that would strip member states of sovereignty (2022, May 25). Reuters Fact Check.

17. Constitution. World Health Organization. https://www.who.int/about/governance/constitution

18. Why do we prefer doing something to doing nothing? The Decision Lab.

CHAPTER 21

1. Canadian convoy protest. Wikipedia. https://en.wikipedia.org/wiki/Canada_convoy_protest

2. Al-Hakim A (2022, January 30). Ottawa soup kitchen staff allegedly harassed by truck convoy protesters. Global News.

3. Rupa Subramanya biography. Asia Pacific Foundation of Canada. https://www.asiapacific.ca/about-us/distinguished-fellows/rupa-subramanya

4. Subramanya S (2022, February 20). What the truckers want. *Common Sense*.

5. Magill G (2022, February 1). Elites are smearing truckers because we're doing their job representing the people. *Newsweek*.

6. Malcolm C (2022, February 10). Trudeau catastrophically underestimated the truckers (featuring Rupa Subramanya). True North podcast. YouTube. https://www.youtube.com/watch?v=AUgice-DCZo

7. Raquel Dancho. Government of Canada. https://www.ourcommons.ca/members/en/raquel-dancho(105521)#work

8. Raquel Dancho gives powerful speech on the current state of Canada (2022, February 7). Parliamentary Precinct. YouTube. https://www.youtube.com/watch?v=ZeHJcw_GrmY

9. Canadian Pandemic Influenza Preparedness (2015). Pan-Canadian Public Health Network. https://www.phac-aspc.gc.ca/cpip-pclcpi/assets/pdf/report-rapport-2015-eng.pdf

10. Gilmore R (2022, January 27). 'Fringe minority' in truck convoy with 'unacceptable views' don't represent Canadians: Trudeau. Global News.

11. Bingham J (2022, January 3). Trudeau calls unvaccinated Canadians 'racists,' 'misogynists' in unhinged interview. Life Site News.

12. Tunney C (2022, February 14). Federal government invokes Emergencies Act for first time ever in response to protests, blockades. CBC News.

13. Aziz S (2022, February 9). 'Snowball effect': Canada's trucker convoy sparks anti-mandate protests globally. Global News.

14. Stannous J (2022, February 14). Trudeau's totalitarian turn. *The Spectator*.

15. Thiessen M (2022, February 17). Canada turns authoritarian to shut down the 'Freedom Convoy'. *The Washington Post*.

16. Subramanya R (2022, August 2). Court documents reveal Canada's travel ban has no scientific basis. *Common Sense*.

17. Malik N (2022, August 17). Understanding the violent attack on Salman Rushdie. *The Guardian*.

18. Trudeau J (2022, August 13). Twitter. https://twitter.com/justintrudeau/status/1558487509277065218

19. Salman Rushdie quotes. Goodreads. https://www.goodreads.com/quotes/17828-what-is-freedom-of-expression-without-the-freedom-to-offend

20. Salman Rushdie quotes about free speech. Inspiringquotes.us. https://www.inspiringquotes.us/author/9509-salman-rushdie/about-free-speech

CHAPTER 22

1. Jefferson T, Heneghan C (2020, April 8). Covid-19—the tipping point. The Centre for Evidence-Based Medicine.

2. Tringle N (2020, September 28). Covid: Is it time we learned to live with the virus? BBC News.

3. Professor Carl Heneghan on learning to live with Covid this winter (2021, September 2). Planet Normal podcast. YouTube. https://www.youtube.com/watch?v=ZvkF6SZrHVA

4. McGee L (2021, July 19). Boris Johnson is taking another huge gamble by lifting lockdowns in England. CNN.

5. McGuinness R (2021, December 20). Oxford professor warns against 'annual winter lockdowns' amid debate on COVID rules. Yahoo!News.

6. Clarke L (2020, October 30). Why scientists fear the "toxic" Covid debate. *New Statesman*.

7. Heneghan C, Gupta S (2021, June 4). Written evidence submitted to the inquiry led by Dominic Cummings (CLL0117). UK Parliament Committees. https://committees.parliament.uk/writtenevidence/36911/pdf/

8. Heneghan C, Jefferson T (2020, November 9). Landmark Danish study finds no significant effect for facemask wearers. *The Spectator*.

9. Powell M (2022, March 26. Twitter bans Oxford academic who shared this Mail on Sunday article—but allows anti-vax rants amid fears over new 'online safety' powers letting tech giants censor legitimate journalism. *The Daily Mail*.

10. Ajana B (2021). Immunisations: defence and sacrifice in the politics of Covid-19. *History and Philosophy of the Life Sciences*, 43, 25.

11. Cardiff C (2020). What went wrong: corona and the world after the full stop. *Medical Anthropology Quarterly*, 34, 467.

12. Vidhi F (2020). Homo Pandemics: Covid ideology and panic consumption. *Crisis and Critique*, 7, 447.

13. Senger M (2021). *Snake Oil: How Xi Jinping Shut Down the World.* Plenary Press.

14. H.L. Mencken quotes. BrainyQuote. https://www.brainyquote.com/ quotes/h_l_mencken_143263

15. Marni J (2022, February 1). Unvaccinated shoppers 'must be accompanied at all times' in big stores in Quebec. *Miami Herald.*

16. Robert A. Heinlein quotes. Goodreads. https://www.goodreads.com/ author/quotes/205.Robert_A_Heinlein?page=7

17. Robert A. Heinlein quotes. BrainyQuote. https://www.brainyquote. com/quotes/robert_a_heinlein_136368

18. Furey A (2021, July 24). Canada's COVID busybodies will never leave you alone—so just ignore them. *Toronto Sun.*

19. Outcomes for hospitalized COVID-19 patients taking immunosuppressive medications similar to non-immunosuppressed patients (2021, November 16). Johns Hopkins Bloomberg School of Public Health.

20. Goldman JD et al (2021). COVID-19 in immunocompromised populations: implications for prognosis and repurposing of immunotherapies. *Journal for ImmunoTherapy of Cancer*, 9, e002630.

21. Oscar Wilde quotes. Goodreads. https://www.goodreads.com/ quotes/445661-selfishness-is-not-living-as-one-wishes-to-live-it

22. Schorr A (2022, January 31). Enough is enough. *Yale Daily News.*

23. Dingwall R (2022, January 13). (Belated) New Year thoughts on the barriers to ending the pandemic. *Social Science Space.*

24. Benn A (2020, October 16). Robert Dingwall interview: the damage done by our refusal to accept disease and death are part of life. *Reaction.*

25. Emanuel E (2014, October). Why I hope to die at 75. *The Atlantic.*

26. Halleman S (2022, September 6). Ezekiel Emanuel on the state of COVID-19 in the US and the 'major issue' of healthcare burnout. *HealthCareDive.*

27. Illich I (2000). *Limits to Medicine: Medical Nemesis, the Expropriation of Health* (updated since 1975 publication). Marion Boyars.

CHAPTER 24

1. Living with Covid (2022, January 21). *Real Time with Bill Maher.* YouTube. https://www.youtube.com/watch?v=8bQ2rctogOs

2. Patten D (2022, January 21). Bill Maher on 'Real Time's 20th season, being "over Covid" & America's upcoming "real day of reckoning". *Deadline.*

3. McDougall AJ (2022, January 23). CNN doc slams Bari Weiss for saying she's 'done with Covid': 'She's acting like a child'. *Daily Beast.*

4. Schaefer S (2022, January 24). Twitter. https://twitter.com/saraschaefer1/status/1485653660700844036

5. Baragona J (2022, January 24). Whoopi Goldberg blasts Bill Maher's Covid dismissiveness: 'How dare you be so flippant'. *Daily Beast.*

6. Sofija E, Bernard NR (2021, September 9). We're sick of Covid. So government messaging needs to change if it's to cut through. *The Conversation.*

7. Cuadrado E at al (2021). Construction and validation of a brief pandemic fatigue scale in the context of the coronavirus-19 public health crisis. *International Journal of Public Health*, 66, 1604260.

8. Yildirim M, Solmaz F (2022). COVID-19 burnout, COVID-19 stress and resilience: Initial psychometric properties of COVID-19 burnout scale. *Death Studies*, 46, 524.

9. Wolfsohn J (2021, October 30). Bill Maher rails against Covid restrictions: it's time to admit pandemic is 'over'. *Fox News.*

10. New rule: panic porn (2020, April 17). *Real Time with Bill Maher.* YouTube. https://www.youtube.com/watch?v=UcvIQJ-QurQ

11. Pandemic Fatigue (2020). World Health Organization. https://apps.who.int/iris/bitstream/handle/10665/335820/WHO-EURO-2020-1160-40906-55390-eng.pdf

12. Petherick A et al (2021). A worldwide assessment of changes in adherence to COVID-19 protective behaviours and hypothesized pandemic fatigue. *Nature Human Behaviour*, 5, 1145.

13. Meacci L, Primicerio M (2021). Pandemic fatigue impact on COVID-19 spread: A mathematical modelling answer to the Italian scenario. *Results in Physics*, 31, 104895.

14. Berg A (2022, September 9). What doctors wish patients knew about pandemic fatigue. American Medical Association.

15. Topol E (2022, May 15). Twitter. https://twitter.com/EricTopol/status/1525923634686328832

16. Miller H (2022, June 7). Why this is no time to ease up on efforts to contain Covid-19. Genetic Literacy Project.

17. Fiore K (2022, August 19). Petition to cut Leana Wen as APHA speaker faces backlash. *Medpage Today.*

18. Anderson C (2022, April 18). Florida Judge voids US mask mandate for planes, other travel. AP News.

19. *The New York Times* (2022, October 16). Twitter. https://twitter.com/nytimes/status/1581626033958445057

20. Lewis T (2022, March 14). People, not science, decide when a pandemic is over. *Scientific American.*

21. Richarz A (2021, December 3). On Covid restrictions, our governments keep firing up the gaslights and shifting the goalposts. CBC News.

22. Hulme M (2021, March 6). Why the old normal needs to be fought for (transcript of February 18 interview). Professor Mike Hulme's site.

23. Restrepo ML (2022, June 16). 'Revenge travel' is surging. Here's what you need to know. National Public Radio.

24. Wolf N (2022, April 28). Oh, OK, it's over. *Outspoken with Naomi Wolf*.

25. Nelson F (2022, August 27). The lockdown files: Rishi Sunak on what we weren't told. *The Spectator*.

26. Editorial board (2022, August 25). The West needs a Covid lockdown debate. *The Wall Street Journal*.

CHAPTER 25

1. Senger M (2022, October 29). The great gaslighting. Brownstone Institute.

2. Ferguson N (2022, January 23). China's Covid victory over America turns out to be Pyrrhic. *Bloomberg*.

3. Wagner A (2022, October 13). Boris Johnson's Covid law took away our rights with a flick of the pen. Don't let that happen again. *The Guardian*.

4. Tucker J (2022, October 6). Why did so many intellectuals refuse to speak out? Brownstone Institute.

5. Leonhardt D (2021, July 30). More Covid mysteries. *The Morning* newsletter. *The New York Times*.

6. Varkey B (2021). Principles of clinical ethics and their application to medical practice. *Medical Principles and Practice*, 30, 17.

7. Greek medicine: the Hippocratic Oath. National Library of Medicine.

8. Pandemics: the ethics of mandatory and voluntary interventions (2020, March 30). The Hastings Center.

9. Sumption J. (2022, August 28). Little by little the truth of lockdown is being admitted: it was a disaster. *The Sunday Times*.

10. Stringham EP (2020, May 21). How a free society deals with pandemics, according to legendary epidemiologist and smallpox eradicator Donald Henderson. American Institute for Economic Research.

11. Five Reasonable Demands (2021, February 1). Recovery UK. Covid19 Assembly. https://www.covid19assembly.org/2021/02/five-reasonable-demands/

12. Cohen B (2022, June 29). Norway was a pandemic success. Then it spent two years studying its pandemic failures. *The Wall Street Journal*.

13. Statement on the ethical principles of public health (2022, August 23). Academy for Science and Freedom.

14. Schulman A (2022, September 15). The dirty war over Covid. *National Review*.
15. Hannan D (2021, January 7). Freedom won't survive a world where every lethal virus triggers another lockdown. *The Telegraph*.
16. Dupont SC, Galea S (2022). Science, competing values, and trade-offs in public health—the example of Covid-19 and masking. *New England Journal of Medicine*, 387, 865.

INDEX

Made in the USA
Las Vegas, NV
27 March 2023

69775598R00187